Hollywood's Vietnam

Hollywood's Vietnam

GILBERT ADAIR

HEINEMANN : LONDON

William Heinemann Ltd
Michelin House, 81 Fulham Road, London SW3 6RB

LONDON MELBOURNE AUCKLAND

First published 1989
Copyright © Gilbert Adair 1989

The filmography on p. 203 was compiled
from the credit listings in the *Monthly Film Bulletin*.
The author and publishers are grateful for the editor's assistance.

British Library Cataloguing in Publication Data
Adair, Gilbert
  Hollywood's Vietnam: from the Green Berets
    to Full Metal Jacket
  1. California. Los Angeles. Hollywood.
  Cinema films, 1947–1987. Special subjects:
  Vietnamese wars
  I. Title
  791.43.'75

ISBN 0 434 04580 2

Photoset by Rowland Phototypesetting Ltd
Bury St Edmunds, Suffolk
Printed and bound by
Richard Clay Ltd, Bungay, Suffolk

For John Paul Getty III

CONTENTS

INTRODUCTION

The subject of this book, as its title and jacket illustration intimate, is the American cinema's treatment of the Vietnam War. It has no pretensions to being about the war itself or the confluence of historical circumstances that determined its escalation: nowhere in the text, for instance, have I discussed the real Viet Cong, only their various, often highly stylised facsimiles in Hollywood movies (most conspicuously, the snake-eyed addicts of Russian roulette fabricated by *The Deer Hunter*). It is not a study of the war's *coverage* but of its *representation*. I have in consequence preferred to concentrate almost exclusively on works of fiction, as I believe them to offer up a far richer vein of ideology than documentaries, which in any event have never loomed very large in Hollywood's history. Similarly, since it would not be easy to name a single American film dealing with South-East Asia in the post-1975 period (or one that, however peripherally, alluded to Pol Pot or the boat people), I have chosen not to take such data into account. Nor have I dwelt, except in passing, on non-American productions. These may be judged contestable limitations, but they are the limitations that I have allowed to define and circumscribe my reflections on the subject.

In the course of the book (a revised, expanded and considerably updated version of its original edition of 1981) I identify two separate and distinct 'waves' of Vietnam films. The first of these may be said to have extended from *The Green Berets* in 1968 to *Apocalypse Now* in 1979. The second and still flourishing wave was actuated, most probably, by *First Blood*, the first of the *Rambo* cycle, was lent added force by the concurrent success, both critical and commercial, enjoyed by *The Killing Fields*, and undoubtedly crested with Oliver Stone's *Platoon*, the movie that did most to revive the controversy with which the cinema of Vietnam had once been surrounded. This latter wave, however, launched almost a decade after the cessation of hostilities and therefore benefiting from the advantage of a political and historical hindsight which the former was denied, may of course prove to be more than just a phase. The evidence suggests, instead, that Vietnam is at long last 'entering the system', so to speak, and starting to acquire its own generic conventions and energies, on which every director and screenwriter will henceforth have a right to call. Clearly, given the increasingly prolific output of films on the subject, neither Hollywood nor its public is any longer afraid of the Vietnam War.

Yet the adjective 'afraid' was all too aptly descriptive of the major studios' initial reluctance during the late sixties and early seventies to come to terms with an issue that, apart from having virtually monopolised the media platforms for national (and frequently international) debate, seemed to offer a host of intriguing dramatic possibilities. While researching the original edition of this book, I became puzzled by the impression that Hollywood sometimes gave of curbing its already tentative handling of Vietnam and related themes by a kind of self-imposed censorship comparable to that which had for over thirty years frustrated any real advance in its representation of sexuality. This self-censorship, if such it was, was only very gradually relaxed (a few, mostly aberrant, exceptions apart, e.g. *The Green Berets*), giving rise to the first, oblique dialogue references to the war, as was the case in a series of exploitation road movies whose motorcyclist heroes were often embittered vets turning skills learned in Vietnam to more overtly criminal purpose (titles such as *Satan's Sadists, Angels From Hell*, etc.). Travis Bickle, the eponymous protagonist of Martin Scorsese's *Taxi Driver* (1976), was also a war veteran; but more significant than the relatively rare occasions on which Vietnam was specifically mentioned in the film's dialogue was a pervasive moral and physical squalor whose reverberations far exceeded what would normally have been justified by its depiction of Manhattan's seamy underside.

Numerous traditional genres were annexed in this way, notably the genial, all-purpose western, which had at least the alibi of a bona fide historical precedent. It often served to allegorise the war (e.g. Ralph Nelson's *Soldier Blue*, 1970, a relentlessly brutal denunciation of the Indian massacres, and Robert Aldrich's *Ulzana's Raid*, 1972, whose Apache warriors were turned into blood brothers of the Viet Cong), as did, though at greater violence to narrative credibility, the medieval romance (e.g. John Huston's *A Walk with Love and Death*, 1969). And when the studios eventually got round to making movies *about* Vietnam, they nevertheless began, by an odd reversal of chronological priorities, with its aftermath, with the reintegration of vets into a society that greeted them as though they had returned from Mars. Or else with the young people who had elected *en masse* to opt out of that society and fight the war (or rather, its advocates) on home territory – on campuses, in demonstrations and even, with the release of *The Green Berets*, outside cinemas.

Though the best of these efforts could be defended as worthy and well intentioned, in general the subject-matter proved too complex, too multilayered, to be comfortably confined within the closed plot structures – a beginning, middle and end in that order – that were natural to the American cinema, and the results more often ran the gamut from the queasily ambivalent to the downright dishonest. It felt like almost the fun thing to be against the war if it meant filling the screen with sit-ins, peace-ins and love-ins in Death Valley, with all the funky psychedelic paraphernalia of the protest movement. And it was much more fun attacking America than defending Vietnam. The Star-Spangled Banner, even when unfurled to ironic effect, is still a jazzy, brightly coloured icon. A hideously maimed infant is less invigorating.

I was reminded of that when I attended a screening of several polemically pro-Vietnam short films by the distinguished Cuban director Santiago Alvarez (*Hanoi, Tuesday 13, April in Vietnam in the Year of the Cat, The Stampede*). The predominantly under-thirties audience, of impeccable liberal credentials, was respectfully atten-tive to these heartening if harrowing documentaries, but one sensed that the angel of boredom, though it had not yet settled on the auditorium, was hovering perilously close at hand. Then his *LBJ* was shown, a scurrilously witty collage of anti-Americana or, in the director's own words, a satirical pamphlet in three chapters, in which the letters of the Presidential monogram also stood for, respectively, *L*uther King, *B*ob and *J*ohn F. Kennedy. Suddenly the house was alert, practically hissing the villains and hooting at the more flagrant examples of doublespeak perpetrated by some of them. However, when this in turn was followed by *79 Springs*, a straightforward tribute to Ho Chi Minh and the resilience of the Vietnamese people, as one man we all sank back into our former lethargic earnestness.

The products born of Hollywood's first brief idyll – more precisely, marriage of convenience – with sixties youth tended, then, to reveal more of the period's contradictions in their trappings than in their ostensible 'substance'; and it is indicative of the relatively marginal status of Vietnam as the raw material of fiction, while the fighting was going on, that the most commercially successful of all youth-orientated movies, George Lucas's *American Graffiti* (1973), more or less turned its back on the war and set its affectionate celebration of adolescent mores on the very edge of the Vietnam era. So that of the two opposing axes of received wisdom concerning the subject of this book (and which were tirelessly communicated to me while I was writing it) – one, that there are too few Vietnam movies to warrant a full-length study and, two, that every American feature film made during the decade of 1965–75 must directly or indirectly reflect some aspect of the United States' political make-up and therefore be relevant to the debate – each may claim to contain elements of truth.

What distinguished the second grouping of films from that preceding it was basically that they had the opportunity to build on a foundation which had already been laid. And what this meant in effect was that the moment had arrived for the 'artists' to move in – where once, with the odd exception (Kazan, Cimino, Coppola), only craftsmen, artisans, journeymen and outright hacks had dared to tread. Notwithstanding the fact that the cycle was re-launched by the transcultural myth of Rambo/Stallone – whose influence on the meaning of the movies enshrining him was far more crucial and conclusive than that of their directors – it was characterised above all by a cluster of prestigious *films d'auteur* (*auteurs* real or self-imagined): Stephen Frears's *Saigon – Year of the Cat*, Roland Joffé's *The Killing Fields*, Stone's *Platoon*, Stanley Kubrick's *Full Metal Jacket*, Francis Coppola's *Gardens of Stone*, even Barry Levinson's *Good Morning, Vietnam*. And because the political, historical and

4

ideological processes responsible for shaping the war, as also the grisly quotidian realities endured by the soldiers in the field, were necessarily transfigured by each film-maker's own particular preoccupations and obsessions as an artist, I have focused my attention in the body of the text on the individual works cited above and consigned those for which Vietnam was simply one narrative component among others (e.g. *Four Friends, Birdy*, any number of thrillers whose heroes' psyches were permanently scarred by combat experience) to a filmography at the end of the book.

A postscript, finally, to the original edition. As it happens, it concluded with a carefully worded speculation that any film hoping to excel *Apocalypse Now* in communicating the *sensations* of the Vietnam War would have to be shot 'on location' – 'if by "on location" we mean that it must be made by the Vietnamese themselves'. Reviewing that edition, the critic Philip French castigated me for my *naïveté*. 'Does Adair seriously believe,' he asked, 'that the studios of Hanoi and Ho Chi Minh City are likely to produce a film on the war that will command international attention?' Well, put like that, maybe not – or not yet. Even so, the *desire*, however wistful, to see a film emerge from the other side still strikes me as a perfectly legitimate one. And though, bowing resignedly to the inevitable, I have, at least in the book's latter section, refrained from censuring any film for having failed to address the Vietnamese cause, or even accord the merest semblance of life or humanity to a single Vietnamese character, though age, temperament and perhaps the onset of a certain conservatism have persuaded me to accept (as, in the war's aftermath, I confess I could not) that American films can only reasonably be expected to reflect American truths, I continue, incorrigibly naïve as I am, to be troubled by the fact that Hollywood's Vietnam appears even now to have rather more to tell us about Hollywood than about Vietnam.

— *Chapter 1* —

APOCALYPSE THEN

In this century the United States has been involved in four major wars: the First and Second World Wars, Korea and Vietnam. In 1918, the year the First World War ended and only one year after America had intervened, D. W. Griffith, the director of *The Birth of a Nation* and *Intolerance*, made his first movie on the subject, *Hearts of the World*, a melodrama so blatantly anti-German in attitude as to cause, in Erich von Stroheim's words, 'hundreds and thousands of men and women in more or less pro-German audiences in the United States to have a complete change of heart'. Thereafter the trenches, bunkers and twisted barbed wire, the imagery by which the First World War is instantly recognisable on the screen, became a familiar feature of Hollywood movies for the next two decades.

By the mid-thirties, however, another World War was all too noisily in the offing; and both before and after America's intervention in the wake of the Japanese assault on Pearl Harbor, the Second World War movie became almost an autonomous genre whose popularity, eclipsing that of the war movie *per se*, has remained constant to the present day.

In June 1950, North Korean troops crossed the 38th Parallel and invaded the Republic of Korea. A few days later, when his appeal for a cease-fire had been ignored, President Truman decided to send in American naval and air forces. In September of the same year a delegation of Hollywood notables was dispatched to the White House to acquaint the President with the industry's unanimous support. They declared, notably, that: 'We are at your service, at the service of the country and the United Nations.' Though, for various reasons, fewer films were made about Korea than about the preceding World Wars, those which did surface (mostly B-movies, like Samuel Fuller's *The Steel Helmet*, 1950) were serenely

7

untroubled by any doubts or disillusionment concerning the American initiative.

And then came Vietnam. It is a delicate matter picking over the ruins to try and locate the precise moment when the Americans first opened fire in Indochina, for the war's origins were all but obscured by the ebbing tide of French colonialism (since 1953 heavily subsidised by the United States), but it is on record that by 1968, the year of *The Green Berets*, co-directed by Ray Kellogg and its star John Wayne, their forces in the region already totalled almost half a million men. Though a commercial success in countries whose geographical proximity to the war made them particularly sensitive to its outcome, such as Australia and Japan, as well as in certain hinterland areas of the United States with a high recruitment rate, the South and Midwest, the release of *The Green Berets* was also the signal for widespread demonstrations – the picketing and even bombing of cinemas exhibiting it – and a merciless critical drubbing. Since then every movie dealing with the American presence in Vietnam has been greeted as some sort of event and the merest hint of ideological revisionism in its dialogue pounced upon.

But to understand why Hollywood was so chary of depicting the Vietnam War within a conventional gung-ho framework, it will be necessary to give brief consideration to its treatment of those which preceded it.

The First World War, in a sense, was not an 'American' affair at all. In 1914, with President Wilson determined to pursue a 'Keep Out' policy, the United States was prey to another of its frequent but never very durable bouts of pacifist isolationism, as witness film titles like *Be Neutral, Neutrality* and *War is Hell*. The rare movies that sought to transcend such cautious abstractions and make what was happening in Europe come alive in terms of plot and character motivation were generally obliged to set the action in one of those reassuringly unspecified countries where over the years so many fictional wars – in novels, plays and films – have been waged to symbolic effect. Thus Herbert Brenon's *War Brides* (1916) had the arrestingly surnamed tragedienne Alla Nazimova playing a young wife who, when her husband is killed in action, refuses to obey a royal decree ordering widows to remarry and bear more children to carry on the war (which, if such long-term planning is any indication, promised to be an unusually lengthy engagement).

If geopolitical frontiers remained undefined, however, the enemy had to be particularised at least to the degree of their not resembling Americans; and since all other signs of national status had been piously expunged, this could be achieved only through racial typification. In both *War Brides* and Thomas Ince's prestigious superproduction *Civilization* (1916) the brutal soldiery is inescapably Teutonic in appearance. Ince's film, which involves a young submarine engineer whose body is invested by the spirit of Christ and put to higher service in the crusade against war, had an ostensibly pacifist premise. But by again locating the origin of the war in question – and, by implication, the origin of War itself – in a thinly disguised racial type, it cunningly insinuated the urgent necessity for taking action against what was presented as an irreformably bellicose nation. Its 'neutrality' was so patently biased, in fact, that Sweden, a country which was truly neutral, banned its importation.

In these films, released concurrently with the war in Europe but prior to American intervention, we can already see taking form a mythologising process that was to suffer very little change in the decades to come. Once and for all, as far as the cinema industry was concerned, this was a 'futile', 'tragic' war in which 'the flower of youth was trampled underfoot on the field of Flanders', and so forth. More than any other, it seemed to lend itself to a vaguely mystical pacifism. So much so that certain directors were apparently unaware of any contradiction in using it as the backdrop for an antiwar tract between filming two conventionally heroic Boys' Own Adventure movies about the Second World War.

A case in point is Lewis Milestone, who made his reputation with the adulated, Oscar-winning *All Quiet on the Western Front* (1930), from Erich Maria Remarque's best-selling novel. Though overrated in its day, *All Quiet* remains a moving enough indictment of the waste and stupidity inherent in every war, however 'just'. The fact that, as far as the film version is concerned, the story is being told from the enemy's point of view, with the doomed young German soldiers being played by attractive American actors, not only humanises its sometimes ponderous didacticism but also makes it more difficult for nationalistic considerations to come into play. Far better than the spurious universality that would have been gained by setting the action on some purely symbolic battleground, such a casting *parti pris* succeeds in blurring our sense of two opposing sides locked in combat and goes some way towards exposing the condition of war itself. This 'fraternisation' of American actors and German soldiers could even be said to mirror that which took place in the trenches during the Christmas truce of 1914 and encourages the spectator to identify emotionally with characters who are often – and in Hollywood war movies, invariably – categorised as aliens, bearing all the racial, social and cultural stigmata of incurable 'otherness'. Its famous last image of the young German hero (Lew Ayres) stretching out his hand to stroke a butterfly and suddenly convulsing in death from a sniper's bullet makes the naïve but affecting statement that aspirations towards beauty have never been the sole prerogative of 'our boys', that Germans too are human, every mother's son of them.

As Milestone's career advanced, though, it became clear that his pacifist convictions were by no means immutable. He was quite prepared to discard them, for instance, in *The Purple Heart* (1944), a straightforward guts 'n' glory Second World War movie marred by a crudely racist treatment of the Japanese, and *Pork Chop Hill* (1959), ditto for Korea. Similarly, the British actor Richard Attenborough, a below-decks veteran of innumerable morale-boosting war films, initiated his career as a director with an all-star adaptation of Charles Chilton and Joan Littlewood's satirical anti-war musical *Oh! What a Lovely War* (1969), then coolly proceeded to film *A Bridge Too Far* (1978), a spectacular reconstruction of the battle of Arnhem for which many of the same stars were required to pull their tongues out of their cheeks and re-stiffen their upper lips in preparation for another 'big push'.*

It would be easy to attribute such ideological volte-faces to sheer mercenary opportunism. To be sure, movies are made to make money and antiwar movies doubtless get made because their producers reckon them to be what the public wants at that particular moment. But, beyond these economic facts of life (which apply to fully one hundred per cent of Hollywood film-making), it is

---

* *A Bridge Too Far* was, to be fair, the account of a British defeat.

probable that whenever an antiwar story was mooted around the studios the decision to give it a First World War setting was taken at an almost subliminal level. (There are too many examples to list here, though mention should be made of Stanley Kubrick's *Paths of Glory*, 1957, and Joseph Losey's *King and Country*, 1964. The exceptions mostly centred on colourful tête-à-tête skirmishes between stylish air aces who 'respected each other' and contrived to preserve a cavalryesque ideal of chivalry high above the carnage, as in John Guillermin's *The Blue Max*, 1966, and Roger Corman's *Von Richthofen and Brown*, 1971.)

Such semi-automatic concordance of theme and period can be accounted for by a combination of factors: the tragically arbitrary set of events which led to the outbreak of war; the monotony of its strategy, with both Allied and German forces dug in along a line stretching from the Channel to the Swiss border; the stark contrast between the insouciance with which the first Tommies left for France, convinced that they would be home for Christmas, and the hideous reality confronting them in the trenches; the unglamorous nature of the fighting and wholesale slaughter of its major battles; the disastrous diplomatic aftermath; and, not least, the widely held belief that it constituted a turning point in history, with the concomitant nostalgia for a *belle époque* soon to be viewed through the soft focus of memory.

The Second World War presented a substantially different picture. If the First World War had been exclusively a game of chance, here was a game of skill with plenty of opportunities (for the film-maker, that is) to dart freely over the board. From jungle combat in the Philippines and Pacific Islands to air strikes over the Rhine, from a North African campaign waged against that gallant 'good German', Field-Marshal Rommel, to undercover activity in the Balkans, it was for Hollywood's purposes very much a tourist's war, with no shortage of local colour for the romantic interludes. It was a relief, too, that the moral and political issues seemed so absolutely clear-cut. In the face of an aggressor as monstrous as Hitler, pacifism was, as it were, disarmed – tarred with the inglorious brush of 'appeasement'. For once all shades of opinion concurred in the necessity for taking up arms. And this solidarity is reflected in the relative good humour and optimism of many Second World

War films (generally perceived by their audiences, even after the period when they were considered an integral part of the war effort, as upbeat entertainments), which were only slightly affected by the postwar revelation of the full extent of Nazi atrocities.

If a few directors had the courage to tackle the highly uncommercial subject of concentration camps (e.g. Stanley Kramer in *Judgment at Nuremberg*, 1961), for the majority – as for many an ex-soldier who had enjoyed a 'good' war – they were oddly detachable from the main event. Nothing in the fairly unproblematic heroics of a film like J. Lee Thompson's *The Guns of Navarone* (1961), to take one example from among hundreds, suggested that its fictional fortress belonged to the same war that had spawned Lidice and Auschwitz.

As mentioned above, the Second World War movie soon became almost a separate genre, encompassing without too much strain such varied approaches as the farcical (Spielberg's *1941*), satirical (*Catch-22*), black comedy (Lubitsch's *To Be Or Not To Be*), musical (the 1944 version of *The Desert Song*), romantic (Vincente Minnelli's remake of *The Four Horsemen of the Apocalypse*), adventure (*The Great Escape*), psychological (*The Young Lions*), melodramatic (*From Here to Eternity*), sentimental (*Mrs Miniver*), biographical (*Patton*), semi-documentary (*Tora! Tora! Tora!*) and even, though any such film would tend to be made long after hostilities had ended, pacifist (notably, David Lean's *The Bridge on the River Kwai*, 1957, from Pierre Boulle's novel). On the other hand, John Huston's magnificent and acutely distressing *Let There Be Light*, a documentary on the psychological rehabilitation of shell-shocked GIs, was for many years banned from public exhibition by the War Department, which had commissioned it back in 1946. Another of Huston's documentaries, *The Battle of San Pietro* (1945), focusing on the struggle of one infantry division for a key Italian village, was cut by a third because of its allegedly ambivalent attitude towards the army's morale, a trace of which may still be found in the suggestion of its commentary (spoken by the director himself) that there were to be 'many more San Pietros, a thousand more, and many of those you see here alive will die'. Likewise, certain sequences of Delmer Daves's excellent *Pride of the Marines* (1945), which dealt with the difficult readjustment to civilian life of a blinded Marine (John

Garfield), were so painfully realistic and the subject as a whole so grim that the Warner Bros. publicity department attempted to mislead the public with a poster suggesting some bright romantic comedy!

In some respects – precisely those which made it so conducive to cinematic re-enactment – the Second World War was rather uncharacteristic of modern warfare. Good and evil appeared encased in the simple black-and-white symmetries of a chessboard; and advances in military technology permitted a liberty of movement which totally reversed the helpless stalemate of the First World War without the attendant frustration, as would later be the case in Vietnam, of sitting on a useless pile of nuclear weaponry while getting bogged down in a kind of tactical fighting for which the enemy was far better equipped. Such is the period's enduring popularity – extending to novels, TV shows, comic strips, toys, fashions, even the perverse boom in Nazi memorabilia – that, if a war movie is mentioned, we immediately suppose it to be about the Second World War. In spite of concentration camps, the saturation bombing of Dresden and Coventry, and atomic razing of Hiroshima and Nagasaki, the thought of it seems to conjure up no especial horrors in the average person's mind. Perhaps conditioned by countless celebrations of American derring-do, British muddling through, French cunning and, for comic relief, Italian incompetence, succeeding generations have been anaesthetised to its more terrifying realities. Like the western, it has become an unquenchable source of myths, sustained by its own set of endearingly predictable stereotypes: Gestapo officers with black leather trench coats and sinister granny glasses, tight-lipped RAF commanders briefing their men with a brisk 'Some of you may not come back alive . . .', etc. And most dramatisations of the Second World War bear as much resemblance to the real event as most westerns do to the real Old West.

As long as the war was being waged in Europe, Hollywood could revel shamelessly in the opportunities it provided for high adventure, but its chronic incapacity to come to terms with defeat, its need to disguise it rather than (like the British at Dunkirk) glory in it, proved a major stumbling block to filming the Pacific war. Though the degree to which Pearl Harbor might be considered a 'victory' for the Japanese was compromised by their failure to officialise the assault by declaring war in advance, there could be no question that it was a defeat for the United States. Within ninety minutes, eight battleships, three light cruisers and four miscellaneous vessels had been sunk or seriously damaged and almost two hundred aeroplanes, more than half of America's air power on the island, had been destroyed. In addition, 2,400 Americans were killed and about as many again were injured, a casualty list whose public release was long delayed to avert a national panic. Roosevelt instantly declared war, but American momentum had suffered a crucial setback and a series of military reverses followed in Bataan, Corregidor and Wake Island.

This unnerving start to the war had a powerfully galvanising effect on Middle American prejudices. Southern California, for instance, discovered to its horror that it had been harbouring a considerable Japanese-American population, both Issei (first generation) and Nisei (their offspring), who were, unfortunately for them, infallibly detectable in any crowd. All at once they found themselves the target of homegrown retaliation. Apart from the petty harassment that they had to endure from some native-born Americans and ethnic minorities not implicated by association in the country's disgrace – restaurants refusing to serve them, insurance policies summarily cancelled – a warrant was issued by Earl Warren, the reputedly liberal Attorney-General of California, authorising the round-up of such 'aliens' and their transportation to other states. Opposition to these measures was duly made by the American Civil Liberties Union but proved totally ineffective. And henceforth 'Japs' were to be portrayed in war movies as congenitally malevolent beings only a few rungs up the biological scale from vermin, their traditional facial inscrutability transformed by heavy underlighting into a cruel mask of atheistic inhumanity. Even their inexplicable indifference to the virginal charms of American womanhood – so untypical of 'the enemy' – somehow counted as a point against them.

Their image was more or less fixed for the next thirty years (almost the only sympathetic portrayals of Japanese in the American cinema of the period were by Occidentals: Marlon Brando's interpreter in Daniel Mann's *The Teahouse of the August Moon* and

Alec Guinness's businessman in Mervyn LeRoy's *A Majority of One*)
and would moreover serve indiscriminately for Koreans, Chinese
and, in a few notorious instances, Vietnamese. In Leo McCarey's
abysmal *Satan Never Sleeps* (1962), a ludicrously implausible melodrama of the tribulations besetting American missionaries in the
Far East, the Chinese protagonist is grossly caricatured so long as
he remains a rabid Communist. Turned capitalist in embryo after
a lightning conversion, he miraculously becomes (in McCarey's
mind, at least) natural, likeable and, in short, a regular guy.

One of the consequences of South-East Asia's progressive Com-
munisation from the forties to the seventies has been, in a certain
knee-jerk mentality, the sublimation of ideology by race, the determination to identify Communism and its spread exclusively with
'barbaric' Asian peoples (among which, of course, are included the
Russians). In fact, the attitude of right-minded Americans toward
Communism has always been fundamentally *racist* in nature,
fuelled by rhetoric no less hysterical in its irrationality than the
crassest anti-black or anti-Semitic rabble-rousing. If, in the mythology of the Ku Klux Klan, Communists have never quite chal-
lenged the supremacy of blacks as embodiments of 'racial'
degeneracy, it can only be because the latter are rather more in
evidence in the Deep South. For Commie-haters, however, the
abusive term 'red' is conveniently colour-orientated, while the
even more derisory 'pinko' (to designate fellow-travellers) evokes
the ambiguous status of the half-caste. Polemical literature on the
subject (in particular, the speeches of the Republican Party's lunatic
fringe) has always tended to portray Communism as a plague, a
mysteriously contagious malady which, having been allowed to
attain epidemic proportions over much of the globe (the celebrated
'domino theory'), must at all costs be halted before it contaminates
healthy Americans. So, just as Communist states make it hard for
their citizens to get out, the United States makes it hard for a
Communist to get in. Visitors risk having their visas annulled if
suspected of 'smuggling in' the unspeakable ideology.

But ideology is precisely what has been drained from such demagoguery. What the majority of Americans hold in abhorrence is
less the theoretical foundations of Marxism-Leninism, of which they
are largely ignorant, than its most disheartening social realities: the

15

Gulags, of course, but also, and perhaps more keenly, the terrifying drabness of life behind the Iron Curtain, the shortage of material goods, *the absence of neon*. Both capitalism and Communism impinge on the American psyche in terms of hardware: on the one hand, the kind of glossy consumerism that is by its very nature conspicuous; on the other, those ghastly East Berlin streets just glimpsed beyond the Brandenburg Gate. Never has the grass seemed greener on *this* side of the fence.

And when, with the Korean War, this irrational fear was grafted on to another – the deep-seated dread of marauding, mosquito-like hordes of Asians – it was evident that paranoia would soon have a whole nation in its clammy grip.

The outbreak of hostilities in Korea was, of course, preceded by an extended period of 'phoney war' with global Communism. After Germany's surrender in 1945 the Soviet Army, entrenched halfway across Europe, had remained more or less on a war footing, with emphasis in the current Five Year Plan abruptly switched from consumer goods back to armaments; in a famous speech in Fulton, Missouri, Churchill coined the term 'Iron Curtain'; and the Cold War may be said to have been declared in February 1947, when Truman received the backing of Congress to send 400 million dollars' worth of economic and military aid to Greece and Turkey, countries devastated by the war and threatening to 'go over' to the other side. As Communism, however, was widely perceived as something so elusive, formless and insidious that, despite the Truman administration's increasingly hawkish foreign policy, it might yet worm its way into the national consciousness, this war had to be fought no less vigilantly on the domestic front.

The McCarthy period, the trials and hearings, the Friendly and Unfriendly Witnesses, the apotheosis of the Fifth Amendment, have all been sufficiently, even exhaustively, documented in case-studies and memoirs not to need recounting here. But though, in relation to the lasting historical significance of the larger context, undue attention has perhaps been paid to the fate of the 'Hollywood Ten' – directors and screenwriters who refused to bow under pressure and perjure themselves – the publicity which their cases received is central to an understanding of the cagily obeisant posture adopted by most studio moguls at the time. If from no other source, this can be gauged from the profound embarrassment of Samuel Goldwyn at having produced, back in 1943 when the United States and the Soviet Union enjoyed an uneasy alliance, a Lillian Hellman-scripted, pro-Russia movie, *The North Star* (directed by the decidedly versatile Lewis Milestone, it was later shorn of twenty-three minutes, to 'de-emphasise' earlier solidarity with the USSR, and retitled *Armored Attack*), and of MGM at having financed an idiotic melodrama directed by Gregory Ratoff in the following year, *Song of Russia*, whose harmless iconography was, in any case, far more indebted to a pre-Soviet mythology of balalaikas, lyrical embraces in cornfields and the opening chords of Tchaikovsky's First Piano Concerto.

When war broke out in Korea, therefore, Hollywood producers would tread an exceptionally wary path, conscious that shifting allegiances might easily cause the most candidly patriotic effort subsequently to rebound in their faces. Not that there was any shortage of product – war has traditionally been good news for both film production and attendances – but few major directors cared to venture into such uncharted, booby-trapped territory. (To be sure, Ford, as later for Vietnam, made a documentary, *This is Korea!*, in 1951.) Also, in view of the undiminished favour enjoyed by Second World War movies, the industry was loath to become enmeshed in a whole new war, one for which it, like the rest of the nation, had been totally unprepared. This caution was redoubled when, in spite of General MacArthur's notoriously rash forecast (seemingly as old as war itself) that it would all be over by Christmas, the American forces were utterly trounced by the Koreans in the first two months of fighting. Or when, with MacArthur's controversial dismissal by Truman in the dark winter of 1950–1, the war lost the only larger-than-life 'hero' it could ever lay claim to.

If the very first Korean War movie, Samuel Fuller's *The Steel Helmet* (shot largely in Hollywood's Griffith Park on a budget of just over 100,000 dollars), had all the rough edges of Poverty Row cheeseparing, it benefited at least from Fuller's own brand of demonic energy and refreshing lack of hypocrisy. (Fuller is a right-wing maverick and doesn't care who knows it.) Thereafter, alas, it was downhill most of the way. An indifferent string of productions followed, dealing with the war either literally (the best of these being again by Fuller, *Fixed Bayonets*, 1951, in which a very youthful James Dean may be glimpsed) or metaphorically (as with the weird if not quite wonderful science-fiction allegory *Red Planet Mars*, directed by Harry Horner in 1952), all of which will have to be crammed into the same tight footnote to cinema history.

What is interesting about them, however, especially with regard to the first halting attempts to chronicle America's involvement in Indochina, is that Hollywood seems to have proceeded on the assumption that Korea was merely a coda to the Second World War, whereas it can now be seen as a full-scale dress rehearsal for Vietnam. Here, as would later happen, American soldiers were fighting a semi-guerilla army in a remote country and for a dubious cause: the immediate welfare of the United States had not been and could not conceivably be imperilled by North Korea. Here, too, they would find themselves gatecrashing a local conflict with North pitted against South. Here, too, atrocities relating to the treatment of prisoners or civilians suspected of sheltering the enemy would be recorded on both sides. And, finally, to paraphrase MacArthur's famous epitaph for old soldiers, this war, like the one to come, never actually *ended*, it just faded away in inconclusive peace talks and a solution with which no one was satisfied.

Perhaps for this reason American opinion has never quite come to grips with the meaning of Korea: as an event, it has remained *illegible*. If Vietnam was to polarise sympathies to such a degree that even the most skull-numbing adventure movies were obliged to pay lip service to at least some of the issues at stake (e.g. David Janssen's 'liberal' journalist in *The Green Berets*), then Korea, except for those directly involved, passed as in a bad dream, one not sufficiently nightmarish to awaken the sleeper. And Hollywood both fostered and slavishly reflected this indifference by turning out a ragbag of duds which, if the spectator half-closed his eyes, could well be mistaken for being about the Second World War. Indeed, the best-known film to be set in Korea is undoubtedly Robert Altman's *M*A*S*H* (1969), whose spaced-out irreverence and callously anarchistic high jinks make it about Vietnam in all but place-names.

The real Vietnam had, on film, a singularly undistinguished

prehistory: a handful of mostly long-forgotten B-movie titles, *A Yank in Indo-China*, *A Yank in Viet-Nam* (how that hyphen dates it!), *Operation C.I.A.* and the regulation shocker from Samuel Fuller, *China Gate*. Considerably more ambitious than the two *Yanks* were a duo of *Americans*: Joseph L. Mankiewicz's *The Quiet American* (1958), which 'revised' Graham Greene's novel by transforming its protagonist (not so ironically played by the Second World War's 'most decorated soldier', Audie Murphy) from a dangerous *naif* into a Communist-betrayed innocent; and George Englund's *The Ugly American* (1963, from the novel by William J. Lederer and Eugene Burdick), a muddled political tract set a trifle conspicuously in a mythical South-East Asian state named Sarkhan and remembered only, if at all, for Marlon Brando as its American ambassador in natty striped pants, silk topper and Ronald Colman moustache.

The war itself, when it had finally been officially conceded that there was one, appeared to offer unlimited opportunities to the film-maker: the pacifist slant of the First World War, the high adventure of the Second World War, the Communist conspiracy of Korea, even a dramatically troubled aftermath recalling that of the Civil War (for this was also a civil war, no less in the United States than in Vietnam, with Kent State, perhaps, as a domestic My Lai). And yet, as I hope to show, Hollywood at first did not simply pass the buck, it endeavoured to bury it.

— Chapter 2 —

GUTS 'N' GLORY

There is a scene in *Holocaust*, a television dramatisation of the
Hitlerian 'final solution', in which the young Jewish hero, concealed in a ditch, is witness to the massacre of 40,000 of his fellow
concentration camp internees. The series had its fair share of both
defenders and detractors (the English dramatist and critic Dennis
Potter referred contemptuously to 'Jews being boiled down into
soap opera'), but few commentators paused to reflect on the un-
wieldy logistics of genocide, even when considered solely in filmic
terms. How, for a start, does one actually depict the killing of 40,000
people? Assuming that one actually had at one's disposal a cast of
40,000 (an improbable eventuality), how would one simulate their
massacre without either boring the spectator, not exactly unused
to small-screen violence, or encouraging him into a kind of vicarious
complicity with the thrilling excesses of Nazi sadism? And if one
cannot assemble such a cast, how then does one convey the
enormity of the crime?

The quite reasonable solution arrived at by the show's writers
and director was: through the eyes of an observer. But here, too,
an unforeseeable problem of dramatic representation arises. On
what resources of talent and experience can an actor call, be he
the world's greatest, in order to register horror so profound as to be
commensurate with its supposed object? In this particular episode of
Holocaust the actor in question proved competent enough – the
pupils of his eyes dilated convincingly, his mouth gaped – but in
no way could he be said to have 'risen to the occasion' of the
atrocity. Had he been watching an automobile accident, the assassination of a President or an oversized primate scaling the Empire
State Building with a hysterical blonde clutched to its chest, his
facial reaction would not have been appreciably different. Like the

threat of nuclear extinction, however, Nazi death camps offer such a difference in *degree* of horror from anything that preceded them that it has become almost a difference in *kind*. What is therefore required of such fiction-producing factories as television and Hollywood, when dealing with such subject-matter, is that they contrive to distance themselves not only from the material but also from their own time-honoured systems of narrative codes. Otherwise, the results will only be grotesque: though the idea of such light comedians as Cary Grant and Ginger Rogers at large in war-ravaged Europe may be, within the Hollywood context, acceptable enough, their presence in a concentration camp, as in Leo McCarey's *Once Upon a Honeymoon*, is deeply offensive – or would be if it weren't so foolish. (In fairness to the film, it should be noted that in 1942, when it was made, the term 'concentration camp' had yet to acquire genocidal connotations.)

Since it was too much to hope that the first Vietnam-related movies would subject the confused political background of the war to any real scrutiny or analysis, criticising them for failing to do so is a futile exercise. Not that a movie like *The Green Berets* is apolitical. On the contrary, it assumes its Neanderthal hawkish stance far less guardedly than most 'liberal' movies, whether or not about Vietnam, have assumed theirs. Moreover, it would be silly to write off John Wayne, as some apologists have managed to do, as a political innocent. The ignorance of these so-called 'innocents' has a habit of steering them straight into the camp of extreme reaction; and, for a hard-liner, almost all of the American cinema must be accounted as reactionary, with a few of its greatest directors – Griffith, Ford, Vidor, Capra, Fuller – flagrantly so.

What is so repugnant about *The Green Berets* is not its politics (nor even, politics apart, its total ineptitude purely as an adventure war movie) but the fact that, in spite of overwhelming evidence to the contrary, evidence that by the late sixties had already filtered through to the United States, its makers were still determined to reduce Vietnam to simple-minded Manichaean antitheses: good guys versus bad guys, cowboys versus Indians, white men versus 'natives'. As Michael Wayne, the film's producer and its star's son, blandly put it to an interviewer from *Variety*, 'Maybe we shouldn't have destroyed all those Indians, but when you are making a picture, the Indians are the bad guys.' Why, naturally. No one – least of all, anyone who works there – expects Hollywood to learn a lesson from the past. And the myths and codes of popular fiction exert a powerful hold on the imagination, even if the intellect struggles to expel them: many a movie buff with irreproachable opinions on race nevertheless continues to harbour a secret preference for the stereotypical black servants and Pullman car attendants of thirties screwball comedies – i.e. when Negroes 'knew their place' – over their emancipation in the sixties into aggressive leading roles. But the offence of Wayne and Son proved a dual one: not only did their movie provide a tritely simplified, almost *nostalgic*, reading of what was in reality shot through with self-recriminations and self-exonerations, prejudice and sheer bad faith, they attempted to impose such a reading while the war was still going on.

Consider, in *The Green Berets*, an atrocity tale recounted by the tough-named Colonel Mike Kirby (John Wayne). A journalist from what we gather is a liberal newspaper, George Beckworth (David Janssen), has flown out to Vietnam to 'see for himself' after being chided by Kirby at a press conference for judging events from a comfortable position of Stateside semi-ignorance. ('Hard to talk to anyone about this country until they've been over and seen it.') A number of little things like bamboo traps have chipped away at the rigour of Beckworth's antiwar stand (that he is in the film at all has, of course, nothing to do with objectivity and everything to do with his eventual and inevitable conversion), but the incident that really clinches matters involves, as always, a child. Beckworth had befriended the granddaughter of a Montagnard village headman and presented her with a medallion. Later, revisiting the village with Kirby, he discovers that the headman has been murdered by the Viet Cong and the little girl raped (or rather, in the movie's coy patois, 'abused') by five of them. And, as though this gangbang were not in itself sufficiently horrible, Kirby immediately switches to hard-sell by describing in gory detail to the shattered Beckworth a similar incident when a chieftain's wife was 'abused' by no fewer than *forty* Viet Cong.

Here we are again in the shadowy area of logistics, though the basic problem is not quite the same as *Holocaust*'s: not how you *film*

22

an atrocity, but how you *invent* one. Why, for instance, forty? Was thirty considered too few? A tentatively suggested sixty laughed out of the writers' room? Or did the calculation proceed along the lines of an auction, with bids steadily rising until forty was settled on as a nice round figure, not so high as to become preposterous but high enough to justify a liberal's conversion to the cause? Though the My Lai revelations were still to come, one is almost tempted to believe that the ante was upped so that American rapine, in the unlikely event of its existing at all, would be vindicated in advance by the comparison.

In a way, of course, this ploy would parallel the whole course of the war itself (viewed from the American side) towards *escalation*, with an inflation of interests leading inexorably to a corresponding inflation of bloodshed; and even if the movie never burdens its clichéd narrative with so much as an atom of scepticism (except in so far as Beckworth is concerned), its pathetic attempts to contain an event as complex as Vietnam within genre structures that once seemed indestructible has lent it a kind of documentary value – and, incidentally, made it more watchable today than in 1968. One of the American cinema's strengths has always been its ability to disarm direct ideological criticism of a character's more dubious motives and actions by the behavioural charm of the performer portraying him. With its comic relief 'scrounger' (Jim Hutton), hardboiled NCO (Aldo Ray), glamorous Oriental spy (Irene Tsu), sensitive black (Raymond St Jacques) and cute local orphan, *The Green Berets* evidently hoped to make the old magic work for it, too. But this time something has gone seriously awry.

Take Sgt Provo (played by the aptly named Luke Askew). Early in the film, before the unit is shipped out to Vietnam, Provo volunteers for front-line duty as 'I'd like to get orientated to the critical area'. (As we shall see, the English language is made quite a meal of by everyone in this movie.) Since Kirby is advised by an aide that Provo is a good soldier, he is duly assigned and dies a hero's death. Now it is wellnigh impossible to watch *The Green Berets* free of bias, but a critic especially must strive to keep an open mind. While viewing the movie, however, it becomes difficult not to believe that the zombielike Provo, with his shorn head, granite features and robotised speech patterns, is being played as a

23

psychopath or, at the very least, a severely disturbed war-lover; that, in the context, he is the token representative (as Beckworth of liberalism) of a marginal but, alas, inescapable element of militarism and will eventually receive his come-uppance in combat. Not a bit of it: it seems he is intended to be taken at face value, even offering with his death the choicest example of the film's elephantine forays into comedy. Provo is obsessively concerned with how his name would sound on a memorial. 'Provo's Barracks, Provo's Commissary. Ya see what I mean – it just don't sing.' As he lies dying, he whispers a last request to Kirby, who commissions a sign that reads 'Provo's Privy', declaring gruffly, 'It sings.'

In a Second World War movie this might conceivably have worked. With William Bendix or Jack Carson as Provo, however implausible or antipathetic the character's eagerness to get to the front, one would probably have accepted it as a genre convention. Here, as with the Bilko-ish scrounger Petersen, whose casual looting around the base is uneasily reminiscent of larger-scale corruption in South Vietnam, the stereotype has simply ceased to function. Equally, when the orphan Hamchunk first endears himself to the audience by sending Petersen sprawling over a trip wire, we have the uncomfortable (and no doubt unintended) impression that he will naturally graduate to playing with just the kind of bamboo trap that skewers Petersen in the end.

It is with the film's star, though, that the gap between intention and realisation widens to become virtually unbridgeable. Unlike Bogart, whose brand of cynical idealism made him the (posthumous) idol of a whole generation of students and middle-class youths, Wayne was a blue-collar hero, the defender of traditional American values and sworn enemy of intellectuals, Communists and (what amounted to the same thing) perverts. Particularly during the turbulent sixties and seventies his appeal to educated young people tended to atrophy the moment they enrolled in college. This disaffection was nevertheless tempered by regular TV exposure to a career that could be considered distinguished by any standards (numerous films by Ford, Hawks, Wellman and Walsh) and by a grudging respect for the mythic figure he seemed to cut with such easy masculine grace and good humour. Many of the student radicals who despised Wayne's politics, his reprehensible political cronies and his deplorable public pronouncements (in a *Playboy* interview: 'I've directed two pictures and I gave the blacks their proper position. I had a black slave in *The Alamo*, and I had the correct number of blacks in *The Green Berets*') retained a sneaking affection for the guts 'n' glory movies on which they had been weaned, so to speak, which had comprised the staple Saturday matinée fare in the neighbourhood fleapits of their childhood, with the white screen serving as a kind of security blanket. Rare was the spectator capable of distinguishing actor from role and who, armed with this distinction (which in the latter, overtly ideological stage of Wayne's career was to become an increasingly fine one), could lace his enjoyment with irony, smugly keeping his distance from some more artless fan beside him. (Sadly, the elevation of Wayne to the status of national myth, consecrated by an Oscar in 1969 for his performance in Henry Hathaway's western *True Grit*, came at the end of his life when a series of tiresome tic-ridden characterisations, all crust and no bread, had contrived to obscure his very real abilities.)

That his film alienated these smart-alecky college kids once and for all was surely of no consequence to Wayne; but even among his more unconditional admirers a certain embarrassment was felt. Since he had never bothered to keep his political sympathies to himself, it came as no surprise that *The Green Berets* turned out so fanatically, illiberally hawkish. It was the very folly of his making a Vietnam movie in the first place that was hard to forgive, as though he had really believed all those frontiersman myths about the taming of the Old West, as though he had never once stopped to wonder, with the offhand shrug of his son, whether 'maybe we shouldn't have destroyed all those Indians'. The Indians, it appears, were still to be typecast as the bad guys.

Nor were Wayne and his screenwriter James Lee Barrett (the film was based on a novel of the same name by Robin Moore) very subtle in the way they went about forging a link between Monument Valley (an Arizona beauty spot at which, before John Ford's camera crew arrived, no particularly memorable event in American history had occurred) and the jungles of South Vietnam. The movie's credit-titles unroll to the accompaniment of a would-be stirring march tune 'The Brave Men of the Green Beret'; over the entrance to a Special Forces outpost is a wooden ranch-style sign-post reading 'Dodge City' (admittedly, this kind of jokey nomenclature was common practice during the war); when he and his men are forced to evacuate the camp after prolonged (and seemingly successful) attacks by the Viet Cong, Kirby merely radios for an air strike, which arrives *à la* 1st Cavalry to polish off the intruders in a matter of minutes; there is Kirby's almost too familiar line 'out here, due process is a bullet'; and the last scene is a final, quietly heart-tugging exchange at sunset between Kirby and Hamchunk, now doubly orphaned by the death of his mentor, Petersen, and obviously doomed to become the regimental mascot. What makes these narrative trappings lodge so securely in the gullet is in part the movie's unerring awfulness; but if Ford, say, had directed it (not an impossible hypothesis, unfortunately), the result might have been even more revolting.

The Green Berets, however, is too inept to be effective, let alone dangerous. It is the film of an old, old man; and the sight of a sexagenarian John Wayne cavorting about the undergrowth in made-to-measure battle fatigues is not one calculated to strike terror in the hearts of the enemy – or the antiwar movement. All the flaws of his ageing physique are cruelly exposed by what would seem to be a pitiful attempt to recapture his youth: the rolling hips, the enormous, top-heavy frame precariously perched on small, remarkably dainty feet, the craggy, weatherbeaten features topped by an implausible toupée. Age and costume apart, the role could have been patched together from a montage of his past appearances, so derivative is every last gesture, every drawling syllable, every quizzical arch of the eyebrow. There is something slightly indecent in his thus personifying so barefacedly the schism of generations that was one of the war's most durable legacies: an old man playing a young man's game, one which many young men were no longer prepared to play. And one is struck by the fact that, except for the just middle-aged Jim Hutton (a refugee from sixties beach party movies), he has surrounded himself by actors hardly less ancient than himself: as Kirby's superior, the bloated Bruce Cabot (who once – a long, long time ago – rescued Fay Wray from the extrovert embrace of King Kong); and bull-faced Aldo Ray hamming it up as the truculent Oirish-American Sgt Muldoon. As for the 'correct number' of blacks, that would appear to be one, on the evidence of the film's speaking parts at least: Raymond St Jacques, the soulful embodiment of Uncle Tomism (or Uncle Samism).

To be sure, one should not forget the representative of youthful unrest, David Janssen. In 1968 the actor Janssen was (and looked) thirty-eight, an age when the opinions of crusading journalists tend to be fully formed and impervious to the kind of abrupt ideological conversion that Beckworth undergoes in the movie, his radical chic finding a none too subtle sartorial equivalence in the Jungle Jim safari outfit he sports on arrival in Vietnam, just as his change of heart is expressed through a corresponding change of costume: he is soon in regulation fatigues. But, having served his purpose by showing up the protest movement to be founded on sheer blinkered ignorance (a premise contradicted by the testimony of numerous vets who returned from 'over there' only strengthened in their conviction that the American presence was both useless and criminal), he is more or less dispensed with by the narrative, which settles down to do its own war movie thing.

Even so, in view of the sluggishly routine combat sequences (which aren't, even if they look like, stock shots) and nonsensical plot thickenings with the aforementioned glamorous spy (which, wherever one's sympathies lie, have absolutely *nothing* to do with any reality of the war), much the most interesting battle being waged is that against the forces of scepticism – as represented, precisely, by Beckworth. And since, in lieu of a clear statement of eventual victory, *The Green Berets* is obliged to conclude with no more than Kirby's unctuously phrased claim that South Vietnam would one day triumph over the Communist threat, it is all the more imperative that a victory (if 'only' a moral one) be recorded against the peaceniks. The Green Berets, at the centre of both conflicts, must therefore prove themselves as nifty with words as with mere weapons.

When conversing among themselves, they employ a macho army rhetoric so elementary as to become almost self-parodic. E.g. ARVN colonel to Kirby: 'We build many camps, clobber many VC. Affirmative?' Kirby: 'Affirmative.' And he adds: 'I like the way you talk.' *I like the way you talk.* Here's cultural imperialism with a vengeance. It is normal, one supposes, for the South Vietnamese to speak in

English; in both a military and an exclusively cinematic context it would raise awkward problems of communication if they didn't. But the infantile slang of 'clobber' and hideous militarese of 'affirmative'? Did the ARVN really talk like that? Are we really supposed to like it? Affirmative, or so it would seem.

When handling civilians and heretics, however, these same roughneck servicemen are transformed into smooth, even glib debaters, well versed in dialectics and oozing quiet, long-suffering dignity from every pore, as is evident in the very first scene.

The movie opens in the USA at the John F. Kennedy Center for Special Warfare, Fort Bragg, North Carolina. A public demonstration of the training and qualities required of the Special Forces is in progress. The first words we hear are disconcertingly spoken in German: a unit leader, identifying himself and his mission, displays this apparently irrelevant gift for European languages to emphasise the truly international role being played by the Green Berets (or maybe just in the hope of distracting his listeners' attention from more tropical and topical parts of the globe). When a number of these leaders have presented themselves in the same fashion (one of them bizarrely boasting a working knowledge of *English*), a question period follows, emceed by Sgt Muldoon. The first question comes from a reporter seated in the front row and it's a biggie: 'Why is the United States waging this useless war?' But Muldoon, a hard man to faze, is not about to give away any secrets: 'A soldier goes where he is told to go, fights where he is told to fight.' Touché.

Soon questions of the same type follow thick and fast, with no one any longer terribly interested in the Green Berets' proficiency in German or Norwegian. Beckworth to McGee (Raymond St Jacques): 'Do you agree with that, Sgt McGee? That the Green Beret is just a military robot with no personal feelings?' Muldoon seethes in the background. But Beckworth has made a serious tactical error in his choice of interlocutor; McGee has 'personal feelings' practically tattooed on his forehead: 'Let me put it in terms we can all understand. . . . If this same thing happened in the United States, every mayor in every city would be murdered. Every teacher . . . every professor . . . every Senator . . . every member of the House of Representatives . . . and their families. . . . But in spite of this, there's always some little fellow out there willing to stand up and take the place of those who've been decimated. They need us . . . and they want us.'

Housewife: 'It's strange that we never read of this in the newspapers.'

Muldoon: 'Well, that's newspapers for you, ma'am – you could fill volumes with what you *don't* read in them.' Laughter, even from the press in the front row.

Beckworth, somewhat miffed that all the witty repartee seems to be coming from the other side: 'That's sometimes very true, Sergeant. But how do you know we should be fighting for this present government? They've had no free elections. They have no constitution. Six months ago, a committee was appointed to form a constitution – still no constitution.'

Whereupon Beckworth, the audience and the camera focus on Muldoon, who is rapidly shaping up into *the* spokesman on American foreign policy. He clears his throat. 'The school I went to taught us that the thirteen colonies, with proper and educated leadership, all with the same goal in mind, after the Revolutionary War, took from 1776 to 1787, eleven years of peaceful effort, before they came up with a paper that all thirteen colonies could sign.' Pause. 'Our present Constitution.'

It is easy to mock the crude didacticism of this scene, which is really in no need of ironic editorial comment. But since later Vietnam movies – in particular, Michael Cimino's *The Deer Hunter* – will use the same basic arguments, even if cloaking them in a calculated and hypocritical ambiguity, it might be useful to examine the mechanism at its most rudimentary.

Clearly, the makers of *The Green Berets* saw McGee's 'Let me put it in terms we can all understand' as their own primary task. This was to be no ordinary war movie. It had a *message*. But, with hindsight, McGee's phrase has unwittingly acquired an emblematic value: American involvement in Vietnam can be reduced to 'terms we all understand' only if we adopt the ignorant, culture-bound view of history that was its root cause in the first place. After all, traditional westerns may fairly claim to have put nineteenth-century American history in a perspective that everyone, even infants, could 'understand'. The Warner Bros. gangster movie cycle, albeit with greater equivocation, put the period of Depression and Prohibition in terms that everyone could thrill to. Hollywood has always traded in the most artless kind of myths, consistently managing to palm them off on the same paying customers who would scorn such shoddy wares if offered them in literature or the theatre. Its advantage (one it has never been reluctant to exploit) is that the myth-makers are generally at work before the historians. When the fullest implications of an event have finally begun to sink into the national consciousness (as, let us say, with the Indian wars), there already exists an established canon of much-loved movies whose very manipulation of historical accuracy is excused and justified *in extremis*, as having contributed an extra layer of sociological significance.

What changed with Vietnam is that, for the first time since the Civil War (a subject treated by Hollywood with perhaps surprising sensitivity), the nation found itself denied the reassurance of a broad consensus of opinion: decisions of urgent matter were openly, violently contested – in the streets, on campuses – as they were being taken; history, as never before, was revised as it was being made. *The Green Berets* attempts to mythologise its heroes – the credit titles ballad, 'Big' Mike Kirby, the climactic sunset – but the myths are stillborn.

The film's overall drift is patent, of course, but in that first sequence a number of precise points are being made, as an 'action replay' will demonstrate.

1. The Green Berets never query or reflect upon the orders they receive: a soldier's job is to obey. In a period of even limited war there can therefore be no excuse for draft dodgers or deserters.

2. They are not, however, insensitive to human suffering, particularly where 'little fellows' are involved. The Viet Cong, buttressed by the vast ideological and military machine of world Communism (and the scene ends with Muldoon producing a cache of captured enemy armaments, of Chinese, Russian and East European provenance, presumably amassed for just such an occasion), do not qualify as 'little fellows'.

3. Given this evidence of massive material aid from the whole Communist bloc, the apparent imbalance of forces engaged in the war is deceptive. What the United States is really up against is

nothing less than, as Muldoon puts it, 'Communist domination of the world'.

4. It *is* America's business to be in South-East Asia, since the inhabitants 'need us and want us'.

5. If, however, the tribulations of a small, insignificant country thousands of miles away leave one uncaring, one should try to imagine a similar Communist insurrection within the United States, with the systematic liquidation of city mayors, teachers, etc. (a ludicrous analogy, invalidated by countless historical and geographical inequalities between the two countries, but one calculated to bring the war home, in both senses).

6. Don't believe everything you read in the newspapers.

7. To Beckworth's reasonable objection that the brutal Thieu regime might not after all prove to be the lesser of two evils, Muldoon offers the eccentric but attractive theory that South Vietnam is fighting for the same freedoms as the founding colonies in 1776 and that any delay in the country's democratisation only confirms its government's seriousness of purpose.

8. With American aid, South Vietnam will surely prevail.

There, in a nutshell, are the pro-war lobby's main articles of faith, as propounded by numerous political and military executives, Washington columnists and a significant portion of the electorate. A few random quotes will suffice as illustration.

General Curtis LeMay (quoted in David Halberstam's *The Best and the Brightest*): 'In the last thirty years we've lost Estonia. Latvia. Lithuania. Poland. Czechoslovakia. Hungary. Bulgaria. China . . .'

Cardinal Spellman in 1966: 'This war in Vietnam, I believe, is a war for civilization. . . . American troops are there for the defense, protection and salvation not only of our country, but I believe of civilization itself.'

Vice-President Agnew in 1972: The Vietnam War 'is perhaps the most moral act the United States ever performed'.

David Lawrence, editor of *U.S. News and World Report*, in 1966: 'What the United States is doing in Vietnam is the most significant example of philanthropy . . . that we have witnessed in our times.'

Future Presidential candidate Edward Kennedy in 1965: 'We have a commitment in South Vietnam' and we 'have to stand by our commitment'.

Senator Strom Thurmond in 1968: 'If we lose in Vietnam, before you know it the Communists would be up on the beaches of Hawaii.'

Major General Moshe Dayan of Israel in 1966: 'The American army as a whole . . . gets satisfaction out of every day it spends in Vietnam. . . . Most soldiers would volunteer for service in Vietnam if they were not posted there.'

Senator Thomas Dodd in 1967: 'If the Administration were to negotiate a settlement that paved the way for an early Communist take-over, then it will mean the total eclipse of America as a great nation and the beginning of the end of the entire free world.'

To do justice to the wilful ignorance that characterised most pronouncements as to the war's outcome made by the political and military Establishment during these dark years, however, would need a chapter of its own, and what follows is only a modest sampling.

Political columnist Joseph Alsop in 1961: 'The good guys have been coming out on top for once.'

Secretary of Defense Robert McNamara in 1965: 'We have stopped losing the war.'

Vice-President Hubert Humphrey in 1966: 'There can be no doubt of our ultimate success.'

General Maxwell Taylor in 1966: 'The Viet Cong will just peter out.'

Admiral John S. McCoin, Jr, Commander-in-Chief, Pacific, in 1969: 'The enemy is beaten.'

And political columnist Joseph Alsop once again in 1970: 'Victory has at last been won.'

As for the accusation often levelled against a partisan press that it deliberately misled its readers, it was very much part of the conventional wisdom of the period, though naturally not given much coverage in print. But it should be remembered that, long before the 'experts' began to temper their optimism (a cautious Gerald Ford in 1972: 'Time is on our side'), a good many ordinary citizens had come to doubt the value and necessity of prolonging American involvement in South-East Asia.

The movie's opening sequence is therefore not only a rather wordy piece of exposition to introduce the Beckworth character but an example of virtually undiluted propaganda (of a type rare in the American cinema), and an indirect measure of how important it was considered for the domestic market is the fact that it was cut from several European prints. Worth noting, too, is that *The Green Berets* is still the *only* Hollywood movie to have tackled the issues of the war head-on (even if with heavily loaded arguments) and from an ideological standpoint that it endorses without flinching (even if its anti-Communism is of the Pavlovian variety). Until quite recently, the few films to have focused on Vietnam from the antiwar angle and whose political discourse was not subservient to the same old apolitical priorities of heroism (for our boys) and human dignity (for the friendly natives) were either documentaries (e.g. Emile De Antonio's *In the Year of the Pig*, 1969, and Peter Davis's *Hearts and Minds*, 1974) or non-American (e.g. the French compendium film *Loin du Viêtnam*, 1967).

After losing game, set and match to the army, Beckworth approaches Kirby who, perhaps in deference to Muldoon, had remained standing on the sidelines throughout the preceding debate.

Beckworth: 'Colonel, your brainwashed sergeant didn't sell me.'

Kirby: 'Didn't sell you what?'

Beckworth: 'Didn't sell me on the idea that we should be in South-East Asia.'

Kirby: 'You ever been to South-East Asia?'

Beckworth: 'No, I haven't.'

Kirby: 'Huh!'

At which point the film, like Beckworth himself, visibly intrigued by that cathartic 'huh!', shifts to the combat zone (and the second unit to the state of Georgia for location shooting). As Petersen, screaming above the roar of the helicopter taking him into the Vietnamese hinterland, hopefully puts it: 'With joyous memories we leave the mystical city of Da Nang. What gay adventures lie ahead? Brother, this trip is gonna make LSD feel like aspirin.'

Wrong. It makes aspirin feel like LSD. For all that the movie's premise is that Vietnam the war can only be judged by someone who has been to Vietnam the country, its portrait of local conditions is geared to confirm the worst prejudices of Middle-American homebodies. Though screenwriter Barrett himself flew out to South

Vietnam for the purposes of research (and, according to Dan Wake-
field's *Supernation at Peace and War*, among the many things that
impressed him over there was the attitude expressed by one officer
who told him that 'These people don't want to be free, but by God,
we're going to *make* them free!' 'To me,' Barrett said, 'that's a new
and exciting concept'), the cursory and implausible results suggest
he might just as well have stayed in Beverly Hills watching old
Korean War movies on TV. The Viet Cong are depicted as a confused
horde of whirling dervishes, milling around the Green Beret strike
camp to minimal effect; the only one to stand out in a crowd being
a high-ranking general, a corrupt tyrant who lives it up in a
luxuriously appointed French colonial villa guarded by uniformed
thugs. As for the South Vietnamese, they are a different race
entirely: dogged allies displaying a faith in American goodwill so
unswerving that one would have to go back to the Liberation of
Paris in 1944 to find its equal.

The only example of Vietnamese culture we are permitted to see
(and whose 'defense, protection and salvation' is supposedly the
Green Berets' *raison d'être*) is an El Cheapo nightclub in Da Nang
which Kirby visits in company with his local counterpart, Colonel
Cai. Its floor show consists of a maudlin Parisian ballad sung by a
young woman in a shantung skirt; and at a nearby table sits Lin,
the Vietnamese Mata Hari ('Besides being one of our country's top
models, she could be most useful to the government'). Subsequently Lin will deploy her top model's charms as bait, in a raid
led jointly by Kirby and Cai, to kidnap the Viet Cong general, a
sequence which, though tediously predictable in its plotting, does
shed a brief light on the nation's overly developed sense of morality.
Lin is obliged to sleep with the general, a sacrifice (especially in
view of the fact that her father was murdered by the Viet Cong)
that nevertheless causes her to be ostracised by Cai, who happens
to be her cousin. It takes a moving little man-to-man speech from
Kirby to persuade Cai to welcome her back into the family bosom.

On the American side the narrative is hardly less sketchy. No
mention is made of napalm (except as a handy means of 'clearing'
the jungle), body counts, body bags, free-fire zones, search-and-
destroy missions, etc. The Green Berets, it is understood, fight by
the Queensberry Rules, all the more commendably in the face

of enemy methods as dastardly as bamboo booby-traps, which somehow come across as the ultimate in destructive weaponry. Though torture is used at one point in the interrogation of a VC fifth columnist, it is phlegmatically condoned by Kirby as a necessary evil to which, in any case, the Viet Cong are more than equal, as an outraged Beckworth is soon to discover for himself. Yet, in spite of its apparently non-committal but in fact wholeheartedly committed blandness vis-à-vis the horrors of the war, the film cannot disguise the fact that a military (and cinematic) mythos is going sour before our eyes. I doubt that it is only liberals who are disturbed by the zeal with which, at the 'Dodge City' outpost, Wayne calls upon the air force to 'move the jungle back' and provide him with 'a clear killing zone'; or by Aldo Ray's mischievous grin when, during the kidnap raid, he blows a bridge full of scurrying Viet Cong to kingdom come; or, in a different register, by the rather equivocal scene where Jim Hutton takes Hamchunk into his bed.

Even if the turgid green-and-brown tonality of Winston Hoch's cinematography makes the whole movie look as though it has been camouflaged, not once does one gain a sense of the lived experience of soldiers at war. The squad is the usual ethnic cross-section, boasting such names as Muldoon, Provo, Petersen, 'Doc' McGee, Jamison (a young lieutenant played by Wayne's son Patrick), MacDaniel and Kowalski. And, notwithstanding Petersen's fleeting reference to LSD and ambiguous use of the word 'trip', there is no hint here of the counterculture orientation toward drugs, rock music and the generalised subversion of authority that significantly altered the public image of the American army in the late sixties. But then, what need was there for the 'good guys' to change, since the enemy had so patently been preserved in amber, the swarthy amber complexion of all wily Orientals from Fu Manchu onwards?

For anyone who has ever mused on what it must feel like for a German or Japanese spectator to be confronted with a Hollywood war movie, seeing *The Green Berets* offers a close enough approximation. Viewed with hindsight, the morale-boosting optimism (if tinged with melancholy for the fallen Provo and Petersen) with which it intends to have us leave the cinema is dispiriting beyond words: one is tempted to interpret the lurid sunset against which Kirby declares to his newest 'recruit', Hamchunk, that 'You're what this war is all about' as the light at the end of the tunnel sinking definitively out of sight.

There is, too, this final exchange between Kirby and Beckworth:

Kirby: 'Whatyuh gonna say in that newspaper of yours?'

Beckworth: 'If I say what I feel, I may be out of a job.'

Kirby: 'We'll always give you one.'

Beckworth: 'I could do you more good with a typewriter.'

One can only speculate as to how the hapless Beckworth would fare in the seventies, a period when investigative journalism (thanks to such media superstars as Bernstein and Woodward, David Halberstam and the Washington muckraker Jack Anderson) was to become the most modish of professions.

In spite of the widespread and also widely publicised picketing of cinemas exhibiting *The Green Berets*, it turned out to be a solid commercial success, grossing more than eight million dollars in domestic returns alone. One should, however, avoid hasty conclusions. Since no direct causal link has ever been established between the political Zeitgeist and cinema attendances, these figures probably tell us more about the popularity of John Wayne than about the breadth of public support for the war. So total, for instance, was the identification of actor with role in Mark Rydell's *The Cowboys* (1972) that the film was actually distributed in France as *John Wayne et les cowboys*; and had *The Green Berets* not opened there, to utter indifference and contempt, in the aftermath of May 1968, it could well have been retitled *John Wayne et les Bérets Verts*. In short, it was very much Wayne's movie: as far as the industry was concerned, his involvement had put Vietnam on the map (even as it blasted it off). Which perhaps explains why, in spite of those eight million dollars, no major studio was willing to undertake another project set in Vietnam until well into the following decade.

But Wayne may after all have had an influence on the immediate course of Hollywood's treatment of the war. There was a vast youthful audience out there just waiting to be tapped. And *The Green Berets* had succeeded in mobilising that audience – if not to the point of bringing them into the cinemas, at least in getting them to stand outside in protest.

── Chapter 3 ──

HOME FRONT

A social historian with data entirely confined to film would be forgiven for surmising that young people, i.e. teenagers, constituted a relatively recent phenomenon, dating at most from the late fifties and early sixties. With rare exceptions, and though boasting every variety of child, Hollywood in the previous four decades had paid astonishingly scant attention to a generation that must have been statistically almost as numerous as it is today. Even the exceptions were deceptive. When, in Busby Berkeley's MGM musical *Babes in Arms* (1939), a youthful Mickey Rooney and Judy Garland decide to put on a show *'right here* – in the barn!', they were both seventeen. But, apart from the fact that the title number 'We're only babes in arms' is given a rather overpowering rendition by the kind of stocky baritone it is hard to imagine in any mother's arms, the very talent and exuberance of the performers, coupled with the innocence and enthusiasm of the characters they portray, were far too remote from all those agonising post-pubertal problems for any young moviegoer comfortably to identify with them.

Nothing could have been further removed from their innocuous capers, however, than the unrelieved torments of fifties movie adolescents, who all appeared to have attended Method acting courses in high school: with Laslo Benedek's *The Wild One* (1954) and Nicholas Ray's *Rebel Without a Cause* (1955) the sleepyhead stumblebum charisma of Brando, Dean *et al.* was unleashed on a startled world. Unlike Rooney and Garland, these young protagonists were intended for an equally young audience and not to indulge the older generation in wistful wish-fulfilment fantasies. Adolescence was depicted pimples and all, with the rocky road to manhood (girls were rarely more than 'girlfriends') abounding in such existential toll-gates as the automobile 'chicken run' in *Rebel*

Without a Cause and the 'loose woman' who, in Elia Kazan's *Splendor in the Grass* (1961), initiates Warren Beatty into the mysteries of carnal love.

These two strains, Rooney and Brando, converged to foster the explosion of movies for, about and on occasion by youth which marked the late sixties (often with the original iconography intact: the prototypical Hell's Angels of *The Wild One* were adopted as consciously assumed models for *Easy Rider*'s Peter Fonda and Dennis Hopper on their gleaming Harley Davidsons). The period also saw a relaxation of censorship, permitting themes of sex, drugs and radical politics to be more freely aired without at the same time subjecting them to the traditional Hays Code catch that conformity invariably triumph in the final reel.

The story has been told too often of how Hollywood, flushed with the mammoth box-office success of a few blockbuster musicals (most notably Robert Wise's *The Sound of Music* in 1965), embarked upon a misbegotten cycle of what were intended to be similar projects (e.g. Richard Fleischer's *Dr Dolittle*, Wise's *Star!* and Gene Kelly's *Hello, Dolly!*), which cost as much and earned far less, just as a relatively low-budget feature made by an untested actor-turned-director, Dennis Hopper's *Easy Rider* (1969), was raking in a fortune for its backers.

With the nonchalance of a tourist changing cable-cars in San Francisco, the major studios coolly proceeded to leap off one band-wagon visibly going nowhere fast on to another headed in the opposite direction. There followed a whole cluster of youth-orientated movies. And if most of these, too, proved commercial disasters, it was perhaps because the very barrage of product denied them the 'sleeper' cult status that had made *Easy Rider* so beguiling to its audience, the sense of a generation long excluded from proportional representation in the American cinema dis-covering and appropriating the movie as its own. Not only were the post-*Easy Rider* films much too aggressively angled at this new, moneyed section of the public, there were too many writers, producers and directors involved whose sole affinity with the subject-matter, unlike Hopper's, was an opportunistic one.

That said, it has to be admitted that *Easy Rider* itself, though indisputably one of the key Zeitgeist films of the sixties, is virtually unwatchable today. It tells of two young dropouts, Billy (Hopper) and Wyatt (Fonda), nicknamed 'Captain America', who sell a consignment of cocaine to a wealthy pusher near the Mexican border, stow the cash payment in Wyatt's fuel tank and set out across America on their custom-built motorcycles (the Harley Davidson became as emblematic of the period as the Hispano-Suiza automobile had been of the twenties), their only goal being to reach New Orleans in time for Mardi Gras. But their long hair, hippie garb and psychedelically daubed machines cause them to be refused by motels and attacked by a lynching party; a commune in New Mexico where they spend some time comes to grief through its members' urban ignorance of basic manual and agricultural skills; their experiment with acid in a New Orleans cemetery turns into a horrendously bad trip; and they both meet violent and pointless deaths.

What *is* intriguing about this See America First odyssey is that, for once, the movie's protagonists appear to derive as much sensual pleasure from the visual exploration of the landscapes they traverse (hauntingly if rather garishly shot by cinematographer Laszlo Kovaks) as, vicariously, does its audience. There, however, is the nub of the problem. Seeing, of course, is a function of the kind of vision one possesses rather than of what there is in front of one; Hopper's direction, unfortunately, never begins to articulate a coherent point of view. The bigoted redneck farmers, the lynching party, even the wan, weatherbeaten hippies have all been co-opted into embodying the moral bankruptcy of a country ready at the slightest provocation to explode into aggression and violence; yet it remains mistily unclear where the two inarticulate, drug-pushing and eventually martyred heroes (filmed – especially blond, blue-eyed Fonda – as though candidates for counterculture canonisation) stand in relation to the general malaise. Hanson, an alcoholic civil rights lawyer who secures their release from prison (played with his usual fiendish charm by Jack Nicholson), muses sadly: 'You know, this used to be hell of a good country. I can't understand what's gone wrong with it.' But the nostalgia which permeates the film is totally unfocused. The country as it 'used to be' would no more gladly then than now have tolerated these misfits who, in any case, are quite prepared to contribute to its potential for violence by dealing in hard drugs.

Easy Rider is fatally pinned between a facile (and slightly premature) *fin-de-siècle* romanticism (Hopper's pet visual trope is allowing the sun to dazzle his camera lens) and an unrealised ambition to conjure the moment when the American Dream also turned into a 'bad trip'. Like some mobile sculpture, the glistening chrome surfaces of its heroes' motorcycles reflect only random fragments of contemporary disquiet; and, ultimately, the movie is undone by its own intrusive narcissism, as though, not content merely to contemplate his navel, Hopper decided to film it in grainy close-up. What it lacks is an objective factor that would concentrate the genuine disillusionment and direct it against a more substantial target than mere small-town bigotry. Vietnam was to be that factor. To a sixties mythology that, even before the turning point of *Easy Rider*, had been exploited by such movies as *The Wild Angels* (1966), about a Nazi-inspired motorcycle gang, and *The Trip* (1967), about a controlled LSD experience, both directed by Roger Corman and starring Peter Fonda, was to be added the war – a war, however, that would at first be cautiously conjugated in the past (returning vets) or future tense (anxieties over the draft), not in the present.

Though the first of the specifically protest movement movies (in which the Rooney–Garland cry was updated to 'Let's put on the war *right here* – on campus!') surfaced only one year later in 1970 (Stuart Hagmann's *The Strawberry Statement* and Richard Rush's *Getting Straight*), in some respects the richest works were those whose relation to the war was more oblique. The movement had its own dynamic, its own heroes and martyrs, even its own atrocities (e.g. the Kent State killings), so that the demonstrations of solidarity at home often appeared curiously unconnected with the antipodean war that had ostensibly prompted them.

A case in point is Michelangelo Antonioni's *Zabriskie Point* (1969), almost universally dismissed as either a cynical exploitation of the youth market or an ignorantly superficial response to the troubled vitality of America's contemporary landscape by an ageing, patrician, European 'art movie' director. How could one take seriously, the argument ran, a film that proceeded from the realistically edgy concourse of a group of radical militants (presided over

by the formidable Mrs Eldridge Cleaver) to the cop-out apocalypse
of its climax, when Daria (Daria Halprin) visualises in her mind's
eye the destruction, in slow motion, of her millionaire employer's
opulent desert villa? American critics doubtless expected an intellectual of Antonioni's stature to have 'something to say' about
student revolutionaries and the deep divisiveness of opinion over
the war. But here campus unrest, almost autonomous of any larger
political context, seems more fixated on the domestic guardians of
the nation's foreign policy (the police) than on the import of that
policy itself. As Antonioni sensed, the war – a pressing problem, to
be sure, for those about to be drafted – more generally served to
centralise a spirit of rebellion that was already, if diffusely, in the air;
at worst to perpetuate and legitimise any confused, half-motivated
violence. But he also saw, and expressed through poetic rather
than analytical insights, the extent to which this disaffection was
itself a child of the conspicuous capitalism that it professed to reject.
For all their well-intentioned cant about 'alternative life-styles',
these young people remain the fauna of America's surrealistically
beautiful urban and rural landscape – where the desert paradoxically offers an oasis from the smog-haloed city and, as in a Magritte
painting, a breathtaking natural vista may be obscured by a huge
kitschy billboard advertising just such a vista. Even in revolt, they
are slavishly dependent on its most sophisticated artefacts: the
private airplane stolen by Mark (played by an unknown, Mark
Frechette, later to be killed in a prison brawl) no less than *Easy
Rider*'s Harley Davidsons stuffed with dollar bills. And the final
explosive destruction is so stylised as to become a Creation in
reverse, a magnificent firework display of America's material
plenitude.

But the uncritical wonderment at this plenitude shared by most
European directors caused them to see both sides alike as part of
the same affectionately or sourly observed set of phenomena.
Jacques Demy's *Model Shop* (1968), about the last mournful fling
enjoyed by a young architect (Gary Lockwood) before his drafting,
emerged as a bluesy hymn to the seedy, peeling labyrinth of
downtown Los Angeles, the war itself being little more than an
offscreen *deus ex machina*. *Taking Off* (1971) was a slight, droll,
over-extended comedy of the generation gap, with both parents

and children viewed as endearing freaks in the distorting mirror of
director Milos Forman's somewhat mean-spirited brand of naturalism (an amateur rock contest entirely peopled by pasty-
complexioned teenage girls, a banquet sponsored by the 'Society
for the Parents of Fugitive Children', during which assorted mothers
and fathers make their first maladroit attempts at smoking marijuana, etc.) and the war, one supposes, just out of earshot. And it
was typical of Forman's softie cynicism that, when his work finally
acknowledged the existence of a war behind all these hallucinatory
high jinks, Vietnam had become, in *Hair* (1979), a suitable subject
for nostalgia, and flower power the sixties' Art Deco.

Another indication of how charily Hollywood broached the subject of the war is the fact that the closest Arthur Penn has ever got
to it (at least, as I write this) is *Alice's Restaurant* (1969), despite the
fact that he would seem to possess all the requisite credentials for
making a serious contribution to Vietnam cinema: his espousal of
liberal causes (*Little Big Man*), his sympathy for marginals of every
hue (*The Left-Handed Gun, The Miracle Worker*, respectively about
Billy the Kid and Helen Keller, and *Bonnie and Clyde*) and his perhaps
over-acute sensitivity to paranoia (the intolerably pretentious fable
Mickey One and tolerably pretentious *noir* thriller *Night Moves*).

Alice's Restaurant, expanded from Arlo Guthrie's twenty-minute
talking blues 'The Alice's Restaurant Massacree', is both the im-
pressionistic celebration and bleakly detached post-mortem of a
small community of misfits who run through a representative roster
of sixties panaceas: drugs, music, communal living and ecumenical,
all-embracing love. All-embracing, however, in a rigorously un-
physical sense, as Arlo firmly declines the advances of his benefac-
tress Alice (Pat Quinn), just as, conversely, the truckdriver who
has given him a lift rapidly cools towards him when he sees his
shoulder-length hair cascading from beneath a Stetson. As Tom
Milne has written, Arlo's more famous father Woody, the Dustbowl
balladeer, 'spent his life going towards life rather than dropping
out of it': vague, universally applicable 'love' all too frequently
risks remaining unrequited.

Vietnam is twice woven into the film's narrative. It first leads
Arlo to Alice's deconsecrated church in Vermont (after being run
out of a college in which he had enrolled to obtain draft deferment);

and it is a Thanksgiving dinner at her restaurant that enables him to avoid military service (having helpfully dumped the Thanksgiving garbage, he is jailed as a litterbug and later rejected at an induction centre as an unrehabilitated criminal). Astonishingly but agreeably, both arresting officer and sentencing judge were played in the movie by the actual functionaries who inspired the 'Massacree'.

Haskell Wexler's *Medium Cool* (1969) – the title refers to McLuhan's distinction of hot and cool media – is the study of a TV news cameraman's progressive radicalisation in the late sixties. Paralleling the course of Wexler's own career from cinematographer of other directors' work (*In the Heat of the Night, Who's Afraid of Virginia Woolf?*) to director and scenarist of his own, it traces its protagonist's political education from his initially uncurious recording of news items ('Jesus! I love to shoot film!') to direct and even dangerous involvement in them – an involvement culminating in an extraordinary sequence in which the two parallels, so to speak, converge. John (Robert Forster) has been assigned to cover a tactical exercise at a National Guard riot training camp, where a group of folk-singing Guardsmen in plain clothes, i.e. hippie garb, confront their bayonet-bearing comrades in conventional uniform, tear gas explodes and, on the soundtrack, an alarmed voice is heard yelling to the director (who was in fact gassed while shooting the scene): 'Look out, Haskell, it's real!' Unfortunately, though, much of this glossy 'photographer's film' is somewhat less authentic, from its facile visual rhymes clicking into place (the movie opens with John dispassionately filming an automobile accident while the mangled victim still groans for help and it ends with his own crash, coolly snapped by a teenager from the back seat of a passing car) to its glib narrative strategies (one routine assignment coincidentally apprises him of the existence of black militancy, another of the horrifying depths of poverty in the Appalachians). There is, nevertheless, some fascinating coverage of the turbulent 1968 Democratic Convention in Chicago and the brutally policed demonstrations surrounding it. And that was where two further parallel lines were to meet. John discovers with indignation that the FBI and CIA have automatic access to his footage: ironically, Wexler's *own* twenty hours of Convention footage was subsequently requisitioned by the Justice Department.

Even if the distribution of *Medium Cool* was handled by a major studio, Paramount, its tyro director, absence of stars and semi-documentary style bracketed it rather with the 'new Hollywood', or with films whose relation to the industry was either marginal or (in the case of Robert Kramer) non-existent. In the seventies, the unlovely term 'movie brats' was coined for a generation of, by Hollywood's standards, extremely young directors whose child-hoods seem to have been spent almost exclusively inside cinemas. Thus they have also been described as 'cine-literate' (implying, though, a very narrow definition of literacy: the movies which they know by heart, quote from or pastiche in their own work are just the kind of popular 'classics' familiar to anyone with a reasonably developed interest in cinema). They live and breathe movies, are animated by a passion for the medium that tends to override any lingering doubts as to whether they might have something significant to contribute to it.

As originally labelled, there were six of them: Francis Ford Coppola, Brian De Palma, George Lucas, John Milius, Steven Spielberg and Martin Scorsese. Some of them were students at USC or UCLA, they regularly screened rough cuts of their films for each other, their professional capacities have frequently overlapped: Coppola helped finance Lucas's *American Graffiti*, Milius wrote the original script for *Apocalypse Now*, Lucas produced and co-scripted Spielberg's *Raiders of the Lost Ark*, etc. By dint of a few early and unparalleled box-office triumphs (*The Godfather I* and *II*, 1972 and 1974, *Carrie*, 1976, *Jaws*, 1975, *Close Encounters of the Third Kind*, 1977, *Taxi Driver*, 1976, *American Graffiti*, 1973, and *Star Wars*, 1977 – only Milius, to his chagrin, has seen such monstrous success consistently elude him), these young Turks all managed prematurely to install themselves in positions of power within the Hollywood system. They acquired freedom. They could take risks (Scorsese's mammoth 'big band' musical, *New York, New York*, 1977, Spielberg's indigest-ible thirty-million-dollar slice of slapstick pie, *1941*, 1979, and, an especial risk for those inflationary times, Coppola's *conventionally* budgeted study of paranoia in the age of electronics, *The Conversation*, 1974). If they had been so inclined, they could certainly have raised financing for movies about the war. But while it would be self-righteously puritanical to censure them for having failed to

44

seize the opportunity of becoming the spokesmen of their contemporaries drafted to (and sometimes killed in) Vietnam, it cannot be denied that their record on the matter was disappointing, to say the least.

From Spielberg and Lucas, hardly a whisper. Spielberg's sole foray into war movie territory (apart from the more recent *Empire of the Sun*) was the epically gross farce *1941*, which focused on an invasion that did not even materialise: the unfounded rumours of further Japanese aggression sweeping southern California in the immediate aftermath of Pearl Harbor. As for Lucas, after an unsuccessful essay in Orwellian science fiction (a film that bore, in lieu of a title, the registration number *THX–1138*), he settled for a career of unreflecting but highly marketable nostalgia. *American Graffiti* was a clever, charming, 'neon-realist' evocation of the sounds, attitudes and mannerisms of the early sixties, a movable feast of junk food following its four young protagonists as they cruised through the streets of a small town in northern California (pieced together from San Rafael, Petaluma and San Francisco) on the last night of their adolescence. An end title card spelling out their respective futures informed us that the unprepossessing Terry (Charlie Martin Smith), nicknamed 'the Toad' and the epitome of every kid's 'loser' friend, would go missing, 'presumed dead', in Vietnam; and it was as much a tribute to the movie's uncanny period reconstruction as to its actors' behavioural charm that the death of one pimpled, bespectacled, good-natured adolescent could with such conviction encapsulate the end of an epoch.

(At the same time, however, Lucas's calculated escapism, his wilful evasion of the divided period in which he was living for one socially and politically so conformist, were scarcely irrelevant to *American Graffiti*'s unprecedented box-office returns, greater even, proportionally to what it cost, than those of *Star Wars*. If the movie's motorised pyrotechnics recalled a dodgem-car race and it should properly be viewed at a drive-in, *Star Wars* itself twitched and blinked across the Panavision screen like a gigantic pinball machine, a resemblance which, paradoxical as this may seem, contrived to set it even further into the past: less because it bore no relation to any of the planet's foreseeable futures, a given of science fiction, than in the greedily systematic way it fed upon the mythical narrative archetypes – westerns, Samurai films, medieval romances, *The Wizard of Oz* and Road Runner cartoons – of childhood reading and moviegoing. In fact, it was just the kind of movie that would have played to packed houses in *American Graffiti*'s boulevard Bijou.)

Six years later, in 1979, having switched from directing movies with the mentality of a producer to producing them with the mentality of a director, Lucas became involved in a purely executive capacity with *More American Graffiti*, directed by a certain B. W. L. Norton. Whereas Lucas's own film could be thought of as 'political' only in so far as it retreated from any too blatant allusion to the politics of the period in which the action took place (*not* a paradox: for apoliticism may also be a codified and sometimes profoundly reactionary ideology), the narrative of its sequel was articulated around four successive New Year's Eves, from 1964 to 1967, and complacently ran the full, by now ultra-familiar, gamut of Sixtiesiana from drug culture to draft-card burning, from flower power to campus activism, and from rock concerts at the Fillmore to the war in Vietnam.

Thus we pursue the misfortunes of Terry the Toad (played, as previously, by Charles Martin Smith), who, on being posted to Vietnam, makes a clumsy attempt to inflict a minor injury on himself in the hope of being discharged. Ever the loser, he fails; only, subsequently, to demonstrate his true merit by saving the life of a gung-ho commander. Then, out of revulsion at the hypocrisy and chicanery depicted by the movie as rampant among the officer class, he fabricates an explosion in some field latrines, as a result of which he is indeed supposed dead. He is last seen lighting out for Europe, presumably intended to arrive Stateside just in time for a further sequel (a threat which, to be fair, neither Norton nor Lucas carried out).

More American Graffiti was as puerile as it was pernicious. For where the nostalgia of its model could at least be justified as an expression of retrospective fondness for the prewar period, perceived by its director as the absolute last gasp of folksy, easygoing Americana, the notion of subjecting a decade as activist and heterodox as the sixties to a similarly superficial overview struck one as tasteless, if not downright offensive. Offensive, certainly, was the sequel's calculated 'halcyonisation', so to speak, of the period, as though, beneath its seething crust, it was as affable and conformist a one as that over which Ike had lazily presided.

Apart from writing a scenario for *Apocalypse Now*, Milius alluded to Vietnam in his own weird surfing saga, *Big Wednesday* (1978), notably in a farcical scene of draft induction. But once again the war, to which the most sympathetic and readily identifiable of the three bronzed friends goes quite willingly, is treated, not as the death knell, but as the culminating point of sixties nostalgia. Though in some incidentals a striking film (the use of a beach gateway, invariably shot from the same angle, to frame the action like a classical portico in Greek tragedy), its faintly theological approach to the hermetic sport of surfing and ludicrous macho posturings tended to limit its appeal to strictly local (i.e. southern Californian) consumption.

Coppola's *Apocalypse Now* and *Gardens of Stone*, the sole head-on confrontation of a founding movie brat with the war itself, and Scorsese's *Taxi Driver* will be treated in subsequent chapters. But one of the best of the 'draft' movies, incongruously from a director who later specialised in hysterical, crypto-Hitchcockian shockers, was Brian De Palma's *Greetings* (1968).

De Palma's background was East Coast, not Hollywood, and the minuscule budgets allotted to his first New York-based films, *The Wedding Party* (1967) and *Murder à la Mod* (1968), did not extend to professional casts (though the former – retroactively, as it were – remains one of his starriest productions to date: three of his friends who appeared in it were Jill Clayburgh, Wilford Leach and Robert De Niro). These juvenile efforts, as though in dual homage to film-makers as dissimilar, even diametrically opposed, as Godard and Hitchcock, confusedly sought to challenge the spectator's perceptions and manipulate his emotions at the same time. As one might expect, there were few spectators.

But *Greetings*, brashly launched on a privately raised 10,000 dollars and finally budgeted at 43,000, brought in more than a million. The film (whose title refers to the deceptively genial first word read by recipients of US Army conscription papers) builds up a surprisingly rich mosaic of sixties fringe culture out of the offbeat obsessions of three New York dropouts during the two weeks separating their draft medical examination from its results. Paul (Jonathan Warden) is preoccupied with a series of inconclusive computer-selected dates; Lloyd (Gerrit Graham), a Kennedy assassination addict, makes contact with a bizarre figure who claims to be the seventeenth and sole surviving witness to Oswald's movements following the crime; and Jon (De Niro), a chronic voyeur, cajoles a shoplifter into stripping for him by professing to be a proponent of what he calls 'Peep Art'.

Such outwardly random pursuits nevertheless mesh to refute the picture of a contentedly complacent society as described by President Johnson at the beginning of the movie: 'I'm not saying you never had it so good. But that's a fact, isn't it?' And much of *Greetings* is irresistibly comic: the friends' mock interviews with draft board officers (in rehearsal for the real thing), Paul pinning his hopes of rejection on flamboyant homosexual mannerisms and neo-Fascistic rhetoric; the loony encounter with a street-corner revolutionary who believes that General Motors' imperialist ambitions are inadvertently revealed by the name of its corporate headquarters, the Empire State Building; or Jon's elaborate pitch to induce the shoplifter to strip while, framed unnoticed in a window behind him, another young woman casually undresses. By the film's end, paranoia has been fully vindicated as by far the sanest response to a society coming apart at the seams. Before meeting with his supposed Oswald witness, Lloyd himself is mysteriously shot; and Jon, whose paramilitary discourse, taken over from Paul, has (not entirely unexpectedly) failed to deter the army, finds himself drafted to Vietnam, where he can freely indulge his voyeuristic proclivities: he forces a Vietnamese girl to strip for newsreel cameramen.*

Greetings, though hardly a major work, was even in its ungainliness manifestly more honest than all of the slick inanities of those 'youth' movies whose widest generation gap was that which stretched between director and subject-matter (e.g. John G. Avildsen's crudely opportunistic portrait of a hard-hat bigot, *Joe*, 1970, whose hippie characters appeared to be impersonated by

---

* In 1969 De Palma completed a sequel, *Hi, Mom!* (the first words addressed to the TV cameras by a returning vet), but I have not been able to see it.

plain-clothes detectives rather than actors, and Stanley Kramer's typically lumbering *R.P.M.* – meaning 'Revolutions Per Minute' – made the same year).

As the resister began to acquire respectability, however, the cinema produced less frivolous treatments of his situation. When Joan Baez's husband, the activist David Harris, was sentenced shortly after their marriage to three years' imprisonment for resisting the draft, a documentary film, *Carry It On* (1970), recounted the couple's life together, his arrest and her subsequent concert tour. And, at the less charismatic end of the spectrum, there was Hiroshi Teshigahara's *Summer Soldiers* (1971), about an ordinary GI stationed in Japan, Jim (Keith Sykes), who casually chooses to desert rather than fight in Vietnam. In *cinéma-vérité* style, the movie follows his progress as an AWOL, from a clandestine sojourn in a prostitute's room (hiding in a cupboard whenever there is a knock at the door) to his involvement with the Tokyo Deserters Aid Committee (to whose ideological debates he is apathetically indifferent and whose request that he give a press conference on TV, as The Singing Deserter, he declines) via the nervous hospitality of a little network of Japanese families sympathetic to the deserters' cause. Finally, after an abortive attempt to work his passage on a ship bound for Sweden, Jim walks into the army base at Kyoto in the hope of obtaining an official discharge.

In its refusal to heighten the deserter's plight or draw hasty (or, indeed, any) conclusions from his abrupt decision to surrender, lie both the strengths and weaknesses of this intermittently fascinating film. So bland, so passive is Jim that he remains a cypher throughout, returning to the army as he had departed from it, almost as a whim – which rather belies the remark made by one of the Aid Committee's earnest young idealists: 'Desertion is meaningful in itself.' One does not ask that the protagonist of such a film be portentously 'representative' of all deserters, merely that he be someone capable of bringing a degree of reflection to bear upon his own predicament.

Though there were a number of marginal productions on the issue – Simon Nuchtern's *Cowards* (about deserters in Canada), Anitra Pivnik's *Prism* (about a lawyer who aids draft dodgers) and Allan Brown's *Outside In* (a deserter's homecoming to his father's funeral) – it was handled by no major studio until Robert Wise's pedestrian melodrama *Two People* (1973, with Peter Fonda and Lindsay Wagner), which had the singular notion of exploiting the deserter's return home for a travelogue tour *à la Three Coins in the Fountain* of the Soviet Union, North Africa and Paris. Other movies dealt with the less fashionable theme of young Americans (generally of rural origin) accepting, albeit for the most part reluctantly, to go fight for their country. The protagonist of David Miller's *Hail, Hero!* (1969) – played, in his screen début, by Michael Douglas – volunteers for a disconnected job lot of reasons: out of respect for his Second World War veteran father; because he had accidentally crippled his pro-war brother; and, perhaps, to confound the enemy with his own pacifist convictions ('What would happen if every soldier on both sides would just try to love instead of hate?'). And Anthony Newley's *Summertree* (1971) concerned a young music student (Douglas again) whose gradual disenchantment with his studies ironically results in his being drafted and killed in Vietnam.

By the start of the following decade the draft had already become fodder for nostalgia, like the faded flower power of *Hair*. In Rob Cohen's *A Small Circle of Friends* (1980), a mail-order catalogue of sixties splendours and miseries as they affected the lives of three Harvard undergraduates (one girl, two boys), including pot, women's lib, the Weathermen, unconventional sexual mores and the token battle between cops and demonstrating students (in the Harvard Yard), it is highlighted in a scene where the friends anxiously await the 64,000-dollar classification number on that obscene TV quiz show, the draft lottery. As the *Time* magazine critic Richard Schickel aptly observed, it came 'to seem less a movie than a picture history of an era – one of those tomes that offer a garble of familiar images held together by a pseudo-historical text'.

But revolution was in the air, precisely where Paul Williams's *The Revolutionary* (1970, based on Hans Koningsberger's novel) was determined to keep it. In marked contrast to the strident topicality of the protest movies, it was set in an unspecified country 'somewhere in the free world' at an unspecified moment in recent history. Unspecified countries, however, are much easier to construct verbally than visually (especially in view of contemporary cinema's dependence on natural locations): here, notwithstanding its jackbooted policemen and absence of traffic, the city was inescapably London, the actors' vocal inflections ineradicably American, and the costumes (Jon Voight in baggy trousers, floppy wide-brimmed hat and tight, rimless spectacles) instantly recognisable as classic revolutionary wear to anyone who has read Conrad's *The Secret Agent* or *Under Western Eyes*. In fact, the film's calm pursuit of metaphoric intemporality removed it so far from the telegenic razzle-dazzle of sixties campus rioting into an almost turn-of-the-century world of anarchist dreamers (one half-expected a big black bomb with a lighted fuse to be concealed beneath Voight's shabby raincoat) that the political and moral issues which it raised seemed to be of historical, rather than universal or topical, import or else were articulated in a void that no amount of Kafkaesque angst (Voight's character is named simply 'A' – surely an exclusively literary conceit) could make resonate.

Robert Kramer, director of *The Edge* (1968), *Ice* (1969) and *Milestones* (1974), has many vociferous admirers (particularly in France), and there is no doubting his work's fundamental honesty of purpose. His films, made without (to my knowledge) any official harassment, nevertheless contrive to appear as objects of bureaucratic suspicion, as though smuggled out of some beleaguered totalitarian state. But they also founder on an oddly puritanical variant of the imitative fallacy, whereby any tedious incident, for the characters, is made no less so for the audience; political debates of stupefying banality are served up raw, without much sign of directorial mediation; and nocturnal scenes (of which there are many in Kramer's work) are rendered virtually invisible by under-exposed 16mm stock.

The Edge took as its subject an assassination attempt on the President in reparation for the slaughter in Vietnam, while *Ice* dealt with urban guerilla insurrection in an imagined period of war between the United States and Mexico (which could be interpreted as either a paranoid foretaste of the future course of America's imperialist expansion or else as a metaphorical substitute for Vietnam itself). And, at 195 minutes, *Milestones* (co-directed by John Douglas) was a mammoth orgy of melancholic self-questioning in which random groups of Americans of mostly WASP origin meet to discuss their lives, projects, ambitions and achievements in the light of their experience of the previous decade: these include an intellectual once imprisoned for aiding deserters, a war veteran, a student activist, a militant cell, some ex-dropouts, members of a commune and a baby who is born in the final sequence. The film is dedicated to Ho Chi Minh and the 'heroic Vietnamese people'.

The ultimate in *noir* cinema, Kramer's movies are pitch black (despite the affirmation of rebirth at the end of *Milestones*); all the more so because, eschewing the neo-expressionist stylistics of forties thrillers, they risk striking the unwary spectator as straight-forward, almost documentary, recordings of a world that is objectively *noir*. But if they have in common with nightmares the quality of preternatural vividness, one tends to find it rather difficult, as also with nightmares, to recall them in detail when they are all over.

As for the New York Underground scene, its conceptualist preoccupations would have precluded any very urgent commitment, to filming the war; the sole example of a Vietnam-related issue figuring in a linear narrative was Adolfas Mekas's *Windflowers* (1968), about a draft dodger mercilessly tracked down and killed by the FBI. But vague allusions crop up in at least two Andy Warhol films: *The Chelsea Girls* (1966), in which a prominent Factory denizen, Mary Might, impersonated the sadistic 'Hanoi Hannah', and *Blue Movie* (1969), where the war represented only one link in a chain of free-association chitchat between love-makers Louis Waldon and Viva (even if Warhol with forgivable disingenuousness defended the movie as 'about Vietnam' when it was prosecuted for obscenity).

Non-American films do not really form part of this study, but mention should be made of *Loin du Viêtnam (Far from Vietnam*, 1967), collectively directed by Alain Resnais, William Klein, Joris Ivens, Agnès Varda, Claude Lelouch and Jean-Luc Godard and edited by Chris Marker. A curious ragbag in which quite good jostled indiscriminately with very bad, it too often resorted to effective but simplistic antinomies: General Westmoreland's outrageous assertion that 'Never has a military nation employed its power with such restraint' offset by images of the obscene havoc wreaked by American bombing, Vice-President Humphrey's glow-ing account of his state visit to Paris intercut with newsreel footage of angry demonstrators lining his path, etc. Godard used his section to accost the audience directly with a string of gnomic utterances on the difficulties facing a European artist wishing to make a statement about the war, a sentiment limply echoed by Resnais in a peculiarly thin-blooded playlet about an equivocating French intellectual.

Vietnam, of course, had always engaged Godard, from the brilliant pantomime sequence with Anna Karina in *Pierrot le fou* (1965) to the fatuous moment in *Deux ou trois choses que je sais d'elle* (*Two or Three Things I Know About Her*, 1967, and a masterpiece, nevertheless) when Marina Vlady's child recalls his dream of twins on a perilous mountain path merging into one person to enable him to pass – 'and, at that moment, I discovered that these two people were North and South Vietnam'. In *La Chinoise* (also 1967) Godard invented for the cinema the political cartoon, with a coolie-hatted, blood-spattered Juliet Berto strafed by toy planes and, forming the background, a giant poster of the Esso tiger; in *Letter to Jane* (1972, co-directed with Jean-Pierre Gorin) he sought to analyse and demystify a press photograph of Jane Fonda in the company of some North Vietnamese, which had been published by the French news magazine *L'Express*. Claude Lelouch's unsalvageably meretricious *Vivre pour vivre* (*Live for Life*, 1967), juxtaposing in true Sunday-supplement manner newsreel images of war atrocities with Candice Bergen blithely riding through Central Park at dawn, added to the period's list of chic jet-setting professions – fashion photographer, international racing-driver – that of TV reporter in Vietnam. And Godard's cinematographer, Raoul Coutard, shot his own *Hoâ-Binh* (1970) in what one imagines to be just the visual style favoured by Lelouch's glamorous hero.

But it was also in 1970 that Metro-Goldwyn-Mayer, the studio which had once been Hollywood's centre court, the temple and bastion of traditional Middle-American values, released Stuart Hagmann's *The Strawberry Statement* (based by dramatist Israel Horovitz on James Simon Kunen's *The Strawberry Statement: Notes of a College Revolutionary*). The film, whose incongruous title refers to a university dean's claim that students were against the war in much the same casually Pavlovian way they liked strawberries, traces the gradual politicisation of young, fence-sitting Simon (played by Bruce Davison with irritating winsomeness throughout), who almost stumbles into the protest movement after being mildly harassed by the police ('What is this – France?') for taking photographs of a campus sit-in, and his on-off-on relationship with the more committed Linda (Kim Darby). And it is perhaps a measure of Hagmann's personal remoteness from the lived experience of campus unrest that the narrative's visual textures seem to have been as lavishly reconstructed as for a period melodrama. This is the nostalgia of 'now'.

In the opening sequence, when Simon comes home to find his room-mate in bed with a girl involved in the occupation of the college administration buildings, the slowly tracking camera 'parenthetically' encounters in its field of vision such archetypical bric-à-brac as a poster photograph of Robert Kennedy, a signpost stolen from the City Zoo, some San Francisco-ish sidewalk pottery, a pair of jeans laid out to dry on the window ledge – in fact, all heavy clues to the protagonist's life-style as carefully planted by the set designer as the football pennant, baseball mitt and Lana Turner pin-up of an earlier generation. Spying a cockroach, he remarks: 'You guys are everywhere, you're like the Viet Cong.' In the Bay Area streets he never *walks*, he idly moons around, transfixed in the shimmer of a wide-angle lens. A cart loaded with groceries 'poetically' runs away with him (a scene influenced by the Redford/ Newman cycling antics in *Butch Cassidy and the Sundance Kid*, which had already been vulgarly cribbed from *Jules et Jim*). And when assigned by the student council to fix the administration's Xerox machine, he cutely wastes time by applying the principal's shaving soap and aftershave to his own (canned) peaches-and-cream complexion. Plus countless similar hints that his youthful insouciance is due to receive some violent political come-uppance in the final reel (as indeed it proves).

The film intermittently provides a useful gloss on the mechanics of a student occupation – demonstrators sneaking out just before dark to obtain food supplies, the local grocer (James Coco) urging them to pillage the most expensive delicacies in his store so that he might claim theft insurance, the sudden enthusiasm of Simon's friend Elliot (Bud Cort) for joining the protest on hearing that among those sequestered inside the principal's office are 150 girls – but the modish curlicues of Hagmann's maddeningly fidgety camerawork render it well nigh unintelligible. With its slow motion, freeze frames, excessive focus-pulling, 'artistic' dissolves and ubiquitous zoom shots, *The Strawberry Statement* is abominably shot. Never for a moment is the spectator permitted to engage directly with the characters, who have to contend with a barrage of arty camera angles as much as with the 'pigs' themselves. And the redundancy of these effects is often compounded by the tenuousness of their links with the narrative: Simon's rowing practice for the college team, for instance, an activity which by the end of the movie he can no longer reconcile with his militancy, is treated to a series of lyrically slow dissolves in which his skiff lazily crisscrosses itself over the sparkling river, whereas the participants of the sit-in, with whom the director's sympathies presumably lie, are filmed (and played) with an almost caricatural lack of warmth. It becomes increasingly clear, moreover, that the various romantic interludes and bouts of campus in-fighting are serving merely as a protracted build-up to the final sequence, a spectacular police bust, which is to this film what the San Francisco car chase was to *Bullitt*.

Watching this set-piece, visibly choreographed to within an inch of its life, I was reminded of another, ostensibly very dissimilar movie, *Footlight Parade*, a Warner Bros. backstage musical directed in 1933 by Lloyd Bacon and starring James Cagney, Dick Powell and Ruby Keeler. Its plot, briefly, is the one about impresario Cagney putting on a Broadway show (in fact, prologues, i.e. those stage presentations that in the thirties preceded the screening of a feature film) against numerous, mostly financial odds; but what makes it, to my mind, the best of Warners' extravaganzas of the period is its unusual construction. Until the final explosion of as many as *three* Busby Berkeley numbers, magnificent revolving catherine wheels of feminine limbs framed in his celebrated overhead shots, we have been privy to no more than mere glimpses of musical numbers, frustratingly truncated and generally in rehearsal. In fact, the whole movie consists of rehearsals (for the duration of which, it should be noted, the chorus girls and boys are locked inside the theatre) in preparation for its triple climax.

This is precisely how *The Strawberry Statement* functions. The only confrontation between cops and protesters prior to the main event, a confused skirmish in a neighbourhood playground which happens to be the students' immediate point of contention (they believe it should be given over to children from the black ghetto), is shot with a clownish disregard for realism. The cathartic release of real violence, we understand, is being saved for the very end.

When the students finally learn that the helmeted and gas-masked National Guard have surrounded the administration buildings, they arrange themselves in circles on the gym floor and begin to sing in unison. And lo! what does Hagmann then do but revert to the overhead shot: the Busby Berkeley resemblance is complete (though, given that they are chanting John Lennon's Johnny-one-note lyric 'Give Peace a Chance', the earlier film is musically far superior). The actual mêlée, with clouds of tear gas prettily disturbing the symmetry of the concentric circles of students and Guardsmen lashing out indiscriminately and with totally unjustified savagery, would have been more impressive if its luridly bloody display of police brutality had not so patently been the sole reason for a studio as conformist as MGM endorsing the project in the first place.

In one of his essays in *The Primal Screen* the American critic Andrew Sarris claimed that Hagmann's original intention, reversed by the studio's boss, James Aubrey, was that Simon be killed at the end; in the version released, he is caught in a freeze frame as he lurches forward to aid Linda. Sarris (who was vaguely sympathetic towards the film) went on to remark: 'The movie is set in some anonymous institution in the San Francisco Bay Area without being either Berkeley (the historical continuity of radicalism) or San Francisco State (the sudden eruption of black power with muscle). Why? (. . .) The book is about Columbia, and no student was killed at Columbia by the police bust.' Which all rather makes one wonder which was the more crassly opportunistic decision: to end the film with a killing or to suppress that killing.

'We'll go to the aquarium and turn on with the fish like we used to.' So one of his ex-girlfriends importunes Harry Bailey (Elliott Gould) at the beginning of Richard Rush's *Getting Straight*, the other campus movie produced by a major studio in 1970. But Harry, who served both at Selma and in Vietnam, is through with political agitation: his one remaining ambition is to complete his MA and earn a teaching credential, whose attractions he succinctly summarises to a black militant friend as 'money and power and little girls to molest'. (Its disadvantages include a practice course of what is disparagingly referred to as 'dumbbell English' – teaching college students to make short sentences with the present participle of the verb 'to be'.) Torn between the demands being made on his activist past and an exasperation with new, computerised teaching methods which may well affect his future, his own personal revolt comes at an oral exam where a rather sweatily insistent professor attempts to coerce him into agreement on what he sees as the latent homosexuality of *The Great Gatsby* and its author. While outside protesters and National Guardsmen have finally clashed, Harry, by impudently kissing this professor on the mouth, effectively kisses his academic career goodbye.

A minor, occasionally witty comedy-drama, *Getting Straight* succeeds where Harry failed: in keeping campus revolution safely in the background (for no precise motivation is ever attributed to the rioting). Its concluding images, with Harry and his current girlfriend (Candice Bergen), their respective identity crises now definitively resolved, exchanging worldly smirks as around them surges an exotic mass of youthful humanity, is pure love-across-a-crowded-room sentimentality. And not even Elliott Gould's prodigious mongrel charm can prevent his valedictory line 'It's not what you do that counts, it's what you are' (addressed to the black militant while the latter is gleefully smashing in windows) from sounding as trite and reactionary as 'Love means never having to say you're sorry'. Well, almost as trite.

— *Chapter 4* —

RETURN OF THE SOLDIER

Following the First World War, a conflict comparable to Vietnam in the widespread revulsion which overtook the event long before the Armistice was signed, in the overwhelming sense of useless slaughter suffered on both sides and in the gradual realisation that it constituted a dramatic and truly qualitative break in the nation's history, the United States plunged into a period of isolationism and political apathy which lasted until the Depression. This was, of course, the semi-mythical era of jazz, flappers and bathtub gin (paradoxically enlivened further by the advent of Prohibition), of the celebrated Lost Generation (no less paradoxically, a term invariably used to describe the victors of the war) and of a compulsive, even neurotic urge to live, love, laugh and be happy 'for yesterday we died'.

But the aftermath of Vietnam granted its survivors no such release, perhaps because the contiguous 'roaring' decade was this time *concurrent* with the war: rock was the sixties' jazz; boys grew their hair long, just as girls had once bobbed theirs, to dissociate themselves from their elders; earnest communal living projects supplanted the legendary sexual promiscuity of the twenties; and the legal interdiction on drugs had precisely the same effect on drug-taking as Prohibition on the consumption of alcohol. Even in films in which the relation of Vietnam to the narrative remained a strictly exploitative one, Hollywood with remarkable consistency contrived to portray the returning veteran as incurably 'changed', almost as much an alien as the faceless enemy with whom he had been in contact. Though not necessarily 'disturbed' in a clinical sense, and often judged capable of functioning in society without the purgatory of hospitalisation, he was depicted as somehow not the same person – mentally, physically or both – who had departed for the war. Consequently, all 'returning vet' movies (which have been surprisingly numerous in Hollywood's treatment of Vietnam-related themes) may be said to be paraphrases of Huston's still seldom screened *Let There Be Light*.

Winter Soldier (1972, with no director credited) was an edited record of the Winter Soldier Investigation held in Detroit in January 1971. It was organised by the Vietnam Veterans Against the War (a group whose membership grew continuously after its formation in 1967), and during three days of hearings sixteen civilians and over one hundred veterans (all of them, it should be noted, *honourably* discharged) testified, publicly though not under any oath, to war crimes either witnessed or committed by them in Vietnam – twenty-eight of which the movie documents. These include the splitting open of infants' heads with cans of food for which they were begging, the dropping of live prisoners from helicopters and the rape of a dying woman with an entrenchment tool. That for obvious reasons the movie can offer little in the way of visual evidence to support this testimony (though one of the witnesses had consented to be photographed in the act of torturing a woman) in no way diminishes its power: men who were self-confessed killers *then* we see, in agonising close-ups, to be ordinary God-fearing if profoundly troubled citizens *now*, painfully straining (many are poorly educated) to articulate the warped rationale behind their crimes.

But (and this is where it most strikingly differs from a documentary like *Let There Be Light*) *Winter Soldier* does not merely aim at providing a filmic record of what was visibly a therapeutic experience, it itself *is* that experience. Here film has been commandeered as a medium of expiation, a confessional, and one would like to hope that the participants in this unique experiment have, if not eased the burden of their conscience, at least in some measure adjusted to bearing that burden, as they must, for the rest of their lives.

In the late sixties, meanwhile, exploitation movies were still following in the deeply rutted motorcycle tracks mapped out by *The Wild One* and its successors, and the integration of Vietnam into this iconography was usually achieved at little cost to the original concept. All it required was to attribute the hero's antisocial disposition, not to the traumatic withdrawal of parental love as in the fifties, but to the collective trauma (as it was already being referred to) of the war. As though to guarantee a veneer of 'significance', allusion would be made to Vietnam in the first few minutes of the movie, which then happily settled for the customary diet of crude trigger-happy violence.

Chrome and Hot Leather, for instance, directed by Lee Frost in 1971, involved four ex-Green Beret instructors (viewed sympathetically throughout) who, to avenge the killing of their leader's fiancée by a Hell's Angel, amass an improbable arsenal of tear gas, rockets, smoke grenades, explosion simulators, not to mention assorted radios, walkie-talkies, field rations and a command-post tent. It was perhaps the most risibly extreme illustration of themes that were constantly to recur in this series of films and eventually be apotheosised in the *Rambo* cycle: the illusory nature of 'peace' for the returning veteran, the blurring of the distinction between Vietnam and gang warfare at home, the effectiveness of combat training as a 'street savvy' course for survival in the urban jungle of contemporary America.

Concurrently, and following the systematic 'blaxploitation' of the thriller and horror genres, the first of the screen's black veterans, 'utilising the skills he learned in Vietnam, etc.', stalked across the screen. As a government agent explains to the eponymous hero (played by former athlete Jim Brown) of Jack Starrett's *Slaughter* (1972): 'You're a Green Beret and you're black. That's good copy.' Such good copy, in fact, that one year later a sequel, Gordon Douglas's *Slaughter's Big Rip-Off*, was laboriously squeezed out of the same thin tube. And, in 1972, Jim Brown turned up as the equally invincible *Black Gunn* (directed by Robert Hartford-Davis), on this occasion avenging his brother's murder with the aid of BAG – a Black Action Group composed of Vietnam veterans.

More pretentious, if scarcely more ambitious, was *Born Losers* (1967), directed by its leading man, Tom Laughlin, under the *nom de caméra-stylo* of T. C. Frank. Laughlin, however, was a special case, an enigmatic young film-maker messianically convinced that he held the key to America's spiritual regeneration, a conviction doubtless reinforced (for him) by the box-office returns of what was basically a high-budget home movie (and those of its glossier sequels, *Billy Jack* and *The Trial of Billy Jack*). Its protagonist, who was to become something of a folk hero, was a sullen half-breed veteran grappling singlehandedly with almost every major problem to have beset the nation over the previous two decades – urban violence, racial prejudice, the Indian question, political chicanery and the defence of alternative life-styles. In the face of such a cannonade of virtuous bloodletting, with Billy Jack meting out karate chops to a motley selection of villains, one is tempted to comment that not since Tet and the notorious American claim that 'We had to destroy the city in order to save it' had there been such a shotgun wedding of brutish methods and pacifist motives.

As for Travis Bickle, the psychopathic hero (played by Robert De Niro) of *Taxi Driver*, the film's director, Martin Scorsese, once described him as being 'somewhere between Charles Manson and Saint Paul'. (But then, aren't we all?) Bickle, an ex-Vietnam Marine plagued with insomnia, drives his taxi on night-shift while his days are spent either scribbling lapidary reflections into a diary or pursuing a frosty upper-class blonde in the shape of Cybill Shepherd. In search of some civic mission by which to exorcise the corrosive rage of his alienation, and deciding against the assassination of the Presidential candidate for whom the blonde is campaigning, he befriends an underage junkie prostitute (Jodie Foster), whose pimp and his associates he will eventually slaughter in an outstandingly violent bloodbath.

Exemplified by a mesmerising first shot of a yellow cab lurching in slow-motion through nocturnal neon-lit streets to Bernard Herrmann's overripe score while clouds of vapour billow from a manhole as from the very kitchens of Hell, Scorsese's ghoulish vision of New York City (and he correctly hit upon *red*, a sanguine red filling every vacant pocket of the frame, as the dominant tonality of a *film noir* in colour) is as stylised as a movie poster and bizarrely reminiscent – in advance, so to speak – of Coppola's brooding jungle landscapes in *Apocalypse Now*. If *Taxi Driver* is not explicitly 'about' Vietnam, if Scorsese and his screenwriter Paul Schrader never sufficiently articulate Bickle's neuroses to tie them in with his combat experience, there are nevertheless numerous angles from which it looks suspiciously like a parable of the war (or Coppola's version of it).

For all his animal physicality, Bickle is as wraithlike a figure as Martin Sheen's Willard. Gliding through their respective jungles, both of them contrive to repel audience identification even as they invite it, by suddenly turning their accusatory gaze on the spectator, a disorienting effect achieved with functional smoothness in *Taxi Driver* since Bickle is obliged to scrutinise his unsavoury passengers (who include Scorsese himself as a jealous husband intent on blowing his wife's vagina apart with a .44 Magnum) through his cab's rear-view mirror, i.e. directly into camera. Determined, moreover, to attain a peak of physical fitness for his chosen 'mission', Bickle inflicts strict military discipline upon himself, even to the point of shaving his head guerilla-style and slapping on war paint. Shots of him posed in front of a mirror and repeatedly drawing a bead on his own reflection recall Sheen hovering between nightmarish reality and straight nightmare at the beginning of Coppola's film. And his climactic raid on the brothel, if necessarily bereft of the sacrificial symbolism surrounding Brando's death in *Apocalypse Now*, is still presented almost ceremonially, a ritualised self-purging and cleansing of pollution – as witness the way he grasps the Magnum firmly with both hands and at arm's length, a posture familiar from those movie apologies of urban vigilantes played by Clint Eastwood or Charles Bronson. The difference is that *Taxi Driver*, unlike these films, offers us no assurance, as we delight in its graphic violence, that Bickle, like so many other movie vets, is somehow 'infecting' America; the blackness of Scorsese's vision easily matches that of his protagonist and his depiction of a foul and festering New York, its manholes like open sores, often seems to detach itself from the subjectivity of Bickle's paranoid fantasies to become the movie's own objective reality.

Significantly, its coda is every bit as ambiguous as that of *Apocalypse Now*, as though neither director knew how to bring his film to a satisfactory conclusion. We gather from a magazine clipping pinned to the wall in his squalid room, without quite knowing what to make of it, that Bickle has been acclaimed as a civic hero, and note that even the cool blonde has started to warm to his freshly acquired macho image.

Not every 'movie veteran', though, would release his pent-up violence through such an all-out assault on whatever it was that threatened the purity of the system he had been enlisted to defend. There existed concurrently with these thrillers a more intimate strain, one which confined the problem of the returning vet to relatively modest narrative dimensions and a closed, often rural space.

It was launched in 1971 with Edwin Sherin's *Glory Boy* (subsequently re-released under the original title of John Sanford's First World War novel, *My Old Man's Place*), about an ex-serviceman, tormented by the memory of atrocities he committed in Vietnam, who returns with two other soldiers to his father's isolated farmhouse in northern California. A conveniently unfocused indictment of the brutalising effects of war, it fatally undermined its thesis by filming the resultant brutalities – the visit culminates in rape and murder – with undisguised relish.

A year later, the first Vietnam film by a generally acknowledged major director, Elia Kazan's *The Visitors* (from an original screenplay by his son Chris), was to make use of a not dissimilar plot. Shot by a five-man non-union crew on location in the director's own house in Connecticut, with a cast of unknowns and a derisory budget of 170,000 dollars, it concerned a sensitive young veteran, now a confirmed pacifist, who lives with his girlfriend and their infant son in a New England farmhouse owned by her father, a middle-aged, alcoholic writer of pulp western novels. Without warning they are visited one day by two of his former army buddies, a polite, easy-going black and a clean-cut if somewhat intense white sergeant, both of whom had been convicted on the evidence of their friend of raping and murdering a Vietnamese girl. Just out of Leavenworth penitentiary, closely cropped hair a grim holdover from prison rather than military rigours, their presence at first seems to forebode no specific thirst for vengeance. But time passes. They kill a neighbour's dog. Learning that the pacifist declined to participate in the gang rape, the leathery old writer, himself a cheerfully uncomplexed veteran of the Pacific war, admits that he always suspected him of being 'half-queer'. Finally, they rape the young woman (an act overly telegraphed throughout the movie by the sergeant's insistent leering at her knees) and depart almost as casually as they had arrived.

The Visitors is a strange film, typically Kazanian in its moral and psychological ambiguities: via the pacifist's remorseful self-questioning ('The Viet Cong do exactly the same thing. Everybody does. Why blame those guys? They were my friends, my buddies') and the sympathy that is gradually generated by the two visitors, it shifts by degrees from apparently endorsing the ethics of informing (and it is impossible not to recall in this context the director's own co-operation with the anti-Communist witchhunters of the early fifties) to apparently condoning war crimes. I say 'apparently' because, though the film is masterfully crafted in its atmospherics – the lonely farmhouse, the uneasily plausible blend of intangible Martian otherness and all-American affability in the rapists – the two Kazans never stand back far enough from the double-edged material to avoid being instilled with their characters' indecisions. And I am afraid Andrew Sarris did have a point when he commented (apropos *The Visitors* and movies of its type): 'The problem is that the characters are all so awesomely awful that they don't really need Vietnam as an excuse to scrape on each other.'

In Richard Compton's *Welcome Home, Soldier Boys* (1972), an account of four vets who set out for California full of illusions but end up in the no-hope township of Hope, New Mexico, a grizzled farmer in a Texas diner mumbles: 'When *we* were in the service nobody came back till the war was *over*. . . . Now they put in a coupla easy months and they come back and nothing's done. No wonder that damn war's gone on for ten years – oughta get the *old* army back there. . . . Shit! You watch television – all they do is kill the damn civilians!' And a theme common to almost all of these movies is the utter alienation of young people, whether draft-card burners, deserters or veterans, from the elders of the tribe, who seem blessed with the total recall of their own combat experiences, mnemonically revived from time to time by dusting off old and cherished army uniforms (as do the gung-ho fathers, both played by Arthur Kennedy, of *Hail, Hero!* and *Glory Boy*). If we are to believe Hollywood, it was mainly nostalgia for the simple no-nonsense heroics of the Second World War that kept the generations so decisively divided over Vietnam.

Very occasionally, this alienation would surface in paranoid allegory or near-allegory (or whatever it was that the film-makers imagined they were up to). *Clay Pigeon*, directed in 1971 by Tom Stern and Lane Slate, opens in Vietnam with an ex-policeman, Joe Ryan (played by Stern), heroically hurling his body on to an enemy grenade, which inexplicably fails to explode. Discharged and disenchanted, Joe returns to Los Angeles convinced that he is living on borrowed time. There he is engulfed against his will in an obscure imbroglio of drugs and thuggery until the moment when, after slaying a trio of gangsters, he finds himself whisked back to Vietnam just as, presumably a second or two after his suicidal gesture, the grenade explodes. Unfortunately, in so updating the ingenious conceit of Ambrose Bierce's *conte cruel* of the Civil War, *Incident at Owl Creek*, the film forfeits all credibility by the preposterous convolutions of the plot inside which, for some unfathomable reason, Joe has elected to spend the last instant of his earthly existence.

Welcome Home, Johnny Bristol, a television film directed by George McCowan in 1971, begins in Hollywood's familiar register of anecdotal naturalism, then seems to veer off into allegorical fantasy before resolving itself as naturalistically as before. To preserve his sanity in the bedlam of the war, Bristol (Martin Landau) conjures up fond memories of an idyllic, affluent childhood in what he imagines to have been his home town of Charles, Vermont. On his return to the States, however, he discovers not only that no such community exists but that he was born in a slum area of Philadelphia at the intersection of Charles and Vermont Streets, whose names he had subconsciously conflated into an idealised America, one for which he was readier to risk his neck.

And in Henry Jaglom's *Tracks* (1976) Dennis Hopper plays Jack Falen, an army sergeant assigned to accompany to its final resting place a coffin whose occupant he variously describes as his best friend, an anonymous hero and a black who saved his life in combat. As his train winds eastward across the bountiful geography of the country for which he fought and his friend died, the somewhat eccentric assortment of passengers encountered *en route* come to appear the fragmented reflections of its most recent history (it is 1973 and American involvement in Vietnam has just been formally terminated), as filtered through his own mental instability: an easygoing political activist, two ingenuously candid young girls off on holiday, a gregarious real estate dealer and his chess-playing companion. But when his rambling Vietnam reminiscences are met with responses ranging from indifference to pity, he breaks down completely – at which point it becomes clear that his sense of betrayal over the war forms only part of the heavier burden of guilt and deprivation he has borne since his childhood (one of his earliest memories is of sheepishly peeking at his mother's garters). That Falen is an emblematic figure, bearing the loss of national innocence on his frail shoulders (and there is a haunting rightness to the notion that Vietnam's Unknown Soldier should be one of its *survivors*), is confirmed by the film's ending, of a type that discourages interpretation since any single reading of it can doubtless be matched by others just as valid: leaping into the grave alongside the coffin, he re-emerges draped in the military gear that, it transpires, is all it ever contained.

Betrayal is still the theme of Jeremy Kagan's *Heroes* (1977) and Karel Reisz's *Dog Soldiers* (1978, and known in the United States as *Who'll Stop the Rain?*), though what has been defiled is not childhood 'innocence' but the illusions of a period endowed – at least, from the vantage point of the decade that succeeded it – with the energy and fragile optimism of childhood: the sixties.

The ebullient hero of *Heroes*, escaping from a psychiatric hospital where he has been undergoing treatment after service in Vietnam (and there's a hint of bargain-basement Jack Nicholson about Henry Winkler's wired-up characterisation), sets out with the pooled savings of his fellow inmates to found a worm farm in California. But though adversity stalks his path – a violent run-in with muggers, the discovery that a buddy he hoped to enrol into his scheme was a war casualty, a painful moment of self-realisation in Eureka, California (the United States is apparently dotted with small towns whose names lend themselves to facile symbolism) – all will end happily for the Fonz in the hospitable arms of a pretty girl.

Not so for the tormented protagonists of *Dog Soldiers* (based on the National Book Award-winning novel of the same title by Robert Stone, who collaborated on two separate versions of the script before withdrawing from further active participation in the project and subsequently disowning the completed film): they inject the poison of Vietnam, in the form of a cache of heroin, into the vulnerably fat American forearm.

The movie's credit-titles unroll over some nightmarish images of the war, which, though projected at normal speed, are shot in such a way as to invest the frenzied, directionless movement with something of the heavy, mastodonic sluggishness of slow motion. A horrified witness to this explosive Armageddon, war correspondent John Converse (the excellent Michael Moriarty), forthwith arranges for a large shipment of heroin to be smuggled out of Vietnam. Not the least of the film's narrative inconsistencies, however, is its failure to provide this significant moral and political volte-face with any plausible motivation: it is never clear whether his decision is a gratuitous one, or made solely for profit, or from a whimsically formulated wish to measure up personally to the insanity of the war (as US Army helicopters circle the jungle, he comments off-screen: 'In a world where elephants are pursued by flying men, people naturally want to get high').

The navy friend to whom he entrusts the mission, Ray (Nick Nolte), is first seen playing a game of football so mud-bespattered as hardly to differ from the war itself. Initially reluctant, Ray leaves for America and manages to smuggle the heroin out of the Oakland shipyards; but when he delivers it as instructed to Converse's wife Marge (Tuesday Weld), he discovers that she knows nothing of the operation. Whereupon *Dog Soldiers* develops into a fairly conventional chase movie in which Ray and Marge (her child packed off to relatives) are pursued through California by a pair of boobishly sadistic thugs hired by a crooked Narcotics Bureau agent. The war surfaces intermittently and in increasingly improbable places. The barbiturate-addicted Marge, for instance, works in a protest book-shop. (So what?) When torturing Converse for information, the thugs switch on television to cover his screams – and, of course, at just that moment there would have to be a news report from Vietnam. In fact, Reisz, an English director of Czech origin, has a tourist's tendency to allow the glittery idiosyncrasies of the American landscape to carry much too much ideological weight: the fact that naked go-go dancers have invaded the bar that was Ray's favourite watering-hole before his drafting seems a risibly light-weight indictment of a society's decline.

In its final sequence, the movie shifts gear into melancholic 'Where have all the flowers gone' nostalgia as the two fugitives (Marge now dipping into the heroin) retreat to a fairy-lit Jesuit settlement in New Mexico that was once a hippie commune. There Ray sacrifices himself for Marge and Converse, who give him what looks almost like a soldier's burial by the roadside, with the heroin scattered over his grave as part of the ritual.

As an oblique investigation into the effects of Vietnam on the American psyche, *Dog Soldiers* is not without its merits (notably Richard H. Kline's fluid and smokily beautiful photography), but is profoundly compromised by Reisz's misguided determination to contain the war within the fuzzy, catch-all notion of a 'trauma', seeping insidiously into every crevice – and the film is mostly concerned with crevices – instead of coming to terms with how it irreparably altered the *whole* nation's perspective on its traditional values and aspirations.

In Ted Post's jejune potboiler, *Good Guys Wear Black* (1977), the element of betrayal, bathetically, never rises above the trusty old double-cross variety. Its hero, John T. Booker (played, if that's the word I'm looking for, by ex-karate champion Chuck Norris), attempts to discover who it was that set him up along with his 'Black Tigers' commando unit during a raid to rescue CIA personnel from a Vietnamese fortress at the tail end of the war (as cease-fire conditions were being negotiated in Paris). Though now earning an unlikely living in California as a lecturer in political science ('The reasons for the war were beyond any kind of logic,' he announces to his spellbound class as the definitive word on Vietnam, then, as though he had said something subversive, facetiously proposes that they all sing patriotic songs), Booker allows himself to be sucked into a turgid maelstrom of plots and counterplots leading inexorably (which is to say, predictably) to the ultra-suave Secretary of State designate Conrad Morgan (James Franciscus) and a boozily self-flagellating aide with the misleadingly evocative name of Edgar J. Harolds (Dana Andrews).

Peddling an interpretation of the Vietnam period so simplistic as to verge on the tautological, this is the kind of movie where the villains obligingly spell out their villainy on every conceivable pretext (Morgan, rationalising with cool aplomb the deal he struck with the North Vietnamese: 'Expedience built this country. The end justifies the means'); the heroes suffer no more than a fleeting twinge of doubt as they ramrod their way through due process ('Whatever happened to the good old days when John Wayne and Randolph Scott were glad to have their asses shot off for the good old US of A?'); and everyone poses the type of ill-phrased question any half-competent scriptwriter would know had to be thrown out ('Are you certain of your intelligence?' Booker hilariously asks the CIA agent who is supplying him with information).

In the Hollywood mentality Vietnam was inextricably yoked to crime, with war-weary veterans attempting valiantly to 'go straight' but unable to shake off the lingering odour of carnage that attracted criminality to them and often brought about the violent death they had managed to escape on the battlefield. John Flynn's sleek thriller *Rolling Thunder* (1977) spun a familiar tale of an ex-POW, Major Charles Rane (William Devane), pursuing singlemindedly – and, as we shall see, literally singlehandedly – the killers of his wife and son. But Paul Schrader's characteristically overblown script did succeed in adding a couple of grisly turns to the screw: what causes the thugs' lethal cupidity is the televised presentation to Rane from a grateful home town of a silver dollar for every day of his captivity; and, after his hand has been mashed by a mechanical waste disposal unit (his prison camp ordeal has fortified him against torture and, it is suggested, even given him a taste for it), he sharpens the hook that replaces it into the deadliest of weapons. Otherwise, it was the mixture as before, with the occasional monochrome flashback of Rane suffering at the hands of his VC captors to remind us of what its makers hoped the film was about.

Oddly enough, *Rolling Thunder* presented one of the few cases of a vet returning to his *wife*: this facet of the question, surely rich in dramatic possibilities, was consistently ignored by the cinema of the period. There was Mark Robson's *Limbo* (1972, with a screenplay by Joan Micklin Silver and James Bridges), but it dealt more specifically with the wives of men taken prisoner or missing in action. And perhaps because Robson was an old Hollywood trouper whose first directorial assignments dated from the early forties, it emerged as the kind of genteel, sometimes touching, melodrama (now with an antiwar slant) that used to star June Allyson or Teresa Wright. Its dénouement, however, a parody of the most traditional type of happy ending, was disquietingly effective: the heroine's just released husband returns to a firing squad of TV cameras and a young wife who hardly knows him and never had time to love him, Robson sealing their uncertain reunion with an ambiguous freeze frame rather than the more complacently reassuring 'happy ever after' fade out.

If by 1972 the antiwar position had already acquired an aura of respectability, Hal Ashby demonstrated that six years later it came blessed with full Establishment approval.

In *Coming Home*, whose critical and commercial success made it *the* 'returning vet' movie, a good dose of radical politics suffices to cure the disabled veteran Luke (Jon Voight) of all his mental, and apparently quite a few of his physical, ailments (almost as though being crippled were somehow a more benign affliction in the climate, both meteorologically and spiritually balmy, of Southern California). Luke, paralysed from the waist down, is first seen in an overcrowded, none too efficiently run, army hospital in Los Angeles, wheeling himself along its constricted corridors on a stretcher bed on which he is obliged to lie face downwards. Though his initial encounter with the movie's heroine, Sally (Jane Fonda), is marked by the kind of realistically squalid grace note that would not have been possible before the seventies – she upsets his urine bag – their mutual involvement is still in the classic novelettish tradition of a wounded soldier's regeneration through the devotion of a beautiful nurse; and one who, coupled with his growing commitment to antiwar activism in the wake of a disturbed fellow patient's suicide, will make a new man of him.

For Luke has soon exchanged his stretcher for a wheelchair which he manoeuvres with such ease, speed and mobility that one almost suffers a twinge of envy watching him scoot around. A few football games, a candlelit dinner at Sally's new apartment, and his embitterment would seem to have been dissipated, as though all along it had been directed more against his admittedly humiliating confinement to a stretcher than against the permanence of his condition and the war that caused it.

Understandably reluctant to slow down while he is ahead, he makes a pass at Sally, whose gentle but firm 'I've never been unfaithful to my husband', whether kindly or literally intended, is in the circumstances a rebuff of truly astonishing tact. Or is it – since, in fact, at this point in the proceedings neither she nor the spectator realises just what she might be missing. When, in protest against his friend's suicide, Luke chains himself to the iron gates of a USMC Recruit Depot (an exceedingly tricky operation from the looks of it even for someone in full possession of his physical capacities), Sally, seeing the incident on television, rushes over and proposes to spend the night with him. No sweat: after a few decorous preliminaries in the bathroom, Luke emerges in his wheelchair, his nudity protected by a small towel over his crotch, clambers into bed (without crucially disarranging the towel) and, in a series of tasteful dissolves, accompanied on the soundtrack by the occasional anxious query – 'What should I do now?' or 'Can you feel this?' – Sally, not without hang-ups of her own, achieves her first orgasm.

Since the movie never chooses to disclose the precise extent of Luke's physical abilities, the audience must accept his sexual prowess on trust. It no longer seems to matter that, in an earlier scene, a crippled black patient complained to Sally about the dearth of advice offered disabled vets on their future sex lives (a delicate problem which was, however, intelligently handled by a less permissive Hollywood in such films as William Wyler's *The Best Years of Our Lives*, 1946, and Fred Zinnemann's *The Men*, 1950, in which Marlon Brando played a paraplegic). Glossing over these potentially awkward practicalities, *Coming Home* opts instead for facile beach-party bucolics, with Luke breezily coasting Sally along on the arm of his wheelchair (as on one of the bicycles in *Butch Cassidy*) to the vapid, Mantovani-like strains of Lennon and McCartney's 'Strawberry Fields Forever'. (It should be said that the movie's soundtrack score is one of the most dispensable in the history of the cinema: an ultra-relaxed medley of popular songs from the late sixties, serving neither to underline nor counterpoint the visuals, as though Ashby had had a huge jukebox placed on the set in which he remembered, from time to time, to insert a coin.)

Then the moment arrives when the film focuses, via a flashback, on the character of Sally herself. When her Marine captain husband, Bob (Bruce Dern), is shipped out to Vietnam – 'Combat City', as he jovially refers to it – she decides to volunteer for unpaid nursing duty in the local veterans' hospital. Sally is a model army spouse: hair stiffly permed and ribboned, make-up unimaginatively ap-plied, skirt worn just above the knees with a neat little blouse, she frets about her husband minding that she has taken a job in his absence and stands to attention for the national anthem on TV. Which adds up to a *character role* for Jane Fonda. In view of an average audience's familiarity with the actress's personal appear-ance and much-publicised politics, she will necessarily be perceived at the beginning of the movie as being in disguise: a disguise, moreover, that most spectators will be unable to help mentally 'correcting', to the detriment of any pretence at realism that the movie might harbour.

But her affection for the liberated Vi (Penelope Milford), the girlfriend of one of Bob's fellow officers, gradually causes her to loosen up. She takes to wearing teeshirt and jeans, moves out of her house on the base into a cramped apartment overlooking the beach, buys a weird little speedster and, most dramatically, allows her hair to adopt its natural frizz. In short, *she turns into Jane Fonda*. It is not only possible to measure her disenchantment with the values to which her dreary life has hitherto been consecrated by these outward changes in fortune, it is absolutely essential, since precious few more resonant clues are provided. (An exception, though, and one of the movie's most sharply observed scenes, is her vain endeav-our to interest the ladies of the camp's gossip-sheet in publishing a spread on the veterans' plight. One contributor even voices qualms about the propriety of any feminine presence in the wards: 'When I was on my diet, I didn't want candy lying about the house.')

Resplendent in her new Jane Fonda hairdo, her external aspect coinciding at last with her long-repressed inner self, Sally runs into Luke on his first exhilarating excursion by wheelchair. Their mutual euphoria is enshrined in the script's sole (probably unwitting) stab at a rhyming couplet: 'You got a chair!' 'You changed your hair!' Both have been freed from straitjackets, as it were, and Ashby appears to regard Sally's curls as no less significant an advance than Luke's graduation to semi-vertical mobility. Later, about to join Bob on leave in Hong Kong, she loyally has her hair restraightened and unearths all those klutzy army wife outfits once so rapturously discarded; luckily, on her return, sex with Luke will practically make her hair frizz back overnight. Sally, it is clear, has had a narrow escape. Had there been no Vietnam, who knows what might have happened to her.

Notwithstanding the movie's emphasis on the Luke–Sally axis, a slightly more subtle characterisation has been reserved for Bob (an excellent performance by Dern in a thankless role). In the parallel montage with which the movie begins, a cynical discussion between the resentful hospital vets is intercut with shots of Bob jogging in preparation for imminent overseas service. His whole professional existence has been a preparation for this moment: such a soldier *needs* Vietnam, if only to justify his choice of career. Later, however, he sees things differently. On leave in Hong Kong, he is asked by Sally what the war is like. 'I don't know what it's like. I only know what it is. TV shows what it's like. It sure as hell don't show what it is.' And in the intimacy of their hotel room he struggles to describe to her how he discovered his own men cold-bloodedly decapitating corpses and skewering their heads on the tops of poles. 'Y'know, that really scares the shit outa the VC . . .' he adds in a half-defensive tone that suggests some of the Viet Cong's fear has rubbed off on him.

Bob's untimely repatriation is prompted by a minor leg wound that may have been accidental or self-inflicted but for which he has in any case been given a medal, as though it were a poultice. (It is one of *Coming Home*'s unintentionally comic side-effects, reinforced by the striking contrast between Bob's chronic rigidity of character and Luke's elfin vitality, that his limp emerges as a rather more serious affliction than Luke's only mildly inconvenient paralysis.) Since the demonstration at the Recruit Depot, the activities of the two young lovers, racing around the beach community in Luke's sports car (with its cute registration number VET 210), have been monitored by the FBI and are eventually reported to an uncomprehending Bob. Though Luke, to whose many qualities one must now add that of sagacious counsellor, persuades him of Sally's unabated love, Bob pulls off his uniform (and medal) and plunges naked into the ocean (an act widely if prematurely interpreted as his suicide, just as in almost any Hollywood film a slight cough will invariably betoken the onset of a fatal disease); and

Ashby employs a second parallel montage here to intercut Bob's symbolic self-cleansing with Luke spouting antiwar platitudes to local high-school kids.

What makes Bob a more complex figure than might be apparent from such an ungenerous résumé is precisely that his psychological make-up rejects the type of glib frog-into-prince metamorphosis that overtakes the others. If Vietnam has significantly altered the lives of Sally and Luke, its influence has been strangely *beneficial* (the latter's disability excepted). Sally has liberated herself from the drably decorous routine of a dutiful army wife; and Luke (over whose pre-Vietnam past hangs a whiff of mindless Southern Californian hedonism, as evidenced by his sports car and poolside apartment) has, with his involvement in the protest movement, 'gained a new purpose in life'.

But Bob, who most badly stood in need of a 'happening' on the order of Vietnam, has ironically seen it drain his life of purpose. He went off to fight one war and returned from another. And Dern's performance clearly intimates that the precarious gung-ho ethos which has hitherto governed the character's life – and which, though dented, continues to support him through the estrangement of his homecoming – is a form of repression too ingrained to be as nonchalantly reversed as Sally letting her hair down, in both the figurative and literal senses. Not least, his presence provides the script with its sole opportunity of alluding to the physical horror of Vietnam, in a movie that otherwise treats the war as though it were a particularly violent game of squash and the enemy as being as flat and indistinguishable as a wall. (But it is a disturbing feature of almost all Vietnam cinema, even a documentary like *Winter Soldier*, that the war's 'victims' are generally understood to be maimed or traumatised *American* soldiery and only incidentally the Vietnamese people.)

To be fair, *Coming Home*'s sincerity is never in question and on occasion fleshed out by the kind of behavioural detail with which Ashby is most at ease: a hospital picnic, with the basketball-playing, guitar-strumming, pot-smoking inmates indifferent to the attempts of a visiting officer to boost their morale, is nicely judged, as is the recreated barracks atmosphere of the crowded wards (even to the traditional accompaniment of a mournful harmonica). But it is a frisbee of a movie, held aloft by sheer weightlessness. It succeeds in smoothing away all the rough edges of the period (*circa* 1968 from the evidence of a Robert Kennedy speech on television) to leave only the pious certitudes of a later decade's positive thinking. In short, a movie to which, with the possible exception of Luke's honest-to-goodness bag of piss, not even the ladies of the base newspaper could raise any very strenuous objections.

Infinitely more thought-provoking was an Emmy-winning TV film made in 1979 by the English-born director David Greene, *Friendly Fire*, which – remarkably for such a late arrival on the scene – succeeded in taking the thematics of Vietnam cinema down several unbeaten paths. Inspired by an authentic case (fidelity to which extended to leaving the characters' names unchanged), it recounted the efforts of an Iowan Catholic family – with the aid of the novelist C. D. B. Bryan, on whose book the movie is based – to circumvent increasingly paranoid bureaucratic opposition, in the form of phone-tapping and mail censorship, and uncover the truth behind the official version of their son's death in Vietnam. For Sergeant Michael 'Mikey' Mullin (Dennis Erdman) is a victim of the morbidly dubbed 'friendly fire' (i.e. fire caused not by enemy action but from the home side), and as such his name has been withheld from all the published casualty lists. With the two hundred dollars sent them by the army to defray funeral expenses, the Mullins take out a half-page advertisement in the local newspaper urging parents in Iowa to join them in protest against the war, a gesture which results in a bulging mailbag, a nationwide TV appearance and participation in the Washington Peace March.

So meticulously detailed is its depiction of how issues often deemed to be of only national concern can with shuddering immediacy be brought home to two bewildered individuals, their initial uncertainties hardening into lonely determination (then, imperceptibly, into obsession), that even with a running time of over two-and-a-half hours this modestly gripping drama seems not a minute too long.

When, for instance, the soldier's mother (a bizarrely restrained Carol Burnett) enquires of an attending army officer when her son's body will be flown home, she receives the chilling reply: 'Just as soon as they have a planeful'; sent a form letter of commiseration from President Nixon, with which is enclosed a dossier of his various speeches on Vietnam, she contemptuously scrawls 'Return to Sender' on the envelope; and, confronted at last with Mikey's body in an open casket, she hesitantly confesses that she would have preferred the waxy corpse to be disfigured '. . . so I could believe he died in a war'. No less poignant is the incongruous set of nail-file and clippers bought by Mikey's younger sister as a going-away present; Mrs Mullin's insistence that her son's tomb-stone read not 'died in . . .' but, with blunt literalness, 'killed in Vietnam'; or the wry observation by a black corporal from Mikey's platoon that the only question ever asked him about his combat experience is 'Hey, man, didya kill someone?'

The film, demonstrating how the war could also transform the *parents* of draftees into social misfits (as Mrs Mullin says of their gradual ostracism by the inhabitants of their home town: 'It's like we're on different roads now'), firmly resists the temptation to portray the Mullins as purely altruistic crusaders, untainted by personal considerations. Worrying away compulsively at the con-flicting testimonies surrounding Mikey's death, they manage to alienate their immediate family, their oldest friends and finally even Bryan himself (Sam Waterston), whose own interest in the case meets with less than the full-hearted approval of his wife and his agent. When, after exhaustively interviewing both Mikey's comrades and his superiors, Bryan is forced to conclude that his death was indeed an accident, the suspected military cover-up being perhaps no more than the jittery reaction of a monolithic organisation ill-equipped to deal rationally with such dogged burrowing into its affairs, the Mullins simply do not want to know. It is as though they had been betrayed.

A final, dispassionate title informs us that between 1968 and 1973 no fewer than 10,303 American soldiers were known to have died in Vietnam through 'friendly fire'.

— *Chapter 5* —

GOD BLESS AMERICA

In the prologue to *Notes*, a rather scatty memoir of the filming of *Apocalypse Now*, Eleanor Coppola catalogues her husband's efforts by telephone, and frequently via agents, to obtain the services of various Hollywood stars for his upcoming Vietnam movie. McQueen, Pacino, Caan, Nicholson and Redford all find themselves on the receiving end of these increasingly forlorn calls, and all either make unacceptable demands (McQueen, offered three million dollars for the seventeen-week shooting schedule necessitated by the role of Willard, insists on the same fee to play Kurtz for *three* weeks) or decline outright (Pacino is afraid of tropical diseases, Caan's pregnant wife doesn't want to have her baby in the Philippines, etc.). Eventually (but only after throwing his five Oscars out of the window in frustration) Coppola, as everyone knows, cast Brando as Kurtz and, following the abrupt departure of Harvey Keitel, the then relatively unknown Martin Sheen as Willard.

Hollywood being one vast (sour) grapevine, this kind of news would circulate fast. The fact that Coppola, in 1977 a man of 38 but still a boy-wonder by the industry's standards, was planning a multimillion-dollar epic on the war, though judged in some quarters as a classic instance of a fool rushing in where angels (in the showbiz sense of 'financial backers') had feared to tread, was nevertheless a sign that the subject was at long last coming out of quarantine. It would be cynical to attribute the sudden rush of Vietnam movies set into motion after, but released before, *Apocalypse Now* (Sidney J. Furie's *The Boys in Company C*, produced by the Hong Kong-based company Golden Harvest, Ted Post's *Go Tell the Spartans* and Michael Cimino's *The Deer Hunter*) less to any urgent moral or political commitment than to the desire to steal the thunder of a movie whose preparatory stages alone had caught Hollywood's imagination – cynical but not necessarily wrong. One should not generalise, of course. While neither *The Boys in Company C* nor *Go Tell the Spartans* is absolutely devoid of interest, each is what one might call a 'quickie', if not a B-movie then resolutely an A-minus, whose existence seems motivated solely by opportunism. But *The Deer Hunter*, whatever one thinks of it, is a different matter entirely, a long, complex and skilfully constructed narrative whose inception could not possibly have been inspired by the hope of cashing in on the much-delayed *Apocalypse Now*.

As we have seen, for almost a decade Hollywood had managed to avert its gaze from the horrors of the war itself, opting instead for such Vietnam-related themes as campus unrest and the troubled reintegration of vets into civilian life. For the movie industry Vietnam had been a trauma, a Zeitgeist, a tragic memory, a scar which in time would heal – anything, in short, except a war where people killed and/or got killed. It was evident that, for the seventies, any project bearing even a vague resemblance to *The Green Berets* was out of the question. Given that the subject-matter was far less charged with the emotive immediacy it had possessed in 1968, certainly no one would come out in protest – but, just as certainly, no one would come out at all. The question was therefore: what should the Vietnam War look like on film? What were the motifs, visual and thematic, that would emerge as dominant, that would recur in film after film – with greater or lesser variations – to evolve into a codified 'Vietnam style'? Only by formulating a set of genre conventions at the outset, conventions which would be developed, refined or, alternatively, superseded by subsequent movies could the Hollywood machine come to terms with this still-sensitive area.

The Boys in Company C was not the film to provide a conclusive answer. It revolves around a bunch of raw recruits to the US Marine Corps in 1967, with each of whom we become individually acquainted by means of a series of vignettes at the beginning of the narrative. Thereafter, we follow them through their basic training, with all its rigours and humiliations, into their tragicomic adventures in combat.

Though the purpose of the vignettes (which centre on the

draftees' arrival at the army base) is primarily to familiarise us with the *dramatis personae* before their identities are subsumed by the merciless levelling process of their training, they can also be interpreted as a preliminary assertion of the film's somewhat self-conscious pretensions to 'realism'. Not for *The Boys in Company C* the melting-pot sentimentality of those ethnically balanced military units so familiar from Second World War movies (or, for that matter, from *The Green Berets*). This company includes Tyrone Washington, a tough black dope peddler (played by *Roots* actor Stan Shaw); Vinnie Fazio, obsessed with sex (Michael Lembeck); Dave Bisbee, whose long blond hair and guitar denote the typical counter-culture Jesus (Craig Wasson); and Alvin Forster, an aspiring writer and, like Richard Dreyfuss's Curt in *American Graffiti*, the company's chronicler (James Canning).

But instead of rejecting the old army-as-cross-section-of-humanity cliché, as it patently imagines itself to be doing, such a (superficially) heterogeneous collection of individuals merely updates it. Having bracketed three of the recruits respectively with drugs, sex and flower power, Furie and his screenwriter Rick Natkin, confident that the film's textures are now securely aligned with the sacred iconography of the sixties, tend rather arbitrarily to leave it at that. And, like some Vietnam-recruiting poster beneath whose peeling surface may be glimpsed patches of an earlier one for the Second World War, *The Boys in Company C* cannot really disguise the origins of its stereotypes. In the forties model, some cheap hoodlum of perhaps Sicilian, certainly non-WASP, descent would have contrived to earn the grudging esteem of both his buddies and his superiors, just as the black drug pusher does here; the same sexual longings as here would have been more innocuously channelled into ogling pin-ups of Betty Grable; and the 'writer', represented here by Alvin, would most probably have been a 'sensitive' Montgomery Clift type complete with pipe and tattered volume of Hemingway protruding from his kit.

The problem is that, by leaning so heavily on these stereotypes, Furie is obliged to turn recent history on its head. As we know, service in Vietnam was inclined, in certain instances, to transform ordinary, basically decent young Americans into misfits, dropouts, drug addicts, petty criminals or whatever – not the reverse. Since Hollywood had already dramatised the kind of situation where vets were treated as outsiders by the very society that had made them so, being denied the automatic respect and respectability to which returning GIs have traditionally been entitled (for a few years, at least), it was surely not too much to expect the first films dealing directly with the war experience to offer some insights into what exactly had changed. But, for *The Boys in Company C*, however much the army might brutalise its charges, however riddled it might be with corruption and incompetence (the movie's judgment, not mine), it somehow remains the institution best fitted to make responsible adults out of confused and callow youths. Here misfits are turned into men, not men into misfits. When our heroes emerge at the other end, ready for overseas duty, it is as a tight, well-knit fighting unit, the pride and terror of the base.

Once it gets to Vietnam, the film marginally improves. Its most impressive feature, perhaps, anticipating Oliver Stone's *Platoon*, is that the enemy remains unseen, a shadowy, eerily invisible presence hovering just at the edge of the screen. In contrast to more apocalyptic Vietnam movies, *The Boys in Company C* comes close to capturing the feel of guerilla warfare: in the way the Viet Cong, advancing through the undergrowth with a sense of self-camouflage so instinctive that even stealth can be dispensed with, become almost part of the jungle fauna; or in the way they exchange signals that, by a disorientating reversal, imitate parrot cries, forcing the hapless intruders (who were trained as soldiers, not hunters) into a paralysing state of permanent vigilance. This approach, making the VC threat a near-abstraction (and therefore untainted by the racist slurs of *The Green Berets* and *The Deer Hunter*), means that the tensions in the film arise mainly from conflicts within the army itself and, later, with the ARVN.

But whereas the attacks on military obtuseness in the first half-hour are rather too scattershot, finding little to criticise beyond foul language and the kind of petty sadism common to all institutions governed by rigid discipline, in the latter half they prove more effective because directed against more precise targets. In Vietnam the company is assigned to a Captain Collins (Scott Hylands), an unstable commander whose overriding concern is with obtaining good 'body counts', no matter the identity of the bodies: he counts indiscriminately Viet Cong and peasants, men and women, adults and children. When, after escorting a trailer through enemy-infested terrain to an inland base (and suffering casualties along the way that are due to Collins's bungling leadership), they discover it to contain, not supplies as they had imagined, but cases of liquor, packs of cigarettes and other luxuries for the General and his cronies, Bisbee protests by blowing it up (apparently at no disciplinary risk to himself). And Pike (Andrew Stevens), a young professional footballer tormented by having advised his girlfriend to abort her pregnancy, is plied with drugs by the megalomaniac Collins, who is anxious to exploit his skills on the field against a crack Vietnamese team.

Meanwhile Washington, the drug pusher, now the company's mainstay and increasingly its conscience (as exemplified by several huge, soulful close-ups), has formulated the idea of smuggling drugs back into the States concealed in the kind of shapeless body bag no customs officer would dream of disturbing. Such a plan, though, would involve the collaboration of the local ARVN security chief, Colonel Trang, who, with his chubby, beringed fingers and one elongated fingernail *à la* Fu Manchu, bears a striking resemblance to the corrupt Viet Cong general of *The Green Berets*; and when Washington learns that Trang's way with suspects is to torture them first *then* give them the third degree, he withdraws from the scheme in disgust.

One last test will suffice to complete Washington's and the company's education in ethics. Captain Collins informs them that, if they beat the local Vietnamese soccer team, they will be removed from active duty and sent on a prestige tour of Japan and other neutral countries of South-East Asia. Even the professional Pike, though deeply resentful of the captain's underhand methods, agrees to participate. At half-time, however, with the Americans easy winners so far and elated by the prospect of ending their service in such enjoyable fashion, they discover that Trang has insisted on the conditions of the bargain being changed: as a means of boosting Vietnamese morale, the team is now expected to lose the match. Jeered by the spectators, and by a gloating Trang in the seat of honour, as they allow the opposition to run rings around them (literally), they suddenly follow Pike's lead and begin playing to win again, though fully realising that it will mean their return to the combat zone.

What is interesting about this sequence is the way it usefully encapsulates the confusion to which the whole movie has been prone, the way in which, to begin with, certain discrepancies of plot and motivation go unexplained. If, for instance, a victory for the host team is intended to boost Vietnamese morale, surely the ludicrously obvious way the Americans go about losing – scoring through their own goalposts, protractedly tying bootlaces, etc. – can only be counterproductive and even insulting to the 'victors'? And if the latter are (as they appear to be) such wretched sportsmen that they are actually unaware of being mocked, why should defeating them in the first place have justified sending the Americans on a demonstration tour?

One would be prepared to forgive such minor flaws if they were not directly traceable to a basic moral ambiguity at the core of the film. In his novella *The Loneliness of the Long Distance Runner* Alan Sillitoe hit upon a fairly indelible image of revolt with his adolescent athlete who, about to win a race for the greater glory of the reformatory in which he is interned, stops a few yards short of the winning tape and refuses to cross it. Already this gesture was coarsened by the American athletes at the Mexico City Olympics in 1968, when they raised their fists in a Black Panther salute only *after* winning the event and securing their medals; and in *The Boys in Company C* what subversive charge it once possessed is further undermined by its taking the form of a refusal to *lose*. Though the reasoning behind the team's defiance is that the half-mad Collins (as well as the evil Trang) receive his comeuppance, the audience cannot help but perceive their act as a positive victory for American *esprit de corps*, an exhilarating expression of Yankee grace under pressure. So what if they flirt along the way with antisocial, un-American behaviour – Washington's drug-running scheme, Pike's wish to have his unborn child aborted – in the end, as one would expect of red-blooded American boys, *they come through*. Notwithstanding unscrupulous allies and incompetent, even corrupt superiors, this war can hardly be the dishonest fiasco its detractors would make it out to be if it enables Washington, Pike, Bisbee,

Vinnie and Alvin to overcome their individual problems and work so well together as a team.

But if the movie fails on all the larger issues it can at least be credited with usefully exploring some of the incidentals. It has a semi-documentary aspect that is not negligible. We learn, for one thing, what body bags look like, of what material they are made, how they zip open. We learn that body counts can be (and often were) artificially jacked up by the inclusion of civilian victims, as confirmed by Peter Brook's theatrical dramatisation of Vietnam politics and attitudes, *US* (subsequently recorded on film by Brook himself as *Tell Me Lies*). And the dilapidated USO base with its improvised bowling-alley and 'Esther Williams' pool, though as spectacle no match for Coppola's strobe-lit pleasure palace rising out of the jungle in *Apocalypse Now*, is undoubtedly far closer to reality. Even the monotony engendered by the movie's self-indulgent insistence on the horrors of Marine Corps training, served up in neatly packaged episodes of 'pre-sliced' life, probably does convey an accurate picture of what an average draftee would undergo (as against the archly humorous treatment of draft induction in *Big Wednesday*, whose artful dodgers hope to pass themselves off as cripples or outrageously effeminate homosexuals). These are secondary virtues, perhaps, but authentic ones.

Go Tell the Spartans is set at the time when the French colonial war was coinciding in its final stages with the full and official assumption of Vietnam as an American responsibility (where before the United States had been involved in an ill-defined 'advisory' capacity). Though this has the oddly nostalgic effect of situating the whole even further back in history than, from the viewpoint of 1978, it actually was (an impression reinforced by the fact that two of its principal characters had already fought together in Korea), it does work to the extent that it focuses our attention for once on an exact juncture of the war. In general, Hollywood has portrayed Vietnam as a kind of phantasmagoric limbo, untrammelled by dates or place names, all 'middle' with no real, definable beginning or end.

The film's protagonist (played by Burt Lancaster) is Major Asa

Barker, a professional soldier and commander of an American Military Assistance Advisory Group at Penang. Barker is a battered also-ran of three wars, whose hopes of promotion beyond the rank of Major were blighted when he was caught by the President and his own general enjoying fellatio with the latter's wife – in the White House. When we first see him, he has just received the order to scout an unoccupied hamlet called Muc Wa (the title of the original novel by Daniel Ford was *Incident at Muc Wa*); judging it to be of doubtful value, he sends in a false report. But when the General insists that Muc Wa's position on the coastal road to Penang makes it strategically important, Barker reluctantly dispatches a group of new 'advisers' who have been assigned to his command. These are Second Lieutenant Hamilton (Joe Unger), naïve, untested, fiercely jingoistic, i.e. a young soldier of the old school; Corporal Courcey (Craig Wasson, a real Vietnam war movie vet – he played Bisbee in *The Boys in Company C*), an intelligent, personable draftee whose presence in Vietnam, at a period when virtually no draftees were posted there, mystifies Barker; the battle-weary and slightly punch-drunk Sergeant Oleonowski (Jonathan Goldsmith), who served under Barker in Korea; and a Corporal Abraham Lincoln (Dennis Howard), whose only resemblance to his namesake would seem to be a perpetually lugubrious mien (probably caused in his case by being so named). Accompanying them is a raggedy complement of South Vietnamese soldiers, peasants (both old and very young) and local mercenaries, led by a bloodthirsty Viet Cong-hater nicknamed 'Cowboy' (Evan Kim).

So, except for the vast difference in stature and temperament between Barker and Captain Collins (aided by Lancaster's 'star quality'), the basic narrative components are similar to those of *The Boys in Company C*; on the other hand, the coolly even tone of Post's movie could hardly be further removed from the calculated hysteria of Furie's. If a sense of disillusionment with both military values and objectives is just as pervasive in *Go Tell the Spartans*, it evolves naturally out of precise, realistic and on the whole convincing character developments. Instead of heroes and villains, Us against Them, the movie is crisscrossed by subtly graded shades of imperfection on both sides. Barker himself is no model soldier. When the black signalman Toffee (Hilly Hicks) persists in employing an irreverent manner of address – 'Hey, Major' – he makes a show of objecting more, one suspects, for the sake of form than out of any faith in military hierarchy. Not that Barker has done anything so pretentious as yield to despair: for him (and this will be the keynote of the whole film) Vietnam is just another war, his third.

The composition of the unit departs from both the Second World War movie cross-section, uniform in its very variety, and the coarsely updated caricatures of *The Boys in Company C*. Its members seem almost *arbitrarily* selected, by which I intend a compliment to the film. In life, surely, army units would resist such facile division into one good-natured black versus one sadistic white bigot, one lecherous second-generation Italian versus one virginal second-generation Pole, etc. Here the draftee, unlike Wasson's smirking, pot-smoking hippie of the earlier movie, is an attractive, rather reserved and completely *straight* young man who proves quietly expert at his job. The reason he offers Barker for having chosen a posting to Vietnam – that, if he had to be a soldier, he wanted to be in the roughest, toughest unit in the whole US Army – does make a kind of sense. Though he never claims, like Alvin, to be a 'writer', we feel that the Vietnam experience has been consciously courted, will be stored away and, who knows, one day put to use. Poor Hamilton, on the other hand, has seen too many movies. Fully intending to pave the jungle of South Vietnam with good intentions, he becomes a tragicomic figure whose gestures, purchased second-hand, are fatally ill-adapted to Vietnam combat. About to leave for Muc Wa, he gives his motley crew the standard pep talk, as stale as a sermon, only to see Oleonowski take over and whip up the required fanaticism by screaming 'Kill Communists! Kill Communists!'; assigned to measure the increase in mosquito bites when insecticide is not applied, he bravely bares his own arm, remarking stiffly to Courcey: 'I never ask my men to do anything I wouldn't do myself'; and, after a skirmish with the Viet Cong, he radios back the message: 'We have met the enemy and they are ours', causing an incredulous Barker to choke on his coffee.

Only Oleonowski's angst seems pitched too high: his eventual suicide, by retiring into his quarters and putting a pistol to his forehead, is undoubtedly the least plausible event in the narrative, because so blatantly derivative, in style if not in substance, of hackneyed, a-man's-gotta-do-what-a-man's-gotta-do heroics.

On the whole, *Go Tell the Spartans* is a decent, average war movie (surprisingly so from the director of *Good Guys Wear Black*), its mostly run-of-the-mill qualities appearing exceptional only in the exceptional context of Vietnam cinema. Its cynical, vaguely absurd-ist attitude to the war prevents it from ever embracing the obscene complacency of *The Green Berets*; and perhaps the highest praise one can pay it is that (while in the cinema, at least) one seldom questions its unfocused attitude to the political ambiguities of American involvement. Like countless minor westerns, it gives the impression of drawing unaffectedly upon a well-worn set of genre conventions – *except that, at the period when it was made, there was no Vietnam War genre.*

This emerges most powerfully in its treatment of both the Viet Cong and South Vietnamese. On a scouting foray Courcey encoun-ters a group of displaced peasants, all women, old men and babes-in-arms. Disregarding Cowboy's vehement protests, Hamilton allows them to shelter in the encampment. ('Our task is also to win the hearts and minds of the Vietnamese people.') One pretty young girl takes to dogging Courcey's footsteps.

Barker (who has helicoptered out to Muc Wa): 'Are you screwing her?'

Courcey: 'No, sir!'

Barker (wistfully): 'Well, somebody ought to . . .'

Later, he is heard to say: 'Better pump that little cunt full of penicillin before the whole barracks come down with the clap.'

When they are finally ordered to evacuate Muc Wa in the face of a massive Viet Cong build-up, Courcey, outraged by the decision to abandon Cowboy and the South Vietnamese, elects to stay behind and Barker, grudgingly impressed by this gesture, joins him. At which point, we discover that Cowboy's hatred of the Viet Cong, even if neurotic in its intensity, has not blinded him: his instinct that the group of peasants befriended by Courcey were Viet Cong sympathisers is proved right. Even the tiniest tots, caught making their escape in the night and gunned down by the mercenaries, are swathed in ammunition belts. And the sole survivor of their massacre is the pretty young girl, who subsequently (a shade predictable, this) attempts to kill Courcey.

Earlier, Barker has resorted to bribing an ARVN Colonel (Clyde Susatsu) to raise artillery and air support for the increasingly beleaguered garrison. The Colonel's venality is patent enough: the elegant French drawing-room, the rather too glamorous interpreter, the cases of cognac guilelessly stacked against the wall, not to mention the unctuous suavity of his own con-man style. But this, once again, is held within strictly credible bounds (even erring on the side of modesty when compared to several well-documented scandals involving the South Vietnamese military) and bears little resemblance to the comic-strip Oriental heinousness of Colonel Trang in *The Boys in Company C*.

The Vietnamese are as usual denied psychological 'equality' with the American characters, but they are at least allowed their reasons. Cowboy may deal summarily with prisoners by decapitating them or potential informants by half-drowning them but, given the circumstances of his own death – shot by one of the refugees – his judgment, if not necessarily the severity of his methods, is validated. If the Viet Cong appear devious in their exploitation of women and children as infiltrators, the uninhabitable devastation around Muc Wa would demonstrate, were no further evidence available, that they have plenty to be devious about. One aged war victim, his features as cracked and rutted as a quarry, hovers ominously on the fringe of the action, slipping unseen into the undergrowth at the approach of a soldier. After the ambush, when the wounded Courcey painfully drags himself to his feet and prepares for the long trek back to Penang, this wizened spectre finally steps forward to point a revolver at him. Courcey, strangely unfazed, just calls out, 'I'm goin' home . . . I'm goin' home . . .' and hobbles off. Whereupon, the wretched old man apparently expires.

Throughout, an almost elegiac strain of melancholy underlies the film's rough-and-tumble surface. It is perceptible in the scene where Lincoln, stoned on opium, scrambles up the watchtower at Muc Wa and proceeds to chant the Gettysburg Address in a sing-song (and oddly 'Vietnamese') voice; in Barker's nostalgia for 'a real war', one in which he might be 'hitting the beach at Anzio', instead of this 'sucker's tour, going nowhere just round and round in circles'; and in the reiterated American rumbles of 'It's *their* war . . .'. Most curious and revealing in this respect is the emphasis placed by the script on a continuity of defeat between the recent French humiliation and the gruff confidence of the American military command. The determination of this second wave of invaders not to repeat the errors of the first (the French, according to Barker, 'got tied down in static defense') finds its *reductio ad absurdum* when he is upbraided by his superior for referring to his company's 'esprit'. ('That's a French word, isn't it?') At the beginning, the link seems ironically intended; but, little by little, the movie is infused with a kind of romantic fatalism, culminating in the discovery of the French cemetery at Muc Wa. On its wooden portal can be read (from Herodotus's account of the Battle of Thermopylae and the 300 Spartans): 'Stranger, when you find us lying here, go tell the Spartans we obeyed their orders.'

More subtly controversial than *The Green Berets*, and perhaps more durably so than *Apocalypse Now*, Michael Cimino's *The Deer Hunter* had as chequered a history after it opened as Coppola's film before. Cimino (who collaborated in 1973 with *Apocalypse Now*'s scenarist John Milius on the screenplay of *Magnum Force*, which was directed by none other than Ted Post of *Go Tell the Spartans* and *Good Guys Wear Black*) had only one previous feature film to his credit, *Thunderbolt and Lightfoot* (1974), a heist trifle with Clint Eastwood. Given this rather unprepossessing pedigree, the movie's pre-release publicity was much less aggressively pitched than that of *Apocalypse Now*, which meant that the subsequent risk of disappointment was that much less great. As it transpired, it became an immediate success both commercially and critically, sweeping the board at the 1979 Oscars. But critics writing in specialised magazines proved less adulatory than daily or weekly reviewers, and the existence of a growing backlash was confirmed at the same year's Berlin Festival, where *The Deer Hunter* was the official American entry. Judging the film an affront to the struggles of the Vietnamese people, the Soviet delegation withdrew in protest, followed by the Hungarians, Bulgarians, East Germans, Czechs and Cubans.

The Deer Hunter, in fact, is a before-and-after advertisement for the USA. 'Before' is a few days prior to its protagonists' drafting to Vietnam; 'after' recounts the efforts of the strongest among them, Michael (Robert De Niro), to piece together the shattered fragments of their lives; and 'during', the most sensational and violent panel of its triptych form, is the war itself. Which, of course, does not automatically make it an advertisement for anything – but that it is I hope to demonstrate in the course of this chapter.

In its attempt to wrest from the Vietnam experience a positive or, at least, tolerable statement, it resembles another lengthy movie, William Wyler's *The Best Years of Our Lives*, about three discharged servicemen – from the army, navy and air force – in the immediate aftermath of the Second World War. Both works deal with the psychologically destructive imprint of war on three male friends (even if the postwar period, covered by only one 'act' of *The Deer Hunter*, occupies the whole of *The Best Years of Our Lives*); in both the theme of psychological infirmity is mirrored by that of physical amputation; and both close with a ritualised affirmation of national values emerging (relatively) unscathed from the ordeal.

Yet the divergences are even more revealing. In Wyler's film the unseen, off-screen war remains pretty much an abstraction, its necessity never questioned, its hurts those inflicted by any war, indeed, by War itself. But for Americans the Vietnam War was not merely the first real military defeat in their history (notwithstanding Nixon's cant pretence of peace with honour), it was their first war, along with Korea, perhaps, that resisted every endeavour to inflate it into War itself.

The First World War, for instance, had been a tragically under-motivated conflict, whose origins could therefore be blandly ascribed to some atavistic urge overcoming humanity every thirty years or so to ravage large areas of the planet: war as global hygiene, helping to reduce population levels and encourage reconstruction. (In any case, the United States had intervened late, mainly in order to extricate its European allies from a debilitating stalemate.) The Second World War had been a 'just' war and, dispensing this time with quotation marks, a necessary one: war as crusade. Both were ghastly but, so the argument ran, inevitable. It was during Vietnam, however, that the whole glassy concept of 'war with a capital W' lost all credibility, a phenomenon which every film on the subject (even *The Green Berets*) was obliged to take into account.

Cimino's film, like Wyler's, is concerned with themes of renewal and reconciliation, and even in an era marked by racial violence, ecological warnings, Watergate and the Vietnam hangover itself, he could still place his faith in the United States to achieve these goals: the final scene finds Michael and his friends singing 'God Bless America' together and only then does Steven (John Savage), whose legs have been amputated, succeed in overcoming his bitterness (whereas in the earlier movie the amputee, played by Harold Russell, appeared to bear no resentment whatever at his disability). The point is that Cimino's intentions were basically the same as Wyler's: to restore his audience's confidence in their country's regenerative powers. His intelligence lay in the fact that, by insisting on just how long the tunnel had been, he was able to make the light, when it first glimmers on the horizon, so convincing.

As with the war, the small town to which, in *The Best Years of Our Lives*, Fredric March, Dana Andrews and Russell return, though less sentimentalised than a *Saturday Evening Post* magazine cover, is hardly less idealised in the iconography of its archetypes. The use of grainy newsreel film stock, for instance, during the scene in which the three ex-servicemen rediscover their home town, points up Wyler's intention to universalise his setting, to ensure that it will be every spectator's idea or ideal, dream or memory, of Small-town, USA. But, with the increasing fragmentation of American society following the convulsions of the sixties, it became no longer admissible to paint small-town existence in purely *symbolic* terms, i.e. with the broad, generalising brush-strokes employed by Wyler. The Pennsylvanian steelworking community of *The Deer Hunter* is therefore particularised to the bizarre point where its inhabitants are mostly of Russian Orthodox extraction. Even so, apart from the fact that the presence of such immigrants from a remote Communist country offers the reverse image of second- or third-generation American sons being sent out to another, equally remote country that Communists threaten to overrun, Cimino cunningly devotes the first hour-long section of his film to one of the codified celebrations of American-ness, a white wedding – precisely the ritual that ends *The Best Years of Our Lives*.

God Bless America

Here, in short, is a close-up of that America which Michael, Steven and Nick (Christopher Walken) have been called upon to defend, and it would be churlish not to admit that Cimino has recreated the texture of a small, tightly knit industrial community with an almost novelistic wealth of detail: the local supermarket where Nick's girlfriend Linda (Meryl Streep) works, the masculine clutter of the bungalow shared by Nick and Michael, the dark silhouette, both ominous and reassuring, of the iron foundry, and the entanglement of television aerials and bulbous church domes peacefully cohabiting the town's skyline. This part of the movie is bathed in the Edenic atmosphere of a huge, extended and classless family (as rarely in the American cinema, one has the impression of everyone knowing everyone else), felt most strongly during the wedding party itself, a spectacular set-piece of dancing (both Russian heel-dance and American rock), singing, eating and drinking, with neatly laundered children, plump Slavic grannies and garrulous old American Legionnaires packing every corner of the screen. And what makes the sequence so effective, given that the spectator has paid to see a movie publicised as being about the war, is that, by dwelling at such length on what is unashamedly a glorification of traditional values, Cimino so completely distracts our attention from the approaching nightmare that when, like his protagonists, we are abruptly transported to Vietnam, the contrast with what has gone before is genuinely shocking.

However, two minor but disturbing occurrences cast a premonitory shadow over the proceedings. When, in accordance with the Russian custom, the newlyweds, Steven and Angela (Rutanya Alda), link arms and drink from each other's goblets during the ceremony, one fateful droplet of red wine spills (unnoticed) on to Angela's gown. And later, at the height of the revelry, a solitary Green Beret walks into the bar. When toasted by the jocular, slightly tipsy, soldiers-to-be and offered a drink, he sourly declines even to acknowledge their gesture of complicity.

After the wedding, that reaffirmation of community oneness, comes a ritual re-enactment of male superiority: the hunt. The hunting party comprises Michael, Nick, Stan, a morosely insecure womaniser and the butt of the group's jokes (played by John Cazale, a fine actor who died shortly after completing the film),

John, the proprietor of the bar (George Dzundza), and the heavy-set and monosyllabic Axel (played by a non-professional, Chuck Aspegren), the latter three not bound for Vietnam. Michael himself is the Deer Hunter, dedicated and deadly serious, for whom hunting is also, and perhaps primarily, a somewhat mystical communion with nature. This, then, is Hemingway country, with civilised man purifying in the wilderness a soul grown soft and flabby (and if the 'wilderness' happens to be located just a few miles out of town, that too is in keeping with the often self-deluding novelist). It is also Fenimore Cooper frontier country (and Cooper's best-known novel was, of course, entitled *The Deerslayer*), 'frontier' signifying anywhere a man cares to make it, anywhere he can practise the frontiersman virtues of independence, self-reliance and an ease with weapons kept as well-greased as racehorses. It is also, alas, Marlboro country, with the whole sequence shot in such a way that it might be advertising some hyper-virile brand of cigarettes. The choir heard on the soundtrack, for instance, as Michael and Nick reach the cold, clean air of the mountains, is not precisely a 'heavenly' one (it reprises the church music of the wedding), but Cimino employs it to the same uplifting effect.

Between the beery, extrovert spontaneity of the celebration and the tight, claustrophobic framing of the Vietnam sequences to come, this scene exudes an almost Bambi-like innocence. A curious allusion, no doubt, yet one less frivolous than might at first be supposed: Disney's *Bambi* was a seminal film for several generations of American children, in whom the death of Bambi's father and his own ascension to leadership of the herd must have tapped quite a few deep-seated, not to say Oedipal, emotions. And the reference also illuminates one of the scene's (and the whole movie's) more sinister traits: its Fascism, latent here but quite consciously assumed in the Vietnam section. When the critic Jonathan Rosenbaum wrote of 'The intense pantheism and towering vistas of the film's landscape shots, the poetic innocence and purity of the heroine, the telepathy and empathy shown by animals (...), the sheer terror of her flight from angry villagers and the sheer intolerance of their persecution, the misty idealism of the blue light shining on a mountain top before it is despoiled by greedy invaders', he was not describing *Bambi* but *Das blaue Licht* (*The Blue Light*), a German film directed in 1932 by Leni Riefenstahl, subsequently the cinema's most celebrated chronicler of Nazism, in whose work he claimed to detect a strong parallel with Disney's. Like Riefenstahl's and Disney's, *The Deer Hunter*'s mountain landscapes are, so to speak, 'white', 'Aryan', a distillation of elemental purity, both natural and, by a subconscious extension, racial.

Even the killing that must take place there is 'pure', a contest of equally matched wills between hunter and hunted. 'Equally matched' because Michael kills deer with a single bullet. This, the movie's pivotal metaphor, to be developed through its scenes of Russian roulette, is unquestionably linked to the historical ideology of Fascism: killing as an élitist, almost Godlike rite, legitimised by a spurious affinity with gladiatorial combat and medieval knight-errantry. It seeks to invest killing with the lonely nobility of suicide, another act requiring no more than one bullet.

Later, on their return, they spend a tranquil moment drinking in John's bar. Overhead, a propeller fan lazily revolves. Suddenly on its rhythmic flap-flap-flap is superimposed a deeper, menacingly familiar whirring. Cut. A US Army helicopter surveys a fire attack on a Vietnamese village. Michael is seen wielding a flame-thrower as expertly as though it were a blowtorch in the iron foundry. A Viet Cong raises a bamboo shelter beneath which cower a huddle of peasants, mostly women and children: he tosses a grenade inside and closes the shelter. Michael, Nick and Steven are captured by the VC and imprisoned in a bamboo cage which is submerged in a rat- and corpse-infested river under a pontoon shack. At which point, the movie turns its back on the war altogether (except for a few incidental images of refugees streaming along a road and, towards the end, the fall of Saigon) to focus on the dual spaces of cage and shack, in which another deadly but now unequal contest is to be played out between captors and captives, with the Viet Cong unceremoniously dragging their American and ARVN prisoners out of the river and forcing them to play Russian roulette while they themselves make bets on their chances of survival.

Now, given the pitch of tension maintained by Cimino through-out (a tension generated as much by his faster cutting and use of close-ups as by the material itself), there is no way this sequence can fail to make an impact on the spectator. The undiluted savagery of the Viet Cong tormentors, the slaps they administer to any victim unwilling or unable to pull the trigger on himself, the ear-grating clicks when a chamber is empty and ear-splitting explosions when it is not, the extraordinarily well-controlled hysteria of the performances (that of Walken, in particular, who in the earlier scenes seemed an improbably orchidaceous creature to have strayed so far from Park Avenue) – all these factors contribute to creating suspense as visceral as one has ever experienced in the American cinema.

But, no matter how skilfully realised, this is still a clear case of crude audience manipulation. So forceful is the imagery in its own right that we are deprived of those critical faculties which, with a less accomplished movie, might have contested the depiction of the Viet Cong (and, in *The Deer Hunter*, they are all the Vietnamese we see) as sadistic tyrants whose gambling mania, an undeniable phenomenon of life in South-East Asia, has found its ultimate gratification in playing with human dice.

Yet, since the movie is not a documentary, why should we worry at its cavalier treatment of recent historical fact? When questioned, Cimino, shamefacedly acknowledging that he had never heard of such a game being played during the war, pleaded dramatic licence. His was a movie about America, not Vietnam, about how the war changed (and, by changing, strengthened) America's appreciation of its most deeply ingrained traditions, most notably that of individualism within equality; and if these themes emerged most vividly through a misrepresentation of facts, he was, he believed, justified in so misrepresenting them. And what complicates one's response is that the invention functions so very effectively, both in its literal enactment and as a metaphor not only for the obscene logic of war itself (where a man's death may result from his being, as fortuitously as a bullet, in the wrong place at the right time) but also, via Michael's dedication to clean killing, for the whole frontiersman myth and its uneasy but still potent application to the twentieth century.

Thus, though *The Deer Hunter* articulates no overtly political discourse – and though, like his protagonists, Cimino never for a moment questions why *he* is in Vietnam – it does indirectly raise a fundamental issue. How far should an artist be free to deform the 'truth' in the pursuit of avowedly aesthetic aims? The problem is especially thorny where Vietnam is concerned, as the racism and political obfuscation of many Second World War movies, even when not consciously designed as instruments of propaganda, were founded on a consensus of American, Western and, indeed, almost global opinion. The Japs and the Krauts *were* the bad guys. As such, they deserved to be held up to the good guys' scorn. But this argument becomes untenable when no real consensus exists, as with the Vietnam War, or when the consensus gradually shifts, as it has over the years in relation to the nation's treatment of its Indian population. Concerning the latter case, a number of films were made during this same period portraying the Indians as the victims of land-grabbing rapacity (e.g. *Soldier Blue*, Arthur Penn's *Little Big Man*, both of which were also viewed as parables of Vietnam) or else, enshrined in a framework of almost religious iconography, as doomed 'noble savages' (Dolores Del Rio's Madonna of the wigwams in Ford's solemnly elegiac *Cheyenne Autumn*). These unsatisfactory works, however, eschewing the myth-making rhetoric of the best-loved traditional westerns, only confirmed that Hollywood's chronic tendency to mythologise virtu-ally everything it touched had rendered it incapable of dealing conceptually with major historical currents.

The Deer Hunter, for its part, is set firmly in the 'classic' mould, which means that in order to inflate its hero to mythic stature – for Michael, after all, when divested both of the actor's charismatic presence and the character's romantic huntsman trappings, is a blue-collar steelworker whose beliefs include the sanctity of mar-riage (Stan hints at the possibility that he might be a virgin) and, presumably, opposition to any form of gun-control legislation – it is obliged to dehumanise the enemy. The question is therefore not whether Cimino has taken liberties with documented fact (which is, by definition, the prerogative of any work of fiction) but whether his distortions represent an adequate response to the factual back-ground that his movie exploits. And here the failure is total. Whereas in Eisenstein's masterpiece about the Russian Revolution, *October* (1928), the gross caricatures of gross capitalists possessed their own crude vitality (one might say, they leapt off the screen), Cimino's Viet Cong cannot even be called one-dimensional. They exist merely to objectify Occidental fears of the yellow race. Their addiction to Russian roulette serves no discernible purpose beyond their own titillation and profit: no valuable information, for instance, is being forcibly elicited from their country's enemies. In a straightforward guts 'n' glory movie, with both sides reduced to the cardboard cut-out dimensions of archetypal hero and villain, such characterisations, if pardonable, would still be reprehensible; here, given the psychological depth of the American characters as well as the enormously detailed canvas of their environment, they constitute an insult not only to the 'heroic struggles of the Vietnamese people' but to the audience's intelligence.

Finally, it is through Michael's steely presence of mind that the trio of friends manage to make their escape. He persuades his bemused captors to grant him first one, then two, extra bullets in the revolver, thereby suicidally raising the odds against his own survival. But the ploy succeeds: the randomly chosen chamber proves empty and with his accumulation of bullets he instantly guns down the Viet Cong. Michael and Nick release Steven (but apparently none of his fellow prisoners) from the bamboo cage and they begin to float downriver. They are sighted by a US Army helicopter. Though Nick is picked up, Michael and Steven lose their grip on its runners and once more plunge into the river, Steven breaking both his legs on a submerged ridge of rocks. Michael subsequently hauls Steven through the jungle and on to the poignantly named Interstate 9 where, in spite of the fleeing peasantry, he finds a refuge for him on the bonnet of an ARVN jeep. Second-act curtain.

The final section properly belongs to Michael – his return to Pennsylvania, his deepening affection for Linda and his efforts to force the embittered Steven into a reconciliation with Angela – but it is perhaps Nick's story that holds most interest from the point of view of this study. Still numbed by his ordeal, he cannot bring himself to call Linda from a public phone booth in the American Military Hospital in Saigon. He wanders aimlessly into the city's congested streets, which the film depicts (these scenes were shot in Thailand) as an inferno of massage parlours and garish clip joints. In one of them, the Mississippi Saloon, decked out with wagon wheels and go-go dancers, he accepts the advances of a prostitute but reneges when he discovers a baby in the squalor of her tiny room. Further on, he notices bodies being surreptitiously ferried through a sombre alleyway and suddenly finds himself drawn into a dimly lit house where two young Vietnamese with scarlet headbands are voluntarily and 'professionally' playing Russian roulette (a short-term engagement, one gathers) amid a crowd of frenzied gamblers. On an impulse Nick seizes the pistol from a startled player and fires an empty chamber into his own forehead.

Very much later, as the city is about to fall, Michael, after greasing numerous palms, will himself be led into that same smoky cavern to confront a drugged, heavy-lidded Nick, wearing the scarlet headband of his new profession.

Nick has, in short, 'gone native', with all the lurid implications hinted at in colonialist usage of the phrase. For Cimino's Vietnam is only a slightly updated version of that poisonous Oriental lotus-land of ineffable pleasures and pains that Hollywood in the thirties (e.g. Josef von Sternberg's *Shanghai Express*, with Marlene Dietrich) would construct on its backlots like a jigsaw puzzle: a world of prostitutes suspended in cages, of waterfronts veiled by fishing nets, of the swish of softly beaded doorways, of coolie-infested bunks in opium dens, of mandarinesque conversations conducted entirely in fortune-cookie proverbs . . .

Vietnam is a hell on earth, but was not made so – the film seems to suggest – by the American presence. If American involvement was wrong-headed and even criminal, it was only because it exposed 'our boys' to contamination by a continent so irredeemably mired in moral corruption and so debilitated by opium-induced lethe that it hardly deserved to be saved. The unspoken question hanging over the movie would seem to be less 'Why are we in Vietnam?' than 'How can the President allow our soldiers to be contaminated by gooks?' For it is just such contamination that causes Nick's death – as, with Michael saying 'I love you' to him across the gaming table and a hint of recognition momentarily flickering in his glazed eyes, his luck runs out at last and a bullet with his name on it finds its way into the chamber. And, if less directly, it is contamination with an insidiously demoralising civilisation that has made Steven only 'half a man'.

To Michael, who alone emerges intact and uncompromised, is

left the Herculean task of binding the wounds and reconciling the survivors to an uncertain but hopeful future. He brings Nick home to be buried, he consummates his love for Linda, he reunites Steven with his young wife. But even he has not wholly avoided infection: returning to the mountains, he finds himself unable to kill the deer he has sighted, almost as though killing for him has been *sullied* by contact with an unworthy prey. 'Okay!' he shouts, perched high on a precipice beside a waterfall, in a florid shot that might have served as an advertisement for *giving up* Marlboro cigarettes.

After Nick's funeral, Michael, Steven, Angela, Linda, Stan, Axel and John gather in the latter's bar for a wake breakfast of scrambled eggs and coffee. Rendered inarticulate by grief, they raise their glasses to Nick's memory and slowly, haltingly, both moved and embarrassed, break into a rendition of 'God Bless America'. This is in many respects an extraordinarily audacious moment, both impressive in its sheer nerve and rather dispiriting in its recourse to such a trumpery, codified, impersonal expression of feeling for the movie's closing image. The naïve patriotism of the hymn's lyrics would at first appear to rule out the possibility of its being used without irony. But, as with military marches, rational objections to the content of patriotic anthems tend to formulate themselves on one level of our consciousness, while on another we reluctantly yield to their dubious but affecting sentiments. So Cimino has it both ways, exploiting the sentimental jingoism of 'God Bless America' at the same time as he undermines it, just as Furie tried to do with the football match that ended *The Boys in Company C*. Even if we do not 'believe' it, even if we decline to submit to what we can plainly see is emotional bullying, some part of us wishes it all were true.

The need to shape fiction, or myth, out of our collective experience is as old as historical awareness itself. Even the pretension to 'telling the truth' about a political reality, be it Vietnam, the Russian Revolution or the American Civil War, becomes part of the myth-making process, since the notion that there can be one indivisible truth about any event is itself a myth (albeit a long-dying one). If film-makers subject the framing of their material to a process of creative sifting and selection, so too do journalists; and since the political Zeitgeist can never be reduced to a mere cluster of facts and figures, fiction-makers arguably do the better job of reflecting it. In the fifties, for instance, ludicrously low-budget horror movies about beasts from 20,000 fathoms were frequently more sensitive to nuclear paranoia than was a heavily loaded message film like Stanley Kramer's *On the Beach*, with all its big guns pointed in the wrong direction. Such movies as *The Green Berets* and *The Deer Hunter* should perhaps be seen less as *about* the Vietnam war, in which capacity their inadequacies are painfully evident, than *part* of it – part, at least, of how it was perceived by Americans – and any history of the period omitting them from its data will necessarily be incomplete.

From this angle, Cimino's film may be the richest mine of what could rather indelicately be termed Vietnamiana. Its attempts to reaffirm the viability of a heroic posture in an unheroic age, revivify the frontier myth when it was being most vigorously contested and, above all, go some way to salving the nation's uneasy conscience, make it a prime exhibit in any dossier of American attitudes to the war. At the same time, a movie should be more than just the servile barometer of its audience's aspirations: for social historians, the ideological subtext of, say, *The Green Berets* may well prove as worthy of study as that of *The Deer Hunter*, even if the latter is much the stronger work. What is required *now*, for the generation that fought or lived through Vietnam, is a work to challenge our perceptions instead of reinforcing them, dismantle our prejudices instead of indulging them. In this *The Deer Hunter's* failure appears all the more dismaying, as the undoubted breadth of its narrative ambition held out hopes that it might be matched in depth of vision.

— *Chapter 6* —

NOW, VOYAGER

As we have seen, the uncharacteristic restraint shown by Hollywood in its treatment of the war during the late sixties and early seventies – which is to say, concurrently with both the escalation of hostilities and that of the campus protest movement – derived in part from its awareness that straight media coverage was daily pre-empting the cinema's power to shock. By contrast, Francis Ford Coppola's *Apocalypse Now*, touted even before it opened as the 'definitive' Vietnam movie, a legend even *before* its lifetime, had become, when it finally emerged in 1979, almost the memorial to a period willed into hazy oblivion by the vast majority of Americans.

In 1976, when shooting began, the national mood was favourable to reconciliation. Passions were cooling, the immediate past was being left to historians. The destitution of Nixon, last and most flagrantly mendacious of all the war's devisers, had been followed (via Ford's 'regency') by the election of Carter, whose principal qualification for the presidency was the wholly negative virtue of having held no previous office in Washington. He was therefore unbesmirched by either Vietnam or Watergate, those terrible twins of American aggression in which domestic and international commitments were inextricably interwoven.

But the war had left scars that could not be healed by the bland, ritualised upheavals of party politics. A sentiment of unease persisted, which was subtly and perfidiously exploited by Cimino in *The Deer Hunter*. When the disgraced Nixon was driven from the White House, his obstinate refusal to utter a single phrase of genuinely felt contrition denied the nation of what would have been, at least, the relative satisfaction of justice being seen to be done. As though to confirm Lyndon Johnson's celebrated crack that he could not pee and chew gum at the same time, Nixon's successor (and sometime Vice-President), Gerald Ford, balked at pardoning both his mentor *and* the half-million young men whose crime was, for whatever reason, to have refused to kill. So the draft dodgers (not all of whom, to be sure, were conscientious objectors) were left out in the cold, while Ford opted to save America from the supposedly greater trauma of bringing a now almost universally vilified ex-President to trial for a miscellany of offences, the worst, though not necessarily the most notorious, of which were those perpetrated on the peoples of South-East Asia. Even as late as 1978, when Carter cautiously proposed a rehabilitation scheme for draft dodgers, it met with widespread apathy and mistrust. If the war had been waged absent-heartedly, without songs or slogans (which throughout remained the exclusive prerogative of the campus rebels), and with a growing apprehension that this time 'we' might have been the enemy, its aftermath was hardly less demoralised.

As Coppola, his wife, his children, housekeeper, baby-sitter and personal projectionist, along with the actors and technicians from his San Francisco-based company, American Zoetrope, flew into Manila for what would turn out to be 238 days of location shooting in the Philippines, no recipes had been established, no procedures laid down, on how to make a Vietnam movie in and for the seventies.

In an interview Coppola described *Apocalypse Now* as 'a film experience that would give its audience a sense of the horror, the madness, the sensuousness, and the moral dilemma of the Vietnam war'. But, from the start, the moral dilemma was also to some extent Coppola's own. The first three 'senses', authenticated by the testimonies of numerous vets, had been vividly evoked in *Dispatches*, a brilliant collection of Vietnam reportages by Michael Herr (whom Coppola subsequently hired to write the voice-off narration of his movie). And even if *Apocalypse Now* adapted none of the episodes that figure in the book, the film's Bosch-like vision of the war was unquestionably coloured by the surreal intensity (as though caught under stroboscopic lighting) of Herr's descriptions of jungle combat. To recreate on film what Herr had achieved in print, however, obviously required a great deal of money. Though budgeted originally at twelve to fourteen million dollars, *Apocalypse Now* finally cost upward of thirty-one million, much of that coming out of

Coppola's own pocket or from funding for which he, as an independent producer retaining ownership of his film, could be held personally accountable. Expensive war movies had been made before, of course, notably Darryl Zanuck's epic of the Normandy landings, *The Longest Day* (1962). But that had celebrated an Allied victory, one which precipitated the end of the Second World War. Even Pearl Harbor, the subject of the equally spectacular *Tora! Tora! Tora!* (1970), had been a premeditated aggression on a still neutral country ('a date which will live in infamy', in Roosevelt's words) and the film had managed to conclude with a concession to American dignity, one of the Japanese admirals declaring morosely that they had 'woken a sleeping giant and filled him with resolve'.

The war in Indochina, on the other hand, was an incontrovertible defeat for the United States, a defeat rendered all the more poisonous by the hindsight realisation that its advent had been written on the wall as early as Johnson's 'abdication' in 1968 and that hostilities had been prolonged for principally electoral reasons. How, then, could a spectacular film be made out of that defeat which would mobilise the public in sufficient numbers to recoup a colossal investment? It is safe to speculate, his politics notwithstanding, that even John Milius had excluded gung-ho heroics from his original 1969 screenplay (much modified by Coppola himself). The vast resources of American firepower had been outmanoeuvred by the Viet Cong's guerilla tactics. Following the Calley trial and similar revelations, the image of the GI as a folk-hero had been perhaps irretrievably tarnished. And film-makers could not even dodge the main issue by resorting to the dramatisation of isolated victories, individual acts of daredevilry plucked from the morass of terror and mindless sadism. These no doubt occurred, but none had ever caught the national imagination.

Thus, like Cimino's exploitation of the war as a backdrop to a peculiarly sixties variant of 'grace under stress', Coppola's Vietnam epic had to be about *something else* as well. And this something else could not easily relate to such moral concerns as heroism, compassion and human dignity, all familiar features of traditional war movies.

The structure of *Apocalypse Now* is that of a quest: the quest of one Captain Benjamin Willard (Martin Sheen) for the renegade

Green Beret Colonel Walter E. Kurtz (Marlon Brando), who is waging his own private war from a Cambodian temple near the frontier with Vietnam. Before Willard confronts his prey at the end of the film, he will, in true picaresque fashion, meet with a succession of adventures, enshrined by Coppola in a half-dozen of the contemporary cinema's most mesmerising set-pieces.

The theme of the Quest can be traced to the very sources of world literature and is often overlaid with intimations of religious or mythological mysticism, such as are to be found in virtually all tales centring on the Knights of the Round Table. *Apocalypse Now*, however, has perhaps closer affinities with comic-strip or adventure-movie paraphrases of the Arthurian legends, where the quest is usually reduced in dimension to the pursuit of some evil, 'fallen' knight, invariably Black. Within the extraordinarily limpid, almost hieroglyphic framework of his plotline Coppola consciously manipulates these and other narrative archetypes (even if they are most effective when most deeply submerged in the verbal and visual textures of the movie). So the classified mission to root out and destroy Kurtz is treated as a solemn pact, a covenant sealed between Willard and two tight-lipped army officers at a (round) table laid for lunch. A third character (whose anonymity precisely *identifies* him as a CIA man) speaks only once: to advise Willard that Kurtz's career must be terminated, in the arresting locution, 'with extreme prejudice'. The general, offering Willard some shrimp, remarks (in a parody of the ritual test of strength submitted to by any epic hero before he embarks upon a perilous enterprise) that if he eats it he will never have to prove his bravery any other way. Then he chillingly reminds him that 'the mission does not exist nor will it ever exist'.

The extremely cramped and claustrophobic framing of this sequence, set in a small room at the Nha Trang base, not only increases our sense of the war as being waged by remote control, by a concentration of power so unlimited as to be almost abstract, it also hints at a view of modern warfare as an extreme form of organised crime: the military as Mafia. (It was the fabulous box-office returns of *The Godfather I* and *II* that guaranteed for Coppola the economic autonomy necessary for a project as grandiose as *Apocalypse Now*.) Willard is a hired assassin, an 'errand boy' in

Kurtz's words, being briefed for his latest job. And, hundreds of miles up the Nung river, Kurtz is to be made an offer that even he cannot refuse.

Just as his protagonist is no knight in shining armour (we learn that he has already been employed on covert missions for the CIA), so Coppola, like Brecht in *Arturo Ui* equating the rise of Nazism with the convulsive power grabs of Chicago gangsterdom, portrays the manners and methods of the military-industrial complex responsible for Vietnam as identical to those of the Cosa Nostra. The cool, civilised room, its table laid decorously with cold cuts, seems as remote from the nightmarish reality of the war as the spacious mansions of the Mafiosi 'brass' with their amoeba-shaped pools and impeccably trimmed lawns from the rain-swept sidewalks and vacant lots where their orders are carried out, those angst-ridden cityscapes immortalised by the *films noirs* of the forties. Only the shrimp mockingly foreshadows what is to come.

But already, in the preceding scene (into which the 70mm version of the film plunges us without the stabilising benefit of credit titles), with Willard emerging from an alcoholic stupor in a hotel room in downtown Saigon, the two dissimilar if related sensibilities of mythical quest fiction and hard-boiled thriller have been edgily reconciled. In a hypnotic series of images slowly dissolving into each other, dreams, memories and hallucinations commingle freely inside Willard's head. A forest landscape straight out of a painting by Max Ernst is crisscrossed by helicopters, whose almost invisible presence is signalled by the whirr of their rotor blades (one of the emblematic sounds of Vietnam movies, cf. *The Deer Hunter*), like the flapping wings of huge, malevolent birds. As Jim Morrison reedily croons 'This is the end . . .' (the first words pronounced in the movie), the forest is suddenly engulfed by flames, as though from a dragon's mouth, and the chop-chopping of blades dissolves into that of a ceiling fan casting its shadow over the prostrate Willard. In this sequence, then, Vietnam is *literally* what it will become figuratively in the rest of the movie: less a precise geographical (or geopolitical) region than a phantasmagoric landscape etched on the inner eye, an underworld in both the Godfather and God-the-Father sense.

Willard's hotel room is a mess. Its overflowing ashtrays, empty

beer cans and rumpled sheets suggest the squalid, vaguely porno-
graphic clutter of some down-at-heel private detective, a Sam Spade
or Philip Marlowe. (Coincidentally, in Conrad's novella *Heart of
Darkness*, which was the direct literary source for the film's scenario,
the equivalent of Sheen's character is of course named Marlow.)
This kinship with forties thrillers is reinforced by the laconically
Bogartian vernacular of Herr's first-person narration and the fact
that, when a pair of MPs arrive to accompany Willard to the
briefing, he groggily enquires what the charges are. Though he is,
to his knowledge, innocent of any 'illegal' violation, he has in-
herited such a legacy of amorality that he hardly knows whether
he is due for a medal or a court-martial.

Even his sporadic endeavours to keep himself fit between
missions, like Travis Bickle's in *Taxi Driver*, spiral into a paroxysm
of violence when he smashes his fist into a mirror (an improvised
moment, apparently, with Sheen taking the production crew by
surprise and inflicting on himself injuries from which the character
of Willard will suffer during part of the film).

But if, from its opening shots, *Apocalypse Now* reveals the influence
of thrillers and fantasies, Samurai films and even westerns, one
genre to which it bears curiously scant resemblance is the traditional
war movie. Coppola rejects the realistic, quasi-documentary approach of Raoul Walsh's *Objective Burma* (1945, actually screened to
GIs during training sessions) or Samuel Fuller's *Merrill's Marauders*
(1961), films which, though close to newsreels in their depiction
of the realities of jungle warfare, nevertheless implicitly endorsed
American superiority, physical, moral and racial. (In the case of
Walsh's film, it should be added that its documentary accuracy was
purchased at the price of wider historical accuracy: no mention
whatsoever was made of the British role in Burma, of Slim or
Wingate.) Denied the assurance of that superiority, Coppola was
to take aim at a very different target.

Several commentators on the movie have pointed out that,
unlike *The Deer Hunter*, with its novelistic 'density', there are no
real characters in *Apocalypse Now*. Kurtz is a concentration of pure
charisma, an aura incarnate and, as the principal bearer of the
movie's ideology, a somewhat platitudinous oracle; as a full-fledged
'character', he is psychologically undermotivated and not a little

risible. With his Cavalry Stetson and canary-coloured dickie, Kilgore (Robert Duvall) resembles a David Levine caricature, all top-heavy head perched on a stocky little body, and owes a good deal to Sterling Hayden's paranoid General Jack D. Ripper in Kubrick's *Dr Strangelove*. And Willard, basically, is a pair of eyes. Eyes, in effect – Martin Sheen's, above all, on whose dilated pupils the whole eerie slipstream of Vietnam seems to drift past – form the movie's most powerful visual motif, one that is extended to nearly all of the minor characters: the patrol boat crew, the bronzed surfers who comprise Kilgore's entourage and the leaderless, half-crazed soldiers shelling an unseen enemy at Do Lung bridge. The war is such a disorientating spectacle that even the most disillusioned 'grunts' – just like spectators in a cinema – constantly stop to register amazement and horror at the sight of it. When, at the height of an attack on a coastal village, Kilgore asks one young surfing champion for his impression, the latter replies that he finds it 'very exciting'. As it happens, Kilgore was referring specifically to the surf, but the surfer got it right nevertheless. Vietnam is a show, the greatest on earth, a mammoth Disneyland with real crocodiles in the Jungle Cruise, real ghosts in the Haunted House. And *Apocalypse Now* is a guided tour of its scariest 'rides'.

If no Second World War movie ever showed its protagonist transfixed in sheer incredulity at the carnage around him, it was mostly because he was just too busy making the world safe for democracy. But it was also that in Vietnam, caught between the monstrous, faceless technology of his own side's military machine and an equally faceless enemy at ease in the treacherously swampy terrain and malarial climate, the average American soldier had become something of an anachronism, an innocent bystander. Only madmen could hope to survive in this war: ostensibly 'sane' madmen like the three wise monkeys at Willard's briefing session; or else a more overtly 'mad' madman like Kilgore, who seems to survive through unswerving faith in his own indestructibility. Even in madness, though, there has to be method and a kind of moderation: Kurtz, possessing neither, will be eliminated.

As a depiction of 'the horror, the madness, the sensuousness' of war, amplified by the visceral you-are-there sensation of its vast 70mm screen tableaux and Dolby Sound (and even more unsettling, perhaps, is what might be termed Dolby Silence, capturing the thousand and one pinpoints of sound of which silence in the jungle is composed), *Apocalypse Now* will be hard to surpass. And, in this light, it might be worth examining in greater detail the film's most celebrated *morceau de bravoure*: Kilgore's air raid on the Vietnamese village. Solely in terms of spectacle, this sequence has no parallel in any previous war movie. Much of its fascination, of course, can be (and has been) attributed to the exceptional financial resources at the director's disposal; but, both in shooting and editing, Coppola organised the material with incomparable brio, from our first view of the phalanx of helicopters (whose low-flying formation has an oddly science-fiction feel to it) emerging out of a pellucid sky to the final, extraordinary moment when Kilgore, attempting to collect his thoughts about the end of the war, steps simply and almost with dignity off-screen.

Certain critics, however, even if they admitted to being dazzled by the purely visual pyrotechnics of the scene, accused Coppola of indirectly glorifying what he had presumably intended to indict. The spectator, they argued, cannot fail to identify with Kilgore's gleeful bloodlust, particularly during the first-person-style shooting (in both senses of the word) of one young Vietnamese woman who, after managing to plant a bomb in the helicopter carrying off an injured American soldier, is herself sprayed with machine-gun fire.

Though it would be foolish to generalise from any mixed assortment of reactions to a film, there seems to be a confusion here between two distinct notions: 'exaltation' and 'exultation'. The helicopter attack is undeniably an exalting experience for the spectator. In this, it does not differ much from such other cinematic set-pieces as the Odessa Steps massacre in Eisenstein's *Battleship Potemkin* and the shower murder in Hitchcock's *Psycho* – both, incidentally, sequences of extreme violence. But exultation? To be sure, few of us are unaffected by what the French critic André Bazin called 'the Nero complex', the vicarious pleasure afforded us by the representation of large-scale destruction (as witness the success of the disaster movie genre). But what kind of spectator finds himself *exulting* in the devastation of a defenceless village (given that he will make an emotive connection between this purely fictional reconstruction and what he knows to have been a frequent occurrence in the war)? The unrepentant hawk, possibly. But, for anyone politically sympathetic to the Vietnamese cause to feel such uncomplicated exhilaration, he would have to be totally insensitive to the ideological signals that the film is clearly emitting (not least in the portrait of Kilgore), as well as deaf to the factual information no less clearly conveyed by the dialogue.

Item: The village itself, though 'belonging' to the Viet Cong, is presented as going peacefully about its business. Indeed, since all we see of it prior to the raid is a neat little schoolhouse from which an orderly column of immaculately dressed infants is being led to safety (with, inevitably, a last-minute rescue of the tiniest of all), Coppola might even be criticised for special pleading. *Item:* The decision to bomb this particular community derives from Kilgore's obscenely whimsical desire to watch Lance, the young surfer, ride the waves at the height of the battle. *Item:* Though doubtless a contributing factor to the spectator's own pleasure, 'The Ride of the Valkyries', turned up full blast to 'scare the shit out of the slopes', has nevertheless been stripped of all but its most blatantly bellicose, even Nazi connotations – questionable as music criticism, maybe, but an unambiguous (if facile) statement of the film's own antiwar ideology.

When it is all over, when the green, purple and yellow smoke clouds have cleared from the beach and the water explosions have ceased, Kilgore takes a deep breath and comments wistfully: 'I love the smell of napalm in the morning.' The gratification in wholesale slaughter is Kilgore's and his alone – the motto on his helicopter reads 'Death From Above'. If the movie has encouraged the spectator momentarily to empathise with his brand of sadism, it has forced him at the same time to draw back, to observe, judge and redefine this sadism through Willard's eyes and his reflection that, 'If that's how Kilgore fought the war, I began to wonder what they really had against Kurtz.' The conceit of basing his own shooting style on Kilgore's hideously 'heroic' vision of the operation, complete with bugler romantically framed against the dawn and stereophonically stirring background music, allows Coppola to demonstrate how a nineteenth-century frontier expansionist programme (already made possible by the trampling underfoot of blacks, Indians and Mexican-Americans) had petrified into a self-sustaining power structure, exclusively bent on suppressing liberty and promoting empire. And one is reminded of Ford and Kissinger, in a notorious photograph, *exulting* over what they patently imagined was the Teddy Roosevelt-like blood-and-thunder of the Mayaguez adventure of 1975. Though the sequence (like the whole movie, like every other movie made about the war) never begins to question why the Americans were in Vietnam, it does go a little way to suggesting, through the specifically cinematic device of spectator identification, why they behaved as they did once they got there.

The character of Kilgore (and Robert Duvall's bold thumbnail sketch of paranoia at ease with itself is far and away the movie's best performance) embodies an inverted Catch-22 situation peculiar to Vietnam: to wage such a war in such a fashion, one would have to be mad; but since this madness appears to assure one a greater chance of survival, perhaps it isn't so mad after all. In some respects, as Willard grudgingly admits, Kilgore has proved to be a good commander. His relationship with his 'boys' is one of affection, a paternalistically protective affection that may be said to verge on homosexuality: in the scene of the beach-party barbecue, with Kilgore softly strumming on a guitar, the movie openly hints at the fraternal homosexuality of all male groups and, by extension, of war itself. Even when he virtually orders the reluctant Lance to surf in waters that are still 'hairy' (i.e. under bombardment), he somehow contrives to guarantee his safety and, indeed, Lance does return safe and sound. Kilgore is visibly fighting the wrong war. From the Second World War he might well have emerged a much-loved, much-decorated maverick in the MacArthur style.

In Vietnam, however, where medals have become an inflationary currency (cf. the one received by Bruce Dern in *Coming Home*), where individual acts of courage are debased by the disparity of military means deployed on either side and where, in the light of the Calley trial, the phrase 'beyond the call of duty' has acquired a new and sinister connotation, his flamboyant gestures and almost mindless disregard of personal security seem disproportionate at best and dangerous at worst.

Interestingly, Coppola does credit Kilgore with a certain showy sense of compassion while carefully exposing its limitations and self-aggrandising nature. If, in the process of bombing them into the Stone Age, he calls the Vietnamese 'fucking savages', this seems a natural response to the sabotaging of a helicopter carrying a wounded American soldier to safety; contrarily, he offers water from his canteen to a dying Viet Cong, only to lose interest in him when he discovers the presence of the surfing champion. The consciously John Wayne stance and postures may belong to an old frontiersman tradition, one for which even liberals have had a soft spot, but what Kilgore fails to realise (like Wayne himself in both *The Green Berets* and his hawkish public position on the war) is that the context has radically and irrevocably changed.

In a way, Coppola's film makes better sense of the title *Heart of Darkness* than Conrad's novella. Here the 'darkness' is visited upon Vietnam (contrary to *The Deer Hunter*'s racist implication that it predated the American invasion), not only by Kilgore's helicopters and two dozen gunships blasting a peaceful hamlet sky-high but also by the cynical and disenchanted Willard, who 'couldn't remember how many people he had killed'. Vietnam (the war rather than the country) is nothing else but the heart of that darkness, an endless psychodrama, half Theatre of Cruelty, half Theatre of the Absurd, in which impulses normally lurking just below or intermittently bursting through the crust of civilisation are granted free rein. (For Occidentals the Orient has always played this cathartic role, from Conrad's *Lord Jim* to Maugham's *The Razor's Edge*.) And Kurtz's Cambodian enclave is no doubt intended to symbolise the very heart of the heart, the inner sanctum of America's collective unconscious.

Since the whole of *Apocalypse Now* is set in Vietnam, without any external reference point of comparison, the spectator is faced with a world from which every trace of genuine civilisation has been mercilessly expunged and replaced by its grotesque parody. One of the film's most pervasive themes is of colonialism as the reverse side of isolationism: the colonialist (or neo-colonialist) never truly leaves home, he takes his home with him, duplicating its values, styles and artefacts wherever he settles. So the South-East Asia of *Apocalypse Now* may also be read as a transposed vision of America: e.g. the whole Kilgore set-up, the California-style surfing and beach barbecue, the disc-jockeys on Saigon radio and the enormous, incandescent supply depot, whose apparition in the middle of an equatorial forest is reminiscent of the spacecraft descending at the end of Steven Spielberg's *Close Encounters of the Third Kind* (only now *we* are the Martians).

It is there, while waiting for the boat to be refuelled, that Willard and the crew attend a USO show on a floodlit outdoor stage. Three Playboy Bunnies effectively if somewhat charmlessly bump and grind until the audience of GIs erupts in a frenzy of sexual frustration and the emcee, Bill Graham, rushes his charges like scared rabbits back into their helicopter. The true obscenity of this sequence derives less from the mechanically lascivious gestures of the performers (who might be considered the army's cheer leaders) than from the bizarre juxtaposition of American-as-apple-pie razzmatazz with the horror we know to be stalking just outside the compound. Framed by the shifting penumbra of the jungle, an alien culture is revealed in all its hyper-realist crassness and vulgarity; and nothing could more forcefully expose the hypocritically permissive ideology represented by Hugh Hefner's 'untouchable' puppets than to see them dangled provocatively in front of a mob of sex-hungry GIs then yanked back at the slightest threat of action. Indeed, the whole garish construction of the base recalls the tourist's first glimpse of Las Vegas as its shimmering spires loom out of the Nevada Desert like some neon-lit mirage.

By the same token, Graham strewing smoke bombs on to the stage to fend off a too-appreciative public is a minor but telling detail that indicates the degree to which, in this version of Vietnam, the twin technologies (and mythologies) of war and show business overlap and feed upon each other. Another such example is Coppola's own brief cameo as a television director, yelling at the soldiers on the beach to continue fighting without looking into the camera lens. Even straight TV coverage ends up by fictionalising the event it is filming. Kilgore shapes his persona out of bits and pieces of old John Ford westerns, and newsreels must serve up a war that looks authentic: i.e. that resembles Second World War movies. Maybe if, Coppola appears to be saying, maybe if just one of those dazed, haggard faces were to confront the camera directly, staring right into the TV viewer's eyes, a human contact would be

111

established which would make the distancing of the war that much more difficult; the reassuring sense of its being waged by 'others', with 'our boys' hardly less anonymous than the enemy, would instantly be undermined. But just as many American soldiers were able to fight (and some were enabled to commit the kind of atrocity typified by My Lai) because they had been programmed to think of the enemy as subhuman gooks, so many Americans at home rapidly learned to live with TV's unrelenting bombardment of Vietnam news by programming themselves to think of their own army as gooks – 'good' gooks, perhaps, yet basically strangers, other people's sons, husbands or brothers.

Occasionally more tenuous, the link with show business is not systematically used to make an immediate point. Its purpose is rather to enrich the film's textures, with the spectral, circussy seductiveness of certain décors (the fairy-lit Do Lung bridge, for instance) serving to point up the hallucinatory horror of the narrative. These thematic parallels, moreover, have not been autocratically imposed on the material from outside, as an extended private joke on Coppola's part. They are most frequently projected by the protagonists themselves, as though they hoped thus to disguise their own inadequacies beneath a more traditional iconography of war. The notion of playing Wagner during the raid on the village is not Coppola's, as it were, but Kilgore's. It does not blast out from the film's soundtrack as much as from a helicopter's loudspeaker system. And if its ostensible aim is to terrify the enemy, it doubtless also assists Kilgore himself in devising a suitable audiovisual ambience for his posturing heroics. (Later, Dennis Hopper as a photojournalist at Kurtz's court, a freakish relic of the early sixties high on the odour of carnage, will be seen swathed in camera equipment like a guerilla rigged out with rifles and hand-grenades.)

Conversely, however, there is the scene when, during a lull in the voyage upriver, one of the crew members, the ex-saucier Chef, decides on impulse to gather some mangoes from the jungle. Willard accompanies him, and together they proceed almost casually through the snarled undergrowth. Suddenly Willard freezes. The spectator expects a Viet Cong patrol; but it is a tiger that silently springs at them from out of the shadows. The startling, slightly comical anguish displayed by Chef at this moment reminds one of

the gag of two small children calmly absorbing all the heterogeneous, multi-channelled violence that is offered nightly on TV –
gangsters mowing each other down, western gunfights, war movie
bombings – only to recoil in terror from a Disney cartoon of the
Big Bad Wolf. For though the intensity of Chef's reaction suggests
the release of an accumulation of pent-up fear – fear of the war
itself, of its consequences to life and limb, which has been present
from the beginning but anaesthetised by its very persistence into a
dull, throbbing ache, no less for those in the thick of it than for
those watching it on their TV screens – it can also be attributed to
the atavistic and even symbolic (i.e. the common anti-American
gibe of 'paper tiger') nature of the danger facing him, against which
the only defences he can call upon are purely instinctive ones.
Confronted with the Big Bad Wolf, he screams and runs.

Just before the boat arrives at the Cambodian frontier, it encounters a sampan which, against the wishes of Willard, the taciturn
black captain decides to stop and have checked over. As Chef is
cursorily upturning barrels and bursting open food-sacks, a young
Vietnamese woman makes an ill-timed movement in the direction
of a suspect-looking basket, causing the jittery crew to rake the
craft and its occupants with machine-gun fire.

Judged as a superproduction set-piece, this short sequence is
small in scale and therefore 'disappointing'. But its value is precisely
in that, for the first time in the film, we are granted a close look at
the 'enemy', at those anxious, delicate faces painfully familiar from
TV and newspaper coverage of the war. In Kilgore's raid the village
was there only to be annihilated, its existence as an autonomous
human community being preceded by its essence, from the American point of view, as a target. With no more than a single long-shot
of the schoolroom prior to the attack, the possibility of spectator
identification, however fleeting, had been thwarted.

Here, by contrast, we have an opportunity to re-establish the
equilibrium of life and death, to reconstruct the continuity between
some inoffensive peasants and their blood-spattered corpses strewn
across the deck of their sampan only a few seconds later. For the
duration of this sequence the perspective of the movie shifts from
the global to the mundane; briefly relaxing his visionary ambitions,
Coppola settles for the more modest, if also more affecting,

dimensions of a newsreel reportage. Except that its aftermath once more reveals his incapacity to deal with the beleaguered Vietnamese on any level but the most tritely melodramatic. As with the row of doll-like children sighted just before the helicopters close in, he fatally loads the argument. The basket towards which the young woman gestured turns out to contain not firearms but . . . a puppy dog! Perhaps Coppola felt that it was not enough to show the pointless massacre of one small group of civilians, that the terrible irony of the confrontation had to be rhetorically inflated until it became a paradigm of the futility of all wars, calculated to draw tears from Curtis LeMay himself. What could better illustrate 'man's inhumanity to man', one imagines him thinking, than a puppy only a few days old? Though the scene possesses the sharp immediacy of a news item, this detail contrives to situate it firmly in the kind of tabloid press for which, as an old newspaperman's crack puts it, there is nothing like a small and cuddly animal for lending a story human interest.

Whatever the standpoint, therefore, Cimino's reactionary cynicism or Coppola's liberal sentimentality, any consideration in the American cinema of the Vietnamese as fully realised individuals continues to remain subservient to their classified ethnic status as 'aliens'.

This weakness mars even the film's treatment of 'aliens', in a sense, closer to home. Two of the crew members are black: the rather sullen captain, Chief Phillips, and a wild, good-natured kid nicknamed Clean, who spends most of the trip languorously swaying to rock music from his radio. It is in the depiction of their deaths, when approaching Kurtz's hideout, that Coppola's uncertainty of tone is most evident. Clean is the first to go, shot during a Viet Cong attack from the river bank. It is Phillips who discovers him; and what should have been quite simply portrayed as the natural and understandable expression of comradely grief – he tenderly cradles the youth's inert body in his arms – is instantly transformed by Coppola's lighting and framing into a maudlin Pietà of racial oneness and brotherly solidarity, investing the scene with a weight and significance totally absent from the subsequent murder of the white Chef. Through his death Clean is thus made to serve as a short-hand symbol for the wrongs committed by

America's white establishment against blacks, Indians and, by extension, the Vietnamese themselves.

Phillips's own death is even more weighted with implications. As the boat nears the temple stronghold it is bombarded with little blunt sticks by the Montagnard warriors under Kurtz's command (impersonated by members of a tribe of Ifugao Indians). This scene, one of the few to survive intact from Conrad's story, gains extra irony in view of the overwhelmingly technological nature of the war as waged by the Americans (and which is foregrounded in *Apocalypse Now* as in no other Vietnam movie). When the barrage turns lethal, it is unfortunate and surely not wholly fortuitous that the one person killed – skewered by a spear – is the black captain. For, whether or not consciously intended by Coppola, there *is* a subtle whiff of racism in this decision to have a character of African ancestry fall victim to a weapon more familiar from conventional jungle adventure movies, as though a submerged link of primitiveness were being forged between these two non-American peoples. (In Tay Garnett's *Prestige*, a 1932 drama about the French in Indo-China, suave Adolphe Menjou arrives at an island garrison after a long and arduous journey upriver. When asked by his host if anything untoward occurred, he mentions 'a spot of bother with some crocodiles' but adds wittily, 'Fortunately, they prefer darker meat.' In essence, it appears they still do.)

If this seems fanciful, consider the whole concept of Kurtz himself reigning, like some existential Tarzan, over an army of 'natives' who worship him in authentic Great White Master style. Or the fact that, when Willard finally assassinates Kurtz and reappears on the temple steps, these same tribesmen shuffle aside in awe to clear a passage for him. Or even that, in a version ultimately rejected by Coppola, the film was to have ended with Willard taking Kurtz's place as their idol. Already in 1899, when Conrad wrote *Heart of Darkness*, Kurtz's brand of one-man imperialism was out-of-date; here, it cannot help but strike us as grotesquely irrelevant to a film with claims to portray, in its director's phrase, 'the moral dilemma of the Vietnam war'.

Throughout the trip Willard has been thoughtfully poring over a voluminous dossier on Kurtz: third-generation soldier, graduated from West Point top of his class, became a Green Beret at 38, etc.

At the briefing session, he listens to a recording of Kurtz's voice, musing about a snail crawling along the edge of a razor. Studying press cuttings, photographs and letters, both official and intimate, he becomes increasingly fascinated by this man he has not met but who is drawing him inexorably along a river that he compares to 'a main current plugged straight into Kurtz'. Never in the history of the cinema, in fact, has a film so mercilessly protracted the introductory build-up to its leading character (true in so far as Brando was by far the most prestigious name in the cast). For almost two hours of running time the spectator is half-consciously preparing himself for his appearance.

There is a story by the Argentinian fabulist Jorge Luis Borges in which a young Indian student, fallen among outcasts, becomes gradually aware of some higher serenity in their manner, a glow of barely concealed exaltation that could not conceivably be emanating from their own flawed souls. He judges it to be the pale reflection of an infinitely greater, saintlike being whom he determines to reach by tracking this glow to its source, a process analogous to that, in Hide-the-Thimble, of 'getting warm'. Which is, with obvious differences, the basic construction of *Apocalypse Now*; a crucial difference being, of course, that for Borges the godlike guru could remain a purely verbal conceit, his existence, if any, wholly contingent on whatever the reader's imagination cared to make of it, whereas Coppola's screenplay clearly required that Kurtz be visualised. And if the undoubted fascination exerted by Kurtz is paradoxically much more tangible during Willard's voyage upriver than when he himself eventually makes his appearance, the question concerning us here is not why this should be so – Brando's inability to make much of the role, the bathetically portentous dialogue (or rather, monologue) written for him, the crude religious symbolism – but what Coppola intended him to represent.

If he is to be considered the vehicle of the film's ideology, as a number of critics have understood the character, the implications are disturbing, to say the least. When he opines, for instance, that the Viet Cong are stronger because more evil, he would seem to be presenting, in a manner brooking no denial, not only the military's case for American involvement in the war but also its failure to bring it to a swift and satisfactory conclusion – even if his argument is embodied in a philosophical (or pseudo-philosophical) rather than political discourse.

'What is said to be ruthless is very often clarity,' Kurtz goes on, echoing Adolf Hitler's sentiments exactly and forcing Coppola into a struggle to keep his mouthpiece (if such he is) on the side of the angels: what is necessary, he takes care to add, is 'on the side of good, the primordial instinct to kill without fear, without reason, without judgment'. But the notion of an outfit of mindless thugs killing in a worthy cause is simply too far-fetched to merit serious consideration. Someone somewhere has to use a modicum of reason and judgment, and a little healthy fear is often a spur to wisdom.

The inspiration for Kurtz's grisly reflections turns out to be an atrocity once witnessed by him, when the Viet Cong entered one of their own communities and lopped off the arms of infants who had been innoculated by the Americans. As with Cimino's totally fictitious attribution to the Vietnamese of a mania for Russian roulette, there is no record of this incident ever having occurred in Vietnam (its details recall the equally unfounded rumours of German rapine in Belgium which circulated during the First World War). That such a tale could be fabricated is disheartening enough; even more so is the fact that, prior to Kurtz's appearance, the movie, though it certainly heightened and coloured the reality of the war, in no significant respect had to distort it.

It is possible, however, that Kurtz's monstrosity is intended to be perceived as such, his dubiously Nietzschean ravings taken no more seriously by the director than by a discerning spectator. Viewed from this angle, he becomes the perfect product of a highly imperfect system and his only fault has been to take that system's methods and values to a logical but extreme conclusion. Yet since the institutionalised violence of the military – of a Kilgore, for instance – is already sufficiently documented in the movie to cause Willard to wonder how it could be surpassed, what need is there for Kurtz's presence at all?

The ambiguity of Coppola's intentions is further underlined by the weight given the character, not only by the casting of Brando (at a fabulous and much-publicised salary) but by the inordinate degree of suspense generated before we are finally permitted to see him. Led through the compound (which is littered with mutilated corpses and impaled heads) into the confines of the ruined temple, Willard finds himself in a room heavy with stale sweat, sperm, blood, incense and presumably Kurtz's own complex vibrations. A few moments pass. Out of the shadows the dome of a bald head slowly materialises. (Another of the film's dominant visual motifs: Brando's baldness, the temple statues, Chef's head tossed into Willard's lap, Willard's head at the very beginning superimposed upside-down on one of his own nightmares and at the very end surfacing from the primeval swamp as he prepares to kill Kurtz.) While massaging the scalp of his (hollow) pate, Kurtz quotes from Eliot's 'The Hollow Men'. He ruminates about his Midwestern home. In a rather too artfully composed still-life shot his bedside reading is exhibited: Jessie L. Weston's *From Ritual to Romance*, Sir James Frazer's classic (if now discredited) study of magic and religion, *The Golden Bough*, obviously designed as pointers to guide the spectator towards a truer understanding of his impending assassination.

For when Willard at last 'terminates' Kurtz, the act is intercut with the ritualised felling of an ox, thus taking on overtones of parricide, both Oedipal and anthropological, the killing of the father, the destitution of a chief whose ebbing powers demand that he be sacrificed, willingly or not, in favour of a younger, stronger, more vigorous man.

Such mythic resonances, unfortunately, never seem more than 'token', planted mainly to bolster a dangerously sagging narrative, an impression reinforced by Coppola's visible uncertainty as to how the film should end. We know that it was screened in various degrees of rough-cut to friends and other film-makers throughout the period of 1978–9; that the version shown at the 1979 Cannes Film Festival (where it won the Palme d'Or *ex aequo* with Volker Schlöndorff's *The Tin Drum*) was even then by no means the definitive one; that Coppola shot, then staggeringly ditched, a mighty ground-and-air assault on Kurtz's base by both American and Viet Cong forces, a final cataclysmic sequence that he hoped would fully justify the movie's title; and that he subsequently reinstated it in the 35mm version intended for general release. That none of these has proved satisfactory – the 70mm ending makes nonsense of the imagery of sacrifice; the 35mm ending provides just one more big bang; the potentially intriguing (if predictable) notion of Willard's morbid obsession with Kurtz toppling over into emulation would require that their relationship be considerably less sketchy than at present – can be ascribed in part to the failure of Brando's Kurtz to live up to the promise of his powerful off-screen presence. But it is also symptomatic, in a curious way, of what went terribly askew with the undertaking from the start.

If, for much of its length, *Apocalypse Now* captures as no other film has done the unprecedented *obscenity* of the Vietnam War, this is due not only to Coppola's unquestioned *savoir-faire*, to the almost foolhardy boldness of his conception and the enormity of the budget he was prepared to allocate to his mammoth pet project. The very real sense of hopelessness that permeates the movie, the sense of things getting out of hand, of *escalation*, would appear to have derived as much from its own horrendous shooting conditions (as chronicled – fitfully, alas – by Coppola's wife in her published *Notes*) as from the nature of the material itself.

Though it would be irresponsible to extend the comparison too far, one is nevertheless struck by a number of correspondences between the war and this epic that set out to record it: the legendary investments of time and money swallowed up in the jungle, the invasion of an underdeveloped country by massive Yankee technology, the fuzziness of motivation, the daily battling with the elements, the sense of a journey undertaken which would end no one knew where, even the reluctance of many of Hollywood's top actors to commit themselves to what promised to be a lengthy location schedule in the Philippines – behaving like so many draft dodgers. When Eleanor Coppola describes her family's provisory return home to the Napa Valley in California after a typhoon had caused the production to be closed down, it is almost as though she were speaking about a furlough. Martin Sheen, who suffered a heart attack during the shoot, has attested to the fact that (like some traumatised vet) he was a changed man after the film. And Coppola, in interviews, admitted that he had begun to identify first with Willard, then with Kurtz (a role in which, for the Hollywood establishment, the installation of his renegade independent company in San Francisco had already cast him).

It is not surprising, then, that he too would be defeated in the end by the intricate network of motives, aspirations and blindly pursued objectives to which the term 'Vietnam' had come to be affixed. And if his error was to believe (so soon, at least, after the cessation of hostilities) that these could simply be strained out of the experience, leaving only a residue of 'tragic grandeur' to serve as the backdrop for a meditation on the eternal verities of good and evil, it is perhaps not so surprising that his own personal defeat mirrored that of the whole American entanglement in South-East Asia and thus could be considered almost a fit conclusion to what had always been a doomed enterprise.

— Chapter 7 —

RAMBOMANIA

In the scale of its ambitions the film which *Apocalypse Now* most resembled was *2001 – A Space Odyssey*; and it established a set of visual parameters applicable to subsequent representations of the war much as Kubrick's epic had done for the exploration of space. Unlike that of *2001*, however, its commercial success (which was considerable, even if compromised in so far as Coppola's own stake was concerned by its original budget having more than doubled) did not immediately foster a cycle of movies exploiting the same basic pool of iconography. It was almost as though, with *Apocalypse Now*, and its direct, though stylised, confrontation with the realities of the war, Hollywood judged that it had finally got Vietnam out of its system. The subject had been dealt with, the boil had been lanced, and the major studios could gratefully, guiltlessly, revert to the business of populist, apolitical moviemaking. And, paradoxical as it may appear, the cosmic canyons and dizzy, M. C. Escher-like perspectives of *2001* turned out to be relevant to the early eighties in a way that was not true of the forests of South-East Asia: relevant, it should be understood, exclusively in terms of the American cinema in its traditional guise as a purveyor of escapist entertainment. (It was, apparently, from the earth itself that the public was now seeking to escape.) With audiences ever more youthful, to the point where the career of a movie became increasingly contingent on its appeal to adolescents, Vietnam began to acquire what might be called a 'period' feel.

To be sure, the war continued to surface spasmodically and in a fairly incidental narrative capacity. It served essentially as a source of easy, catch-all motivation – the motivation of a (minor) character's neurosis, schizophrenia and, in general, antisocial behaviour. Thus the principal suspect in Peter Yates's *Eyewitness* (1981), a

121

somewhat confused thriller about the killing of a Vietnamese diamond exporter, was an edgy war veteran, resentful at being treated as a second-class citizen, a home-grown 'gook', as he defines himself. In Arthur Penn's *Four Friends* (1981), a fractured, discontinuous retreading of sixties milestones, one of the eponymous quartet duly returns from service overseas. Through a rare reversal of conventions, however, he not only emerges quite unscathed and untraumatised by the experience but is married to a Vietnamese woman and father to a pair of delightful Asian-American children. And one of the more eccentric by-products of the war's aftermath, an unprepossessing mongrel of a movie, was Michael Pressman's comedy-drama *Some Kind of Hero* (1981, based on a James Kirkwood novel), in which Richard Pryor played a draftee held captive by the Viet Cong for six years; on his homecoming he is sucked into (relatively minor-league) criminality by the gradual realisation that he has been 'left behind' in more than the topographical sense. Basically, it was a clownish heist movie, of a type for which Pryor had already been teamed up with Gene Wilder, and one can only assume that the intrusion of a Vietnam theme represented an endeavour to invest its formulaic plot with a spurious 'conscience'. In this it was reminiscent of those modish, so-called 'wrong note' compositions written by sub-revolutionary musicians of the twenties, who would spike the conventional tonality of their style with the odd ambiguously harmonic shiver. In the context of *Some Kind of Hero*, the Vietnam War constituted just such a deliberate and ultimately frivolous 'wrong note'.

Indeed, in a growing number of movies, the war became not much more than a narrative excrescence, its 'token' vets replacing the token blacks of previous decades. The role played by a vet could be just as inconsequential as that of some evocative 'golden oldie' on the soundtrack or (relegated to a corner of the frame) a TV screen on which the image of John Kennedy, say, might be half-glimpsed. His presence served as a facile, instantaneous signifier of the period during which the movie was set, thereby usefully dispensing with expositional dialogue. Such was the case with works (most of them serenely indifferent to the reverberations of American military involvement) as diverse as Richard Rush's *The Stunt Man* (filmed in 1978 but not released until 1980), a genuine sleeper of a success about a disturbed young veteran who stumbles on to the location shooting of a First World War movie; Ivan Passer's *Cutter's Way* (1981), a strange (and, in some quarters, extravagantly admired) paranoid thriller in which John Heard personified the disabled vet as Demon King (black eye-patch and stump of a leg – a choice example of Hollywood's morbid partiality to what might be described as 'tragic cuteness'); John Badham's *Blue Thunder* (1982), which featured Roy Scheider as an LA helicopter patrol officer haunted by memories of the war (of which the chopper was, as we have seen, an emblematic artefact); Bruce Beresford's *Tender Mercies* (1982), with Tess Harper playing a spunky, weather-bleached war widow; and John G. Avildson's *The Karate Kid* (1984), which confronted its teenage hero (Ralph Macchio) and his elderly Okinawan mentor (Pat Morita) with a dojo of swinish, black-garbed karate aces trained as though for imminent posting to South-East Asia by a gruesomely sadistic ex-Green Beret.

These films were variable in quality, to say the least; but what is interesting about their appropriation of Vietnam-related particulars is that, with the passage of time, the presence of a veteran, a war widow or a Green Beret in a Hollywood production no longer, *of necessity*, emitted any very strong politico-ideological message. Each risked becoming, for the first time since the end of hostilities, a mere stereotype, requiring no lengthy justification. The Vietnam War, which before had resonated through the narrative of any film into whose ken it swam, however peripherally, was now being reduced to the level of an *anecdote*.

Of another dramatic mode – the allegorical – employed by Hollywood as a means of coming to terms with the war while it was still in progress, the aftermath proved short-lived. Understandably so, perhaps, since the force of allegory (whose absolute legibility, in any case, sets it at odds with the almost aleatory profusion of signs in a visual image) depends to a great degree on a sense of sometimes perilous topicality. As a manner of speaking about one thing while appearing, or feigning, to speak about another, it may be characterised as a selective and dissident form of 'euphemism'. Which implies, in turn, that there exists some interdiction, even outright censorship, prohibiting any more overt expression of the issue. With the war over, the subject to all intents and purposes closed, the need for such subterfuge would seem to have been removed.

One film, however, was widely interpreted as an allegory of Vietnam: Walter Hill's *Southern Comfort* (1981). It dealt with nine National Guardsmen who set off into the bayous of Louisiana on a routine excursion (the year, for no evident reason other than that of reinforcing the allegory, is 1973). As an unofficial bonus upon completion of the exercise, Rifleman Spencer (Keith Carradine) has organised a visit to a nearby whorehouse; and, in their impatience to sample its merchandise, they 'borrow' three canoes belonging to the local Cajun inhabitants. Thereupon – not in the middle, but on the outside edge, of nowhere – they find themselves enmeshed in a lethal variant on guerilla warfare with the Cajuns. The Louisiana swamps are transformed into an eerily malignant, uncharted territory (or almost uncharted: in truth, their misadventures bear more than a superficial resemblance to what befell the hapless urban dudes of John Boorman's *Deliverance*) from which the survivors are rescued *in extremis* by, wouldn't you know, a helicopter.

If contained within an exclusively generic framework, that of the American action movie, *Southern Comfort* is doubtless quite well made. But such a remark savours of the type of compliment paid to a sexual partner for having been 'good in bed': it remains a matter of pure performance. The question ought rather to be: was it really worth making? As an allegory of the war (and that is not only a critic's interpretation but intrinsic to the way in which the movie functions), it is crucially flawed by Hill's reluctance to make up his mind whether the Cajuns are to be portrayed as hopelessly irreclaimable 'aliens' (akin to the Viet Cong of *The Deer Hunter*) or as more 'exotic' manifestations of ourselves, estranged from us by cultural and ideological incompatibilities, maybe, but members of the same human community and entitled to the same, precisely 'inalienable', rights. The indecisive Hill would appear to have been itching for the coin to land on both sides at once. When, for the purposes of the plot, the Cajuns have to seem menacing, then menacing they obligingly are. And when, later, it must transpire that (as true native-born Americans, after all, whatever their

124

ancestry) their values and priorities coincide with those of the Guardsmen, most of whom are local boys, they no less obligingly shed their more sinister idiosyncrasies – their habit, for instance, of materialising, cat-like, from behind trees and beneath frondage – until they are barely distinguishable from the callow but well-intentioned soldiery whom a 'tragic misunderstanding' has pitted against them. As with many a movie of allegorical pretensions, for approximately half its running time the two interconnected layers of meaning lie neatly folded up together like sheets in an airing cupboard – at which point, however, as narrative incidentals start to proliferate at the expense of a rigidly linear plotline, one of the layers fatally disengages itself from the others.

It could be argued, I suppose, that Michael Cimino's *Heaven's Gate* (1980) also contains elements of allegory. If so, they operate less in relation to the film's historico-western foreground (i.e. the Johnson County Wars) than to the public image of its director and the fact that he had earlier been responsible for *The Deer Hunter*. The troublous (indeed, near-suicidal) history of *Heaven's Gate*, one of those 'titanic' works built to last forever but which sink on their maiden voyage, has made it Hollywood's most infamous cautionary tale: so much so that the memory of its contemptuous critical dismissal and cavalier dismemberment by United Artists is probably more familiar, even to the few spectators who actually contrived to catch the thing in one of its many different versions, than its own obscurely elliptical narrative.

But what concerns us here is how a director who, in *The Deer Hunter*, demonstrated his readiness to depict the Vietnamese in the racist and bellicose terms of a comic strip could proceed to focus on another doubtful episode of American history – the liquidation of alleged 'thieves and anarchists' among the immigrant settlers of nineteenth-century Wyoming by a band of mercenaries – from an unequivocally liberal standpoint (with the film even managing to implicate the President in the massacre). Despite obvious hints of genocide, one would not normally seek to establish any analogical connection between the two wars, Johnson County and Vietnam, were it not for the disturbingly obstinate afterimage of the director's previous work. And there is the poser. Did Cimino's ideological volte-face constitute an authentic, or opportunistic, change of heart? (The latter does strike one as an unlikely hypothesis, in view of the current political conservatism of the United States.) It is all very baffling; and it simply will not do to propose, as did John Pym in *Sight and Sound*, that *Heaven's Gate* 'decisively gives the lie to those who claimed its director was a right-wing apologist'. Had Cimino's two movies, by some chance, been shot and released in the reverse order, would that also have reversed the order of the 'lie'? And what should we make of the same director's *Year of the Dragon* (1985), with Mickey Rourke as a Vietnam veteran turned New York police detective whose targeted gooks are now the city's complement of Chinese drug barons (a film widely judged racist, and not only by the Chinese-American community)?

As for James Glickenhaus's *The Exterminator* (1980), a startlingly repellent specimen of the urban vigilante cycle (the prototype being Michael Winner's *Death Wish*), it featured a Vietnam vet protagonist (Robert Ginty) who wreaks death and disfigurement by a grisly assortment of methods and implements – a mincing machine, a blow torch, a gun with mercury bullets, man-eating vermin and good old-fashioned incineration – in his crazed crusade to delouse the sidewalks of New York City of a particularly ferocious swarm of muggers. (The movie became the object of legal action in Ohio, where it was supposed to have prompted the vicious killing of a spectator during a performance.) Here again, the tenement jungles of the Lower East Side served as a crude simile for the more literal kind with which the hero had been acquainted by combat duty: e.g. the muggers baptise themselves the Ghouls, a name which, enunciated, deviates from the word 'Gooks' by nothing more sub-stantial than a single consonant. And, at one point, recounting to a buddy how he had trounced his adversaries, our hero observes, 'It was like we were back in 'Nam. It didn't matter whether it was right or wrong, I just did it,' an observation that would appear, interestingly, to imply not only that, in Vietnam itself, it had also ceased to matter 'whether it was right or wrong', but that the activities of the US forces there might, with hindsight, be considered as equally illegitimate – in any case, as questionable – as those of vigilantes at home.

Where *The Exterminator* significantly differed from a number of movies on the theme of the returning vet, however, was in its unduly grandiose pre-credits sequence (on which the director claimed to have spent one third of his entire budget). Set in South-East Asia, this sequence actually succeeded in *parodying* the most spectacular visual effects of *Apocalypse Now* and *The Deer Hunter*, as also their predominant coloration of rust, green and red (the fiery vermilion of napalm), thereby providing latecomers with a handy recap of Vietnam imagery to date. (In 1984, a sequel was released, entitled *Exterminator 2*, directed by Mark Buntzman and produced by Cannon Films. Still on the rampage through a New York now so wormy with hoodlums of every hue as to have acquired a distinctly futuristic feel, Ginty has taken to wielding a flame-thrower and sporting a lurid metal helmet. 'The war's not over yet,' his black accomplice declares between gritted teeth. But he could hardly be further in error: in this routinely apocalyptic context, Vietnam seems as distant in time as in space. Typical Cannon fodder, the whole sorry enterprise.)

To return to the war itself: as suggested, *Apocalypse Now* represented a temporary cease-fire. Shying away from any fictional reconstruction of combat conditions, Hollywood continued to dwell instead on the plight of the veteran (a word which, as perhaps in the wake of every such conflict, had gained a melancholy connotation of youth rather than age). Yet such dramatic potential could not be allowed to remain for long unexplored and unexploited, and it must have occurred to more than one film-maker that, whatever their various critical fortunes, the three most famous, or notorious, Vietnam epics – *The Green Berets*, *The Deer Hunter* and *Apocalypse Now* – had all enjoyed a huge commercial success.

Initially testing the water were two movies made by the Canadian-born director Ted Kotcheff: *First Blood* (1982), starring Sylvester Stallone, and its companion piece *Uncommon Valor* (1983), starring Gene Hackman. Their interest was, I should add, socio-economic rather than aesthetic in nature since, if divested of a few incidental but not quite irrelevant ruminations on the meaning of the war (and, specifically, of the American defeat), either film would have worked no less and no more efficiently as a straight-forward, uncommitted action movie. Nevertheless, for the first time since *Apocalypse Now*, here were two mainstream productions consciously rejecting such circuitous approaches to Vietnam as the

127

allegorical and the metaphorical; capitalising on 'normal' – which is to say, large – budgets and the presence of major Hollywood stars; and, above all, appearing to confound the industry's conventional wisdom (at that particular period) with some excellent box-office returns. From the point of view of our study, these factors may be at least as worthy of attention and analysis as any strictly intellectual or aesthetic ones; for, arguably, the movies which tell us most about a period are those which make the most money during that period, not those which purport to address themselves to whatever significant problems might have beset it. (For that reason, *American Graffiti's* nostalgic escapism, let us say, could be regarded as a more indicative product of the Vietnam years than the head-on collision with the war in *The Green Berets*, whose inflammatory chauvinism whole sections of the cinema audience – not excluding returned veterans – refused to recognise as their mirror image.)

Based on what is, by all accounts, a reputable novel by David Morrell, *First Blood* revolves around John Rambo (Stallone), a Vietnam veteran who, as the movie begins, has just paid a visit to the last surviving member of his former unit (only to discover that he has died from cancer: 'Brought it back from 'Nam, all that orange stuff they're spreadin' around'). He then drifts, aimlessly and disconsolately, into the neighbouring township of Hope(!), from which, however, he is forthwith evicted as an undesirable alien by the local sheriff (the type who never strikes a man when he is up). But John Rambo is conditioned to accept orders only if issued by a superior army officer. And when he stubbornly retraces his steps back to town and is beaten up by a deputy as a cautionary measure, the beating has the same effect upon him as the 'petite madeleine' dipped in tea had on Proust: it awakens his memory. His memory, to be precise, of having been tortured by the Viet Cong. Enraged by such treatment, he proceeds to run amok, promptly putting a trio of cops out of commission and fleeing to a patch of forest land on the edge of town. A full-scale manhunt is instantly under way; and before Hope has rid itself of Rambo, the aforementioned deputy pitches out of a helicopter to his death, a squad of National Guardsmen are co-opted as reinforcements, Rambo snipes at his pursuers and the town centre is all but consumed by fire. The fact that the fugitive happens to be an ex-Green Beret, as well as a

128

recipient of the Congressional Medal of Honor, draws a contingent of newsmen to the scene, followed by a certain Colonel Trautman (played in pretentiously stolid fashion by Richard Crenna), who was originally responsible for fabricating the cold, robotic killing machine that Rambo has become and who, even amid the mounting debris of human life and property which his protégé leaves in his wake, perhaps retains the perverse hope that this fairy-tale ogre will vindicate his training by outwitting the superior forces aligned against him.

It is in Trautman's stout, paternal arms that Rambo collapses at the end; it is in his arms, too, that he delivers a lengthy — and, for those of us untutored in classic Stallonese, pretty incoherent — speech, which concludes with the cry, 'How do they know what it was like unless they've been there?' (Word for word, almost, John Wayne's complaint to liberal journalist David Janssen in *The Green Berets*, and one, of course, that might with profit and pleasure be turned against the makers of both movies.)

A number of potentially promising ironies intersect here; but *First Blood*, alas, takes these on as excess baggage without properly squaring accounts with them. The irony of the reversed image, most notably: stalked through the forest by law officers and Guardsmen, dogs and helicopters, at one point nearly buried alive in a dugout, Rambo finds himself engaging in just that kind of guerilla warfare in which he was trained, not so much *for* the Vietnam War as *by* it — save that, on this occasion, *he* has been transformed into a guerilla, a loner and an underdog, his advantage deriving from his superior familiarity with the terrain. (One tends, as the film progresses, to lose sight of the fact that it is set in the United States, with the consumerist urban-ity of a Western capitalist society gradually surrendering to an untamed landscape more characteristic of the Third World.) Then there is, obviously, the irony of a soldier (like a malevolent computer in a science-fiction film) utilising the data he has been programmed with, in a sense, against the very administration that programmed him. Yet, too obsessed with constructing a relentless crescendo of violence towards the climactic devastation, and too subservient to the imagined 'charismatic' properties of its inexpressive leading man, *First Blood*, I repeat, never begins to probe its own subtext. And there can be little doubt that, however earnest its director's intentions might have been, the movie was assimilated by audiences primarily – and perhaps exclusively – as a 'rip-roaring actioner', as they say in the trade.

Such thematic simplification is even more flagrant in Kotcheff's second Vietnam work, *Uncommon Valor*, whose original screenplay (by Joe Gayton) was clearly influenced by the mercenary and much-publicised exploits inside Laos of Lieutenant-Colonel 'Bo' Gritz, reputedly financed in his search for secret prisoner-of-war camps by the actors Clint Eastwood and William Shatner. More than a decade after his Marine son was listed MIA (Missing in Action) in Vietnam, a retired US Army colonel, Jason Rhodes (played as a Dean Jagger for the eighties by the usually more subtle and resourceful Gene Hackman), remains convinced that he is alive and in captivity somewhere in South-East Asia. The movie recounts Rhodes's endeavour to organise a private air strike on one Laotian camp, with the aid of other ex-military men as embittered as himself; the active opposition to his project which he encounters from the military and political Establishments; the enlistment and mobilisation of his outfit of mavericks; and, after countless odds have been overcome (to employ a formula beloved of synopsis writers), the successful raid itself and consequent liberation of a quartet of bewildered and emaciated GIs.

If it does not hesitate to overtax one's credulity along the way (e.g. the ridiculous ease with which Rhodes prevails upon his recruits to risk not only their livelihoods but their very lives in the undertaking of so whimsically quixotic an enterprise), *Uncommon Valor* does at least have the sense to allow for one serious misconjecture on the part of its protagonist. For though he was indeed held prisoner in exactly the POW labour camp of which Rhodes managed to obtain an aerial reconnaissance photograph ('grasping miraculously at the correct straw', as the BFI *Monthly Film Bulletin* reviewer Paul Taylor phrased it), it transpires that Rhodes Jnr succumbed to a fatal illness prior to the arrival of Dad's rescue party. Hence, in the final shot, with a frenzied press corps snapping at the heels of POWs and relatives as they joyfully reunite, Rhodes is left to ponder the relative efficacy of his adventurism – just how much it has contributed to both his own and the general welfare. As about the only ambiguity to which *Uncommon Valor* is ready to subscribe, this is naturally conveyed by Hollywood's codified signifier for all such ambivalent last-minute double-takes: the freeze frame.

Here and there, other ambiguities can be noted, but they are either undeveloped or simply unintentional. For starters, the fact – a fact corroborated by the whole history of the American cinema and central to the vision of film-makers as important as Capra and Vidor – that, within such a narrative, the 'system' exists solely in order that *an individual will come to its aid*, not vice versa. (There are exceptions, no doubt; yet they only confirm a rule that can be taken as almost axiomatic.) And a more immediate, certainly more disturbing, irony is implicit in the gap – or rather, chasm – which opens up between such routine generic representations of the Vietnam aftermath as *Uncommon Valor* and *First Blood*, and whatever realities they are claiming to represent. These are movies at peace with themselves, with the cinema and with the world. No matter that lip service is paid to a few of the more contentious issues raised by the war ('You're criminals because you lost!' is Rhodes's comment on the slow rehabilitation and ill-defined social status of many Vietnam vets), it is never permitted to ruffle the smooth narrative fluency that the majority of paying customers expect from mainstream war movies. There is barely a hint of that half-formulated guilt, that pervasive bad conscience, that played havoc with the climaxes in particular of *The Deer Hunter* and *Apocalypse Now*.

In short, with these two films, and unlike the veterans themselves (at least, such as Hollywood had portrayed them), the *cinema* of Vietnam seemed to have been rehabilitated and reintegrated, i.e. it had at last succeeded in securing for itself a commercially viable place within the movie industry of the eighties. While, paradoxically, the same political vacillation, the same ideological equivocation, as had been evident in the American cinema's first maladroit attempts to turn the war to account as fictional material could be seen in a sprinkling of contemporaneous movies about US military involvement in Latin America (one thinks of Roger Spottiswoode's *Under Fire*), Vietnam appeared at last to have come in from the cold, as the cliché has it.

But though, as commercial successes go, *First Blood* and *Uncommon Valor* were comparably solid and respectable, neither could exactly be termed phenomenal. Curiously, it was by the appropriation from the former of its star, and from the latter of its theme, that a genuine sociocultural phenomenon of contemporary cinema was sired. This phenomenon was the clumsily titled *Rambo: First Blood Part II*.

There is, to begin with, a peculiar rightness as well as a piquant irony to the fact that one of the key movies of the decade (from an ideological standpoint, at least) should happen to be a sequel. The sequel is a genre, perhaps the one original genre of the eighties, and its organisational principle is that of inflation. The prototype, like a wad of bubble gum, is blown up in each consecutive instalment so that, even if its proportions change (in *Rocky*, for instance, the genre's *locus classicus*, the ante is raised, the dramatic conflict is rendered more and more momentous, the blows exchanged become ever more prodigiously violent, bloody and resonant), the basic narrative structure remains miraculously intact. A different sameness – therein lies the secret, the universal remedy, the philosopher's stone, that the indefatigable alchemists of the American cinema have been pursuing for wellnigh a century now, and the eighties sequel is without question the most perfectly achieved and exemplary fruit of their labours, the quintessential Hollywood product.

Several years ago, in his cramped, Oscar-bedecked bungalow at Universal Studios, where he was preparing that strange and anachronistic melodrama *Fedora*, the veteran director Billy Wilder confided to me that he was thinking of calling it *Fedora II* 'to make it sound more fashionable'. He was joking, of course; the joke, though, was a serious one. For, as Wilder well knew, there is nothing that terrifies the movie industry more than the ideogram 'I', denoting as it does both the first person singular and the primary unit in what might be considered the numerical 'alphabet'. On the one hand, such glorious and tragic first persons singular of the American cinema as Stroheim, Welles and Nicholas Ray all found themselves mercilessly and systematically muzzled, neutered, reduced to exile and silence; on the other, it is still those projects that commit the unpardonable offence of rejecting stale, second-hand stereotypes of character and situation that are the least likely to find financial backing. Hence, far from constituting an admission of failure, an abdication from the artist's prerogative to invent, to innovate, to explore hitherto uncharted territory, the *II* of *First Blood Part II*, like the *IV* of *Rocky IV*, is actually perceived by the makers of the film and its spectators alike as a form of security or collateral, an assurance that it will be the same, only different.

The commercial success of *Rambo* (as, from here on in, I shall refer to *Rambo: First Blood Part II*) was considerably in excess of *First Blood* and *Uncommon Valor* combined. In the United States alone it earned more than a hundred million dollars and generated a mania for Rambo comic-books, Rambo toys, Rambo vitamins and even Rambograms, delivered by beefy messenger boys who would apparently sling them at their hapless recipients as though they were paper grenades. It propelled its star, Sylvester Stallone, to an eminence of bankability matched by no other actor in Hollywood's history: for *Rambo III*, the second of the two sequels to date, he was paid fifteen million dollars plus a sizeable percentage of the film's gross earnings; for the projected third and fourth sequels* he is reported to have signed a contract guaranteeing him the unheard-of fee of fifty million. And, of course, it prompted one of President Ronald Reagan's infamous off-the-cuff but on-the-record apothegms. In the aftermath of the Libyan hostage crisis he playfully remarked to incredulous journalists that 'After seeing *Rambo* last night I'll know what to do next time this happens.'

What precisely was it that induced such an improbable infatuation? Or, to paraphrase the same question, why Rambo? Particularly at a period when, following *Apocalypse Now*, the cinema had seemed to weary of the themes and images of the Vietnam War, how could one isolated film make such a forceful impact?

Rambo is, in the debased sense in which this word is currently to be heard bandied about, a myth. The myth in question may be as distasteful as the brutishly simplistic ideology underpinning it, but myths operate on a plane on which complexity, intelligence and taste cease to have any real purchase. Belonging as he does to

---

* In view of the disappointing box-office returns registered (in the domestic market) by *Rambo III* — set in Afghanistan and released, inopportunely for the film's credibility, in the summer of 1988, just as the Soviet occupying forces were at last withdrawing from the country — it is now very possible that these sequels will never be made.

the pure realm of the symbolic, Rambo's interpenetration with a documented politico-historical reality (the Vietnam War, the United States' 'civilising mission', the equivocating attitude of successive American administrations vis-à-vis its outcome) serves only to accentuate the almost unfordable gap between fact and fiction.

Thus, significantly, neither of the two Vietnam-related Rambo films fictionalises a straightforward, factually based combat experience. In the first instance, the war is displaced, transported to the American hinterland as though to vindicate *in extremis* homegrown fears of the domino theory; in the second, it is protracted artificially and far beyond its historical conclusion. In both cases, patently, the objective is to forestall the inevitable – to forestall, if one may say, *the past*. The premise of these films is that the Vietnam War has not in reality ended; or rather, having constituted an American defeat, that it cannot be permitted to end. In this kind of populist fiction defeat is as much an impossibility as victory had been in fact. The war has to be detached from its anchorage – first in a geographical reality (*First Blood*), then in a historical reality (*Rambo*), in both of which the United States is condemned inexorably to relive its ignominy – and allowed to free-float, to become a timeless, stateless fiction, a symbolic abstraction of itself. What remains of the historical Vietnam War is merely a certain guerilla iconography: an iconography, it should be noted, that is specifically *Vietnamese* in its trappings, that derives from the combat tactics of the Viet Cong and can therefore dispense with the kind of glossy Yankee weaponry so lovingly detailed in a movie like *Top Gun*; an iconography, finally, so generalised, so nightmarishly formless, that it can (as in *First Blood*) be inverted, turned inside-out and planted anew on American soil. And given that the real war tended for the non-combatant to be deficient in dates and place names, it itself may be said to have unwittingly conspired in its own dehistoricisation.

For the cinema's purposes, then, this has become a war that can be waged virtually anywhere and at any time. It has been reduced to a 'style', a set of visual, thematic and ideological parameters, a semi-abstract chequerboard arena in which light contends with dark, white with black, good with evil.

Vividly illustrating Rambo's wilful disjunction from, and irrelevance to, the real war, the fact that he stands instead as the living repudiation of its history, is the fundamental paradox of the myth. With someone like John Rambo fighting on their side, how on earth did the Americans ever manage to lose the war in the first place?

For American audiences, lulled into 'feeling good' about themselves by the amiable snoozer in the White House, the image of Rambo/Stallone associated with a national defeat (at whatever remove from his own on-screen presence, and even if only by implication) would be not only unpalatable but untenable. Either the myth of the invincible Rambo – such as it is promoted, in particular, by the second film of the cycle – or the reality of the defeated American forces has to be negated: one cannot co-exist with the other. Which is why, even though in both *First Blood I* and *II* Rambo accepts the commission of testifying personally to the betrayal and abandonment of his disillusioned fellow veterans, he himself is never shown to be less than indestructible. Otherwise, he could hardly be absolved of all responsibility in their defeat. 'The old Vietnam is dead,' sermonises one of his superiors. 'Sir,' he replies, with that extraordinary, otherworldly delivery of his, 'I'm alive. It's still alive.' Rambo, that pure myth, has quite clearly *become* the war, the long dormant genie of the whole Vietnam period uncorked, unstopped and by now unstoppable. As long as he is alive, the Vietnam War is alive, for he and it are one. What Rambo/Stallone incarnates (since between them, too, the identification seems ever more complete and irreversible) is a sort of Protean god-warrior in whose monumental physical immanence each of the four natural elements will be invested. During the course of the narrative he will be assimilated in turn with the earth (he will stalk his prey slathered with mud from head to feet), with water (he will be seen more than once surfacing head first from a river), with fire (he will suffer, unflinchingly, the branding of his cheek from the point of a white-hot sword) and with air (he will swing, in ecstatic Tarzan fashion, from treetop to treetop). There exists (and here, no doubt, we pierce the very core of the film's appeal) a seamless equation between a mythicised war and the mythical hero who, in the most literally corporeal sense, embodies it.

What, in this light, is perhaps most remarkable about the film is its deliberate artlessness, its rigorous, almost superstitious, avoidance of narrative sophistication.* Rambo is a monosyllabic creature with a bisyllabic name, one of those without whom the American cinema as it currently functions could not survive. Think of such emblematic figures, for instance, as Rocky (Stallone again) and E.T., neither of them any more articulate than our deranged and enigmatic vet. The film's plot, too, is a monadic construct, as elemental (or elementary) as a fairy-tale.

Delivered by his mentor, Colonel Trautman (played as before, and as imperturbably as ever, by Richard Crenna) from the prison in which he was interned following the events related in *First Blood*, Rambo is offered a free pardon in return for accepting a covert, almost suicidal mission into Vietnam to establish once and for all whether any American soldiers reported 'Missing in Action' are in reality still being held in Viet Cong prison camps. He is parachuted into the jungle, where he instantly locates the presence of a score of POWs and, with the aid of a young Vietnamese rebel, Co Bao (Julie Nickson), rescues one of them in defiance of instructions that he merely provide photographic documentation. When Murdock (Charles Napier), the sweaty, shifty-eyed officer in charge of the mission, learns of this uncalled-for initiative, he forthwith aborts the rescue operation and leaves both Rambo and the liberated POW to the mercies of the Viet Cong; at which point it transpires that the raid was undertaken solely to demonstrate that no American prisoners remained in Vietnam so that, without fear of further reprisals, the US government might tranquilly renege on its promise to pay fifteen million dollars worth of war reparations. (Paradoxically, this calculated sneakiness on the part of his superiors turns out to be to Rambo's advantage, since it enables him to wage war, so to speak, *in peace*, no longer accountable to the pettifogging dictates of historical accuracy.) Very much as one would expect, however, Rambo outwits his tormentors (both Vietnamese and, in a less predictable plot development, Soviet), liberates his shrivelled and skeletal fellow Americans, brashly commandeers a Soviet helicopter and returns to base. His own personal crusade accomplished,

---

* The film's director, incidentally – and it is an incidental matter – is George Pan Cosmatos.

he warns Murdock that if the military does not exert itself to the maximum to have the remaining GIs freed, it will be obliged to answer to John Rambo. Which is quite a threat to have hanging over oneself. . . .

Clearly, the spectre of yet another myth is being raised: that of the prolonged incarceration and maltreatment of American soldiers in South-East Asian prison camps. (The use, here, of the term 'myth' is intended less as a categorical denial that such a situation may indeed obtain* than as the acknowledgment that in a movie like *Rambo* it necessarily functions at an irrational level.) The myth is analogous to that of an aged, unrepentant Hitler leading a clandestine existence in the depths of some South American rain forest; or, perhaps more appropriately, to that of the celebrated handful of Japanese soldiers who refused to accept late into the forties that the Second World War had ended. And it is not too fanciful to envisage a subsequent episode of the cycle in which Rambo would be doggedly alone in the whole world in continuing to believe that the Vietnam War was still to be fought and won.

Rambo's solitude, in fact, is central to his mythology. Though the direct consequence of a betrayal – a double betrayal, that of America, the country he has come to personify, by its own liberal intelligentsia (who, having once been against the war, have now chosen to forget it) and that of himself and his fellow grunts in the field *by* America (in the guise of the behind-the-scenes duplicity practised by Murdock and his like) – it also represents the source of his strength. Confronted at every turn by an eternally ungrateful world, his hypertrophied instinct for self-preservation has ended by making him impervious to both pain and paranoia, as equally to the hopes, illusions and expectations that might otherwise vitiate his capacity to bear them. It is, in short, the solitude of the professional survivalist who can scarcely wait to be tested in the crucible of the Apocalypse.

For there is, curiously and anachronistically, a bold, spacey

---

* There currently remain, according to an official estimate, 2,393 Americans unaccounted for in Indochina, 1,757 of them in Vietnam. There have also been 119 unresolved reports of first-hand sightings of Americans in Indochina, 58 of whom are said to be held as 'prisoners' and 61 'non-prisoners'.

post-Armageddon atmosphere in the movie – post-Armageddon, at least, in relation to the way such a myth has been handled in the cinema: e.g. John Carpenter's *Escape from New York*, the *Mad Max* cycle. And, in the wake of these films (also the *Star Wars* trilogy), *Rambo* is caught up in the so-called 'post-modernist' vogue for manipulating and synthesising a number of mythic and fictional archetypes (an achievement of sorts, considering how very limited, by comparison with those of George Lucas's interstellar jamboree, are the narrative co-ordinates of the Vietnam War), which range from the seriocomic Samurai adventures of Kurosawa to Edgar Rice Burroughs's jungle romances.

It is, in effect, Burroughs's Tarzan, that brooding comic-book vulgarisation of the Noble Savage (considering his aristocratic ancestry, he ought perhaps to be thought of rather as a Savage Noble), who provides us with the most plausible analogy. With his shoulder-length, permanently matted hair framing his archly schematic comic-strip features, Sylvester Stallone actually bears, as Philip French observed, an almost eerie resemblance to Elmo Lincoln, the first of the cinema's many Tarzans; and even the fact that Lincoln was a *silent* actor finds a sort of latterday corroboration in Stallone's chronic taciturnity. Rambo, moreover, refers to 'coming home' when he is shipped back out to Vietnam, as though, in common with Lord Greystoke, the abandoned infant of Burroughs's original plotline, his natural habitat were the jungle. In consequence, it has become impossible to imagine him at ease in the American society for which he is fighting and from which he presumably issued, impossible to imagine his very existence, indeed, prior to the Vietnam War. It was in *First Blood*, after all, that his arrival on the scene proved so instantly disruptive that the placid township of Hope was transformed overnight into a theatre of guerilla combat.

In both films Rambo is rather complacently described as a 'killing machine'. Yet his bearing partakes less of the machine, of the half-human automaton *à la* Robocop, than of some humanised and purified savage beast *à la* Tarzan. A feral, shiny-skinned Narcissus of unblinking watchfulness, he slinks through the undergrowth with even his hands on tiptoe and is shown to be considerably more adept with such primitive weaponry as knives and bows-and-arrows than with the mighty arsenal of American technology. Like Tarzan, too, he contrives to communicate with his environment despite (perhaps because of) a severely restricted repertoire of monosyllabic grunts; and, at the film's climax, when he has utterly trounced his adversaries, he lets rip with a half-human howl as though to underline the resemblance.

As in the very best of the *Tarzan* cycle, there may be detected in this film a dialectic (one that operates to bizarrely sensual effect within the narrative) between, on the one hand, the breathtaking speed and quasi-permanent aura of violence that characterise the action and, on the other, the weird, preternatural stillness with which the protagonist is enhaloed. For a hero of the eighties Stallone is so incredibly *slow*. He has been compared to Elmo Lincoln; but he also bears a striking physical likeness to another grotesquely bulging, glistening, lazy-lidded actor – to wit, Victor Mature, the Samson of Cecil B. De Mille's pseudo-Biblical extravaganza *Samson and Delilah*, of which Groucho Marx famously commented that he didn't 'want to see a movie where the man has bigger tits than the woman'. His is the physique both of the classical god-hero and of its contemporary, populist avatar, the comic-strip superhero, Batman, Superman or the Incredible Hulk. In contrast to the drifting, disoriented grunts of such films as *Platoon*, *Apocalypse Now* and *The Deer Hunter*, Rambo is totally at home in the jungle; he is, in fact, an American Viet Cong, just the kind of soldier the United States would have needed to win the war. Thus, again, no less than the programmatically simplified landscape in which he moves and the reductively sentimental cause for which he is fighting, Rambo's own near-supernatural self-mastery (not to mention, self-aggrandisement) commits him firmly to the realm of myth and allegory.

Myths, as a rule, are non-verbal entities. For the mythical being, the verbal discourse, whether it be expressed in debate or more casual forms of conversation, is one of the less noble human functions, an effete, decadent practice, the frivolous art of those 'who can do nothing but talk'. In the rarefied sphere of the larger-than-life, talk undermines action and, via its inherently democratising tendencies, leads to diplomacy and compromise, both of which are anathema to myths. Unlike Elmo Lincoln's Tarzan movies, however, *Rambo* could not escape being burdened with a sound-track. And yet, though it would be preposterous to call him the film's 'nominal' star, Stallone must have had fewer lines of dialogue to memorise than virtually any leading performer in a major pro-duction, which made it all the more crucial that each of these lines be as eloquent, terse and unconditional as though it had been chiselled on marble. Consider:

Of the prison quarry in which he is discovered at his enforced labours in the film's opening scene:
Trautman: 'I'm sorry they've sent you to such a hellhole.'
Rambo: 'I've seen worse.'

On the covert mission itself:
Rambo: 'Do we get to win this time?'
Trautman: 'That's up to you.'

On finding himself back in Vietnam:
Rambo: 'In here at least I know where I stand.'

On taking his own initiative in the field:
Co Bao: 'But I thought you were only supposed to take pictures. Orders.'
Rambo: 'No more orders.' (Myths, even those of a crypto-military nature, place themselves beyond the influence of a mere chain of command.)

On finding Co Bao riddled with machine-gun bullets:
Rambo: 'You all right?' (Under the circumstances this is perhaps a slightly less hilarious line than it strikes one at first, since Rambo himself would probably have been not at all inconvenienced by the same volley. The young Vietnamese, however, being a creature of flesh and blood, happens to be dead. No one must be permitted to share in Rambo's solitary triumph.)

Finally, attempting to articulate the motivation which spurs him on:
Rambo (in the film's closing scene): 'All I want, and all every

guy who ever fought in Vietnam wants, is for our country to love us as much as we love it.'

There is one last myth remaining to be mixed into the batter: that of Ronald Reagan's 'Evil Empire', the insidiously eternal myth (for the United States) of the Soviet Union. When, the Americans having perfidiously elected to abort the mission, Rambo is taken captive by the Viet Cong and returned to the prison camp that he had previously reconnoitred, lo and behold, a pair of Russian advisers fly in with a small detachment of troops to interrogate and torture him. As a laconic fellow prisoner sighs, on seeing the Soviets arrive, 'He's dead now.' Wrong, of course, but the implication is clear: no matter how heinously sadistic has been Rambo's treatment at the hands of the Viet Cong (notably, crucifixion and immersion in a swamp of pig manure), what the Russians are about to cook up for him will necessarily be worse. The Russians have always been worse, globally and since time immemorial (i.e. since 1917). They are the enemy *par excellence*, the ultimate, definitive Other.

Such a direct and unambiguous identification of the Soviet Union with the distillation of pure and strangely unmotivated malfeasance (save, of course, for its sheer, pig-headed and practically existential anti-Americanism) serves not merely to lend credence to the aberrant Reaganite epithet cited above, it also represents yet another alibi by which the military defeat in South-East Asia may be rationalised, minimised, then magically negated.

An immediate Soviet on-the-spot presence in Vietnam may be contrary to historical fact but it is far from irrelevant to myth. More than one American administration, at least prior to the advent of glasnostic *détente*, has proposed the quaint thesis that over every single geopolitical conflict since the Second World War, be it in the Middle East or in Central America, there has been cast the sinister red shadow of the Soviet Union. The proposition is of course as ludicrous as it is profoundly offensive, ignoring as it does the entirely localised significance of any number of religious, social, political and territorial issues. It remains a potent one, nevertheless (which explains why certain right-wing politicians, including Mrs Thatcher herself, having had their bluff ingeniously called by the Russians, now find their own instinctively bellicose attitudes hamstrung by just the kind of ideological relaxation they had been demanding so vociferously); and in the specific context of Vietnam, and of such examples of its filmic apocrypha as *The Green Berets* and *Rambo* (as well as that poor man's *Rambo*, the cretinous *Missing in Action* series featuring Chuck Norris), its point is to encourage one to view the war as, ultimately, only a skirmish, a minor altercation in the *really* serious Hundred Years War between the superpowers.

At a stroke the US withdrawal from Vietnam ceases to be the unmitigated, irreversible disaster we had always thought it was and becomes instead a mere setback along the way, a picturesquely quixotic reversal – in short, *an American Dunkirk*. The war, as Rambo himself insists in his dozily autistic manner, is not over yet. More to the point, the Americans are still in with a chance to win. The unexpected involvement of the Soviets in *Rambo* – irresistibly reminiscent as they are of the pantomime mega-villains of SMERSH in the James Bond thrillers of the sixties – is therefore not at all gratuitous, since it emits a clear signal that the essential priorities have not been forgotten.* (Such primary anti-Communism would appear, surely not by coincidence, to be something of a constant in Stallone's work. *Rambo III* finds him fighting on the side of the rebels against the Soviet occupying forces in Afghanistan; *Rocky IV* pits him against a blond steely-eyed Soviet bruiser stereotyped in everything but his outlandish physique, even if there, to be sure, glasnost *oblige*, Stallone concludes by making a plea for international peace and harmony – having first battered his opponent to a pulp.)

With its lovingly, lingeringly filmed violence, its oily sadomaso-chism, its pornography of blood and biceps, the red meat pornogra-phy of Stallone's naked torso and the white meat pornography of young, delicately olive-complexioned, gun-toting beauties in coolie hats and Thai silk pyjamas, with its pidgin-English dialogue and

---

* All of which is whimsically reminiscent of the Dogs' Theatre invented by the composer Erik Satie and described by Cocteau in his *Opium*. The canine public would file into the auditorium and hunker down on all fours in front of the stage; the lights would dim; and the theatre curtain would rise on an enormous bone. Subsequent productions mounted by the Dogs' Theatre would almost certainly grow more and more sophisticated . . . but there would continue to be, by public demand, regular revivals of the Bone. In Rambo's world, as in Reagan's, the Soviet Union is the Bone.

crudely racist Chinoiserie (or Chinese restaurant Chinkoiserie), *First Blood II: Rambo* is a nauseating artefact, the kind of movie one is tempted to think only the 'public' could enjoy. Yet, as we have already seen, a film doesn't have to be *good* – subtle, accomplished, richly textured, whatever – to be generative of meaning. For social historians, if for no one else, *Rambo* is a document of inestimable value, a compendium, a veritable archive, of Reaganite attitudes and aspirations.

Then again, perhaps not only for social historians. . . . At the period of the film's release those critics addicted to puns (and they are legion) made a good deal out of an incongruous phonetic correspondence between the name Rambo and that of a certain revolutionary French poet of the late nineteenth century. Yet even if not one of them then proceeded to remind his readers that it was this same Rimbaud who was prescient enough to encapsulate, in a celebrated verse, *'Je est un autre'* or 'I is an other', what most of us have too cavalierly tended to categorise as an exclusively twentieth-century species of sociopsychic alienation, it can be ar-gued (at the risk of trivialising Rimbaud's poetic intuition) that from the very outset – which is to say, from *The Green Berets* – Hollywood's Vietnam has proved most interesting and revealing as the unconscious (or semi-conscious) exposure of just such a dislocation of the self. Practically the first into the field, *The Green Berets* already, and *against its will*, disclosed the powerful resistance that the Vietnam War offered to the venerable ethos, an ethos both military and cinematic, of heroic individualism. And succeeding movies have done little else but reaffirm that resistance, to the point where the real tension generated in their various narratives arises out of the uncertainty this time around as to who precisely, the Vietnamese or the Americans, constituted 'the *other* side'. It is, therefore, because a movie like *Rambo* endeavours so hopelessly, so schizophrenically, to circumvent and even negate the historical reality without which it could not have come into existence in the first place that it emerges as less the controlled expression than the irrepressible (or un-repressible) symptom of a schism that was not only national but individual, not only political but moral, not only social but psychic.

— *Chapter 8* —

I AM REALITY

If there is one movie to which responsibility is due for the return
in force of the Vietnam War genre, it is Oliver Stone's *Platoon*,
released in 1986. With amazing swiftness its earnings surpassed that
talismanic figure of a hundred million dollars in the United States
alone; it won its director a Silver Bear at the following year's Berlin
Film Festival; it was rewarded with a cluster of Oscars by the
Hollywood Academy; and, perhaps the topmost feather in its cap,
it had no fewer than seven pages devoted to it by *Time* magazine.
What is more, the film definitively established the reputation of its
director, who had previously scripted three highly conspicuous and
diversely controversial films (Alan Parker's *Midnight Express*, Brian
De Palma's *Scarface* and Michael Cimino's *Year of the Dragon*) and
directed a trio of his own, of which the only one to have made any
impact was *Salvador*, a semi-fictionalised account of the peregrin-
ations of the American journalist Richard Boyle in El Salvador.
The unforeseen commercial and critical favour enjoyed by *Platoon*
immediately elevated Stone to the prominent niche that he currently occupies in the Pantheon of the new Hollywood and enabled
him to follow it with *Wall Street*, a chronicle of rapine and butchery
closer to home, of (relative) innocence despoiled and ultimately
redeemed. (As I write this, Stone is preparing his second film on
Vietnam, titled *Born on the Fourth of July* and starring Tom Cruise.)
And *Platoon* received a commendation from the distinguished political commentator David Halberstam, which read in part: '*Platoon* is
the first real Viet Nam film . . . a picture like *Rambo* diminished the
soldiers who were actually over there; if one Stallone can conquer
the enemy, why couldn't *they*? It understands something that the
architects of the war never did: how the foliage, the thickness of
the jungle, negated US technological superiority. You can see how

the forest sucks in American soldiers; they just disappear. I think
the film will become an American classic.' And: 'The other Hollywood Viet Nam films have been a rape of history. But *Platoon* is
historically and politically accurate.'

These remarks by Halberstam are revealing in their very confusion, and a commentary on the film could do worse than start
by extrapolating from them.

First, the comparison of Rambo with real soldiers in the field, to
the evident disadvantage of the latter, might initially strike one as
so elementary as not to need stating, especially in the context of
an American defeat. Yet, even if such stalwarts of Second World
War movies as Errol Flynn, John Wayne, William Holden *et al.*
performed feats scarcely less supernaturally audacious than those
of Stallone, it would have been unimaginable for a journalist of the
period, of Halberstam's stature and unimpeachable patriotism, to
have made a similarly disobliging comment about the immense
abyss separating them from any historically documented acts of
heroism. It has always been in the nature of fiction, not merely
Hollywood fiction, to heighten and intensify reality, and the most
basic, primitive method of achieving such an end is the creation of
a hero.

Who is this hero? He is someone who assumes unto himself all
the various courageous acts that have been or might well have
been performed by the humanly imperfect heroes whose idealised
proxy he has become; but also, more significantly, those acts which
they could not quite bring themselves to carry out or which they
were never given the opportunity to carry out and which were
therefore destined to remain for most of them (and for the rest of
us) as potent yet as unattainable as dreams. Soldiers obscurely
realise this, and it is far from certain that they resent heroes or feel
in any real sense diminished by them (though, to be sure, there is
a scene in *The Short Timers*, the novel by Gustav Hasford on which
Stanley Kubrick's *Full Metal Jacket* is based, in which a cinema
audience of Marines is reduced to helpless giggles by the tub-
thumping absurdities of *The Green Berets*). A greater likelihood, all
things considered, is that the movies most at risk from the censure
of the common soldier are those daring to insinuate the notion
that exceptional bravery was *not* the wartime norm. Halberstam's

remarks, then, turn out to mean that a 'real Viet Nam film' is to be recognised by its absence of both heroes and heroism, which leaves him open to the charge of being rather more offensive to 'the soldiers who were actually over there' than the delirious and irrelevantly self-vaunting fantasies of Rambo.

When he goes on to speak about 'the foliage, the thickness of the jungle', he certainly pins down what is most vividly memorable about *Platoon*. If there had been an Oscar going for foliage, no question but that Stone would have carried it off. But Halberstam appears not to be a connoisseur of Vietnam War movies, since the visuals of *Apocalypse Now* and even *Rambo* had already illustrated the extent to which it was the jungle, and the enemy flitting through it as spectrally as though they were nothing but the shadows cast by their own shadows, that 'negated US technological superiority'. If *Rambo*, indeed, had a genuine polemical point to drive home, it was that only by adapting completely to these conditions, by frankly modelling their tactics on those of the Viet Cong, could the Americans ever have won the war. Moreover, given that a fair number of the 'architects of the war' had themselves, twenty-five years before, contended with the jungles of Burma and the islands of the Pacific archipelago, they certainly had sufficient cause to understand the precise nature of the problems that would be met with by the soldiers under their command.

Oddest of all is Halberstam's championship of *Platoon* as 'historically and politically accurate'. Even if one succeeds in figuring out exactly what the phrase is supposed to mean, it is difficult to know how any work of art can be *politically* accurate. Politics, surely, cannot be reconciled with any pseudo-Platonic ideal of measurable 'accuracy'. As for historical accuracy, the most unanimously acknowledged fact concerning Stone's film is that it was not about history at all but about *geography*. What crucially distinguished it from its predecessors in the canon is that it defined Vietnam not as a time or an event but as a place, a geographical and even meteorological location, and when one remembers that the movie is set in 1967, such an achievement was by no means negligible. In the majority of films whose overall visual style is contingent on a decorative nostalgia for the recent past (*American Graffiti, Chinatown, The Right Stuff*, etc.) those scenographical-cum-sociological co-ordinates that one is initially tempted to believe are indicative of *place* (e.g. the main cruising boulevard of an American small town, a seedy tenement office in downtown Los Angeles, the clinical green chambers and corridors of Cape Canaveral) are in reality signifiers of *time*, of period, of a particular decade (respectively, the early sixties, the thirties, the middle fifties). That is how nostalgia functions, by conflating time and place; and it was Stone's unique and distinctive achievement in *Platoon* to have drained the Vietnam War of all the passéist and nostalgic connotations with which, by the eighties, it had come to be encrusted. He made a film of the second wave of Vietnam films that could be inscribed, without any major revision of tone or style, within the first, a film that actually felt as though it had been made in 1967. For though the war was experienced by those who fought it as a moment of living history – conducted, moreover, under the intense scrutiny of the media – yet, as there could be no certitude for any of them that they would survive to look back on their collective pain, it also represented the essence of the present tense, which is to say, the instant when an infinitude of possibilities is reduced to a single one. That instant, that living present tense, is what Oliver Stone recaptured on film.

The Vietnam of *Platoon* is a neo-Boschian Garden of Eden, an Eden bereft of Eves but rife with serpents. The country is so foully, so viscerally, present as an all-enveloping environment (and not, as in most other Vietnam War movies, as a three-dimensional backdrop in front of which the action unfolds) that one tends to receive the film not with one's eyes alone but with one's whole being. As Halberstam said, the foliage 'sucks in the American soldiers'; but because Stone has contrived for most of the running time to dissolve the distinction between representation and reality, the spectator feels that he too is being sucked into the film, that he too runs the risk of leaving the cinema as dank, sweaty and malodorous as the characters on the screen. Even the climate, with its festering humidity and glazed, clinging drizzle, becomes almost tangible. The movie's imagery (as visualised by Robert Richardson's virtuoso cinematography) is never *clean*. It is not, as is often the case with the cinema of Vietnam, the pellucid mirroring of something that is not pellucid, but so permanently swathed in mist or obscured by rain that one begins to fantasise equipping the screen with a set of enormous wipers. Here, the weather is no mere atmospheric and expositional given, rapidly established then just as rapidly consigned to the background. Rather, it insidiously edges itself between the characters and the spectator. When darkness falls, we are prevented from seeing any more than the soldiers themselves do; our own perception of the action is never privileged in relation to theirs. Which means that if, for instance, they have not yet sighted the presence of an enemy, then neither have we. The camera is always *inside* the setting, inside the jungle. As rarely in a war film, we experience the sensation of being wholly surrounded by an environment, we have the distinct impression that, when the camera (which, if memory serves, is not invariably hand-held) effects a forward tracking shot, it has to *penetrate* the very imagery that it is in the process of generating.

That is the primary, ground-level stratum of *Platoon*'s realism: the spectator's increasingly intense conviction that he is in some sense *there*, vicariously sharing the average grunt's own experience. But even if it is a stratum whose primary concern is with surfaces and textures, with the hard-core materiality of a specific location, it also carries with it a clear moral and ideological charge. There is a democratic or egalitarian ambition in the idea of positioning the spectator's view at the level of a grunt's eye, so to speak. In war movies the spectator's place has always tended to be a privileged, on occasion impossible, vantage-point, shifting between a loftily detached overview of the field of conflict (i.e. the commanding officer's view) and a direct headlong plunge into the mêlée (the grunt's view). Stone, however, rejects such a hierarchy. Just as, in the narrative, the American soldiers are depicted as having no longer much need of the officer class (the sole officer of consequence in the movie, the platoon's commander, Lieutenant Wolfe, played by Mark Moses, is an ineffectual college-boy milquetoast barely tolerated by the two sergeants under him), so, in the auditorium, the spectator is denied the Olympian omniscience to which he has ever been accustomed.

On that level *Platoon* is brilliantly effective. In Vietnam, to use a sporting metaphor, the Americans were 'playing away from home', and no movie (not even those in the forties and fifties, praised for what was then held to be their unparalleled and unsurpassable realism, of Walsh, Wellman and Fuller) has ever conveyed with such physical force and immediacy the impression of soldiers at odds not simply with a hostile people but with hostile surroundings ('surroundings' in the most literally exact sense), with insects and reptiles, heat, dust and malarial, sub-tropical temperatures. No movie before *Platoon* portrayed Vietnam as, simultaneously and inextricably, a war and an environment, one rendering itself gradually indistinguishable from the other, an evilly resorbent miasma in which the characters on-screen – and the spectators off – are equally ensnared.

But even such a film will ultimately aspire to being more than a newsreel with a plot. And it is when the near-hallucinatory realism sought by Stone is obliged to rise above the superficially descriptive that problems start to occur.

The trouble is that, in their eagerness to explain how Oliver Stone arrived at this almost unprecedented degree of naturalistic verisimilitude, how he succeeded more graphically than any director before him in persuading us that this was 'how it was', few commentators on the film felt the need to look much further than the fact that he himself had once served in Vietnam (which is probably a first for the genre). By Stone's own account, *Platoon* is more than loosely autobiographical. The *Time* article consecrating the movie included a lengthy description of how, like his protagonist, Stone volunteered for the army in 1967 and spent fifteen months in Vietnam (precisely the film's own chronology); and how a real military camp was constructed for rehearsal purposes and a fellow veteran, Captain Dale Dye (who makes a cameo appearance, bearing his own rank, in the film), was recruited as a technical military adviser to guide the cast of young actors through a rigorously unsimulated course of combat training. Not one page of *Platoon*'s publicity, whether paid (studio handouts) or unpaid (newspaper and magazine reviews and interviews) omitted to stress the relevance of the director's own experience and the seamless manner in which it coincided with the ordeals undergone by his hero.

The widely shared belief that the film consisted for the most part of raw, unmediated chunks of autobiography was further reinforced by the uncanny way in which several of Stone's own ruminations on the war (most notably, on the reasons for his, a comfortably-off middle-class youth's, apparently aberrant decision to volunteer) were echoed by those of his protagonist, named Chris for the purposes of the fiction. Thus: 'I saw myself as a product – an East Coast socio-economic product – and I wanted to break out of the mold. . . . I felt the solution was total anonymity. I had to atone. So I joined the Army,' and, 'I guess I've always been sheltered and special. I just want to be anonymous. . . . Maybe from down here I can start up again and be something I can be proud of, without having to fake it, be a fake human being.' The first is Stone himself, the second Chris, but clearly they could be inverted without disruption of meaning or effect in either context.

Stone's own tour of duty handily served as a certificate of authenticity for *Platoon*'s realism, as a persuasive argument for the film to be considered neither more nor less than the transparent reflection of what he himself actually went through. It thereby lent the whole concept of realism (which is, after all, an artistic mode like any other, possessing its own feints and strategies) a supplementary layer of veracity. Whereas, if they are honest, most practitioners of cinematic realism aim simply to convey the plausible *appearance* of a reality few of us will ever have known at first hand (an extreme instance of this approach was Jean-Jacques Annaud's *Quest For Fire*, admired for its 'realistic' evocation of the Stone Age!), *Platoon* was judged as presenting a totally unbiased and irrefutable truth.

On what might be termed the pragmatic level, the level of natural, botanical textures, the movie's realism is extremely convincing (even if somewhat compromised by the basic falsehood – which ought not to be ignored merely because it was unavoidable – that it was not of course filmed in Vietnam at all). But what about the 'historical and political accuracy' lauded by Halberstam?

The sole orientation granted the spectator at the beginning of the movie is a title card: 'September 1967/Bravo Company, 25th Infantry, somewhere near the Cambodian border.' *Platoon* therefore starts as it will end – in Vietnam itself. Nowhere else exists. The United States is an intermittently absent/present off-screen abstraction, alluded to, dreamed of, reminisced about wistfully or lubriciously; it is never the object of anyone's overtly patriotic impulse. If the callow young soldiers have a natural tendency to divide the world into 'us' and 'them', 'our side' and 'their side', the frontiers of that world remain coextensive with those of the terrain itself, with their fellow grunts on the one side and the half-glimpsed, hologram-like silhouettes of the Viet Cong on the other. The larger political debate – generally couched in such grand rhetorical questions as those posed by Frank Capra ('Why We Fight') and Norman Mailer ('Why Are We in Vietnam?') – does not enter the equation. They are in Vietnam because, with the single and singular exception of Chris, they were drafted there. And they fight because their sole ambition is to survive long enough to complete their tour of duty and return to the States. Nothing else is shown to concern them. As the French critic Charles Tesson put it in *Cahiers du Cinéma*, the movie's motto might be, 'I came. I saw. I survived.'

In the many interviews he gave at the period of the film's release Stone insisted that he had been patriotically pro-American in 1967 and hoped by volunteering to distance himself from what he resented as the parasitically liberal attitudes of his middle-class parents. And he has Chris, in a slightly portentous voice-off narration, muse of his mostly underprivileged, working-class comrades, 'They're the poor, the unwanted – yet they're fighting for our society, our freedom.' (Note the ineradicable class distinction hinted at by the nearly imperceptible halfway shift from 'they' to 'us'.) Yet, as a film-maker, he actually seems to relish the heady mixture of anti-authoritarian laxity and moral ambiguity peculiar to the war.

The film's first image finds Chris* stepping forth from the bulging underbelly of a transport plane (as though he were being born or reborn in Vietnam) on to a dust-caked landing strip where he is confronted with a pile of body bags that have been unloaded on the runway (as though he were accorded a premonitory vision of what might be the circumstances of his own eventual departure from the country).

---

* He is played by Charlie Sheen, the son of Martin Sheen, whose best-known screen role was of course as the demeaned, bewildered antihero of *Apocalypse Now*. Not only does this father-son continuity underscore *Platoon*'s claim to be the true heir to the first wave of Vietnam movies but the fact that *Apocalypse Now* and *Platoon* are still the two most intelligent and relevant products of the genre seems to denote the Sheen face (Martin's and Charlie's features share a strong family resemblance) as the cinema's Identikit portrait of the American soldier in Vietnam.

Chris hates it already. Though *Platoon* was widely interpreted as yet another account of a young man's baptism of fire, his rite of passage into manhood, there is in the movie virtually no 'honeymoon' (in the electoral sense), no period of blithe innocence and well-being before the day-in, day-out bestiality of war sets about corroding youthful ideals and convictions. Chris volunteered for reasons that he left behind him in the United States. He appears to have expected no more from Vietnam than those who were forcibly mobilised. The cynical fatalism endemic to that time and place has entered his system practically before he steps off the plane. He soon learns that the rules which count are the unwritten rather than the written ones. An unwritten rule, he discovers (the narration is articulated around a series of letters to his grandmother), is 'a new guy's life isn't worth as much because he hasn't put his time in yet. And they say if you're gonna get killed in Vietnam it's better to get it in the first few weeks. The logic being you don't suffer that much.' And again, a shade improbably, in another communication to that no doubt mystified old lady, 'Somebody once wrote: Hell is the impossibility of reason. That's what this place feels like: Hell.'

The soldiers around him are to varying degrees disabused; but, in a crucial difference with Second World War films, there does not exist the one naïve and likeable Lon McCallister type who is not. Even in Vietnam, even before their return to an America that is probably not about to honour them as they expect and deserve, they have in common the paradoxical fact that they are already *vets*. ('Maybe that's why they call themselves grunts – because a grunt can take it, can take anything.') The neurotic, antisocial autism with which the American cinema had previously stigmatised the *returning* vet (in such movies as *Rolling Thunder*, *Taxi Driver* and *First Blood*) seems somehow to have infected the grunts of *Platoon* merely hours after their arrival in Vietnam. Unlike that depicted by Walsh or Fuller, whose humdrum, stoically borne horrors are ultimately transcended by the ennobling agents of courage and moral purpose, Stone's war uniformly degrades those who find themselves enmeshed in it. And because of the moral and spiritual void at the centre of the film, the alienation and despair that overcome every single character, the atmosphere of *Platoon* is closer to that of, say, a prison drama than a traditional war movie.

In fact, the grunts of Bravo Company are doubly lost, since, if for them America no longer really exists, neither does Vietnam. It is relatively late in the film that Stone treats us to the first (and only) close-up shot of an enemy's face, and the impact of the image is as powerful and startling as it is because, until then, the Viet Cong have been depicted as an *absence*, dangerous precisely because invisible.

To be sure, this kind of visual ellipsis was by no means a novelty in the cinema of Vietnam, but no other film-maker dared to take the conceit to such extreme lengths. In the majority of war movies the enemy might be described as *he who enters the frame*, his sudden materialisation on the edge of the screen often jolting the spectator into a reaction of shock, of momentarily suspended horror; the hero, traditionally, is already within the frame, since it is with him that we have been invited to identify. Here, the situation is reversed. It is the enemy (camouflaged by the lush, dense foliage that itself is on the side of the Viet Cong) who is already concealed in the frame; and, by contrast, it is the hapless Americans who, groping and very un-Rambolike, are forced gingerly to enter it, like so many live targets obligingly setting themselves up to be shot at. (The suspense of war in *Platoon* does not arise during its battle scenes but in their interstices.) The Viet Cong resemble pieces of a jigsaw puzzle whose particularity is to be always bafflingly out of focus. When isolated, viewed singly, not yet integrated into an overall pattern or design, they tend to be quite indecipherable; once inserted into the picture, though, and possessed of the infallible instinct for subterfuge of stick insects, they have a knack of so blending into their immediate surroundings that it becomes no longer possible to distinguish individual outlines. It is only when they finally prepare to pounce that they detach themselves from the puzzle – and by then, of course, it is too late.

Thus, without the slightest supernatural undertone, the jungle of Vietnam is transformed into the forest of Dunsinane, advancing invisibly towards the fragmented American army; consequently, and this is what makes those apparently passive scenes of waiting so terrifying, every American character who happens to find himself within the camera's field of vision is *already* in danger.

The scenes of American barbarity, too, are described in a tone of cool, matter-of-fact dispassion and with an unfussy, unheralded abruptness that does not allow the spectator the time necessary to register shock or even surprise. It is as though, for the director, such scenes had become an integral, by now ultra-familiar, element of the thematics of Vietnam movies, neither more nor less than what we have come to expect. Stone's grunts conduct themselves with the kind of casual, routine savagery that in earlier war movies were always reserved exclusively for the enemy – notably, in a sequence of senseless butchery that was obviously designed to remind us of the My Lai atrocity. After discovering the mutilated corpse of one of their comrades impaled on a tree, the platoon enters a Vietnamese village and rounds up its inhabitants. One man is beaten to death with a rifle butt; an elderly woman, screaming at the soldiers to stop brutalising her husband, is shot dead by the sergeant who is in effective command; in a frenzy, Chris himself empties his machine-gun at the feet of a weirdly smiling and possibly retarded peasant, though he also rescues an adolescent girl from a gang rape as the village is being torched.

The scene (to which a speciously funereal veneer is applied with the deployment on the soundtrack, its effect exactly analogous to that of slow motion, of Samuel Barber's too famous 'Adagio for Strings') reflects a curious ambiguity of intention on Stone's part, an ambiguity with which *Salvador* and the three screenplays mentioned above were also infused. On the one hand, a liberalism of attitude is evident both in his readiness (as a former veteran himself) to expose the kind of mindless savagery most Vietnam movies have chosen to gloss over or altogether ignore and in the fact that the film's nominal spokesman, Chris, though understandably influenced by the prevailing amorality, nevertheless ends by recoiling from its most revolting excesses. On the other hand, the latent neo-Fascism for which movies like *Midnight Express* and *Year of the Dragon* were upbraided finds an outlet here in *Platoon*'s fundamental pessimism, its nihilism, its assumption that the world, nature and mankind are alike in their intrinsic malevolence, that atrocities spring out of the conditions of war like weeds out of turf and that it would be futile to condemn them in the name of some misguided, namby-pamby moral criterion. War may be Hell, says the film, but the damned are not all sinners.

Even so, when one considers the razing of the Vietnamese village (as also, at the very end of the film, the mounds of corpses, from both armies, being shovelled pell-mell into a giant crater), Chris's assertion that 'We did not fight the enemy, we fought ourselves – and the enemy was in us' seems almost solipsistic in its heedlessly cavalier disregard for the massacres to which we are made to bear witness. It does reflect, however, the central theme and only real narrative thread of the movie – the struggle by two diametrically opposed and self-consciously emblematic figures for, to quote Chris again, 'possession of my soul', and, by extension, that of America. These are his two sergeants, the messianic and battle-hardened but at heart Jesus-gentle Elias (played by Willem Dafoe, an interesting actor who went on to play the Saviour Himself in Martin Scorsese's *The Last Temptation of Christ*) and the diabolic, literally battle-scarred Barnes (Tom Berenger, whose face, though disfigured by crisscrossing weals, does indeed suggest a sinister mirror image of Dafoe, to the point where it is occasionally difficult to tell them apart).

While Stone's intention to have them personify respectively the doveish and hawkish currents of American politics (not only of the Vietnam War) is patent enough, there is unfortunately something a trifle ludicrous in the solemnity with which they hover about Chris like some diminutive comic-strip angel and devil perched and proselytising on the shoulders of the strip's indecisive hero. In a sense, they represent the conflicting impulses of the character played by Brando in *Apocalypse Now*, under whose baleful and supposedly spellbinding influence another Sheen fell a half-willing victim. Both of them, if by different routes, have explored the heart of darkness and been expelled, physically intact, from the asshole of the world; and, flayed to the depths of their souls by the experience, each of them has seemingly emerged as a pure, unadulterated essence of Good or Evil.

Happily, the rather grotesque schematicism of this conflict within the platoon is fleshed out by a mosaic-like wealth of naturalistic detail inserting Chris and his rival mentors in a grittily observed and wholly credible recreation of day-to-day life in occupied Vietnam. Stone admits to having deliberately pointed up, in the characterisation of the two sergeants, the kind of split he recalled from his own service, and it further subdivides the generational abyss separating him from his parents: 'On the one side were the lifers, the juicers (heavy drinkers) and the moron white element. Guys like Sergeant Barnes . . . were in that group. On the other side was the progressive, hippy, dope-smoking group: some blacks, some urban whites, Indians, random characters from odd places.' Chris himself, though torn between the two, ends by aligning himself with the latter; whereas Barnes, contemptuously mocking the opiates that help his opposite numbers to face up to their quotidian grind of sweat, fear and unreflecting brutality, snarls at them the movie's most memorable line of dialogue: 'You smoke this shit to escape from reality? Me, I don't need this shit. I *am* reality.'

Like Rambo, if less sensationally, Barnes embodies the war. His very face has been branded with a map of Vietnam. While never discouraging us from savouring the character's demented energy and warped charisma and the seductively thuggish gusto with which he has charted out a space for himself in a hostile world (as will equally be the case with Michael Douglas's Gordon Gekko in *Wall Street*), Stone appears to intimate on that more symbolic plane without which his film cannot be understood that it is Barnes's demonic bigotry and bloodlust that constitute the reality of the war and that it is only when *he* is destroyed, rather than the increasingly marginal Viet Cong, that both it and the film can end. And, in view of the fact that the most powerful tensions generated by the narrative are those which exist between individual members of the same platoon, and that the enemy is absent both literally and, in a way, metaphorically, the agent of Barnes's destruction clearly has to be a fellow American.

Platoon, in which America is never seen and in which the botanical and meteorological textures of Vietnam are brought to life in all their venomous sensuality, is nevertheless, deceptively, a movie about America, not Vietnam, an allegory of the profound schism that the war opened up within the collective American psyche.*

* Allegory, according to the *OED*, is the 'description of a subject under the guise of another subject of aptly suggestive resemblance' and may be compared, as an experience, to probing at some hard, firm object through a transparent wrapping: though embracing the contour of the object, the wrapping conveys a quite separate and distinct tactile sensation. In *Platoon* America is the hard, firm object, Vietnam the transparent wrapping.

This allegorising tendency is, as I have suggested, held in balance throughout the narrative by the strong sense of a lived reality. There is an equivocal, never fully assumed, sexual insinuation to the ardour with which Barnes and Elias pay court to their fresh-faced, handsome new recruit, making it hard to believe that it, too, does not reflect an aspect of Oliver Stone's own experience. In a scene of soldiers dancing together one catches a potent whiff of the *louche* homosexual bar which takes us some way beyond the customary depiction of buddy-buddy affectivity peculiar to every all-male society. And when, with a maliciously enigmatic smile on his face, Elias persuades Chris to insert the end of his (Elias's) rifle in his mouth then coquettishly blows marijuana smoke along its barrel, the phallic analogy could scarcely be rendered more explicit.

As Chris said, '. . . the enemy was in us'. Most of the deaths recorded in the movie are of Americans, and all of these are inflicted wittingly or unwittingly by fellow Americans. On a nocturnal ambush raid two grunts are killed when a third falls asleep on his watch. ('Excuses are like assholes,' sneers an unforgiving Barnes, 'everybody got one.') During a Viet Cong attack on their bunker complex following the torching of the Vietnamese village, several members of the platoon are gunned down by 'friendly fire' when their fumbling commanding officer sends out the wrong co-ordinates to the supporting artillery. Considerably more reprehensible than 'friendly fire', however, is outright murder. At the height of the raid, with the situation still in total confusion, Barnes cold-bloodedly shoots down Elias and prevents Chris from going to his aid. Then, while the survivors are being lifted out by helicopter, Chris is forced to look on helplessly as, pursued by VC forces, the agonised Elias finally expires, his two outstretched arms straining heavenwards in that codified posture of Christly crucifixion for which his ethereally macho presence had always destined him.

At these moments *Platoon* reflects and articulates a mythopsychic conjunction of cannibalism and the labyrinth such as one finds in certain classical legends of Crete (but also, for instance, in the grisly misadventure of the Uruguayan soccer team whose aeroplane crashed in the Andes in 1972, as chronicled by Piers Paul Read in *Alive!*). Simplifying grossly, one might propose that, because the grunts are unable to discover the mouth of the labyrinth, they find themselves compelled to devour one another. Except, implies Stone, that America, not Vietnam, is the true labyrinth.

When, at the movie's climax, an air strike is ordered over the ambushed American compound, the wounded Chris stumbles across Barnes, laboriously dragging himself through the under-growth, along a fine slick of his own blood. There is an instant of hesitation before his former protégé finishes him off.

This unrepentant slaying, condemnable in a court of law, is justified by the film as an act of release, of social hygiene, almost of euthanasia, as though Chris (or Stone) were putting Barnes out of *our* misery. It is Barnes, we now see clearly, who constituted the serpent in the garden, and it is by utterly destroying him (and what he represents) that Chris can eradicate the only Vietnam that ever truly mattered: the Vietnam that was written on Barnes's face. When that cleansing operation has been carried out, Chris will return home and the war – for him, as for his fellow grunts, an internal, civil conflict – will be brought to its conclusion. (There is, however, a poisonous sting in Barnes's tail. Chris, like Adam in the Biblical Eden, has for ever forfeited his even relative moral and spiritual innocence, since, as one of the recruits earlier mumbles, 'The only thing that can destroy Barnes *is* Barnes', and the act of killing a killer ironically implies a posthumously symbiotic complicity with the homicidal urges by which he himself had been driven.)

It may seem cranky and perverse, when writing of a film that was widely commended for the harrowing intensity of its realism, to dwell with such insistence on the symbolic pretensions of its narrative (an approach that also tends to leave one vulnerable to accusations of interpretative delirium). The two levels, however, the concrete and the abstract, are non-detachable; for what, after so many years, has made possible such a degree of realism about the actual horror of the Vietnam War is the very absence of a historical consensus as to what precisely it symbolised to Americans. In this light, *Platoon* is a quite fascinating artefact, one of the richest and most complex of all the films discussed in this book. Yet, while its 'meaning', though well concealed beneath the mimetic surface, is really limpidly clear, it is paradoxically its stylistic foreground, the extreme you-are-there naturalism which attracted so much attention (and which, unlike its 'background', its secondary, symbolic layer, requires no operation of decipherment to be understood and is therefore the only level of the narrative likely to be perceived by the majority of spectators), that both poses and begs a few significant questions.

To begin with, I would have to argue that, notwithstanding that symbolic undertow and no matter how legitimate its ultimate ambition, *Platoon*'s scenes of paroxysmatic physical violence (for instance, the raid on the Vietnamese village) are basically as gratuitous and exploitative as those of any film. It is surely time that film-makers learned that the meticulously detailed aping of an atrocity *is* an atrocity; that the hyper-realistic depiction of an obscenity cannot avoid being contaminated with that obscenity; and that the unmediated representation of violence constitutes in itself an act of violence against the spectator – of lesser violence, necessarily, than that which it is calculated to represent, but a form of violence, nevertheless, that cannot be dismissed as merely 'vicarious'. (Like the on-screen victim, the off-screen spectator – the sensitive spectator, at least – will tend to close his eyes, lower his head, avert his whole being from the aggression being committed.) As for the outwardly reasonable counter-argument that it would make no sense, that it would even be inconceivable, to film the Vietnam War without reconstituting the horrors that continue to make it a burning issue, it strikes me as blinkered, hypocritical and applicable only to the strictest canons of that surface realism to which much of the contemporary cinema imagines itself to be existentially yoked. Brecht, to cite only the most obvious and persuasive example, more than once dramatised the corrupting agency of war in plays that never descended to any slavishly complacent imitation of 'the real'; Godard, similarly, in a wittily corrosive masterpiece like *Les Carabiniers*. Is it, then, so quixotically naïve to hope that a *cinéaste* (though probably not an American) will one day make a cool, reflective, neo-Brechtian film about the Vietnam War?*

* That was precisely what was attempted, of course, if in a generally maladroit and laboured fashion, by Peter Brook in his pseudo-Brechtian stage and film spectacle *US*.

The question, however, is not one exclusively confined to the representation of violence, naturalistic mimicry in its most excessively *onomatopoeic* expression, but implicates realism in general as an aesthetic mode. In the course of this chapter I have already argued that the principal hazard attached to such a mode is that it prompts the spectator to assess what he sees as an unprejudiced and impartial reflection of an objective truth. The judgment he brings to bear on it will thus be fatally less critical, less sceptical, than that which would normally be applied to a horror movie or a musical or a flamboyantly stylised melodrama; and, in the case of a film like *Platoon*, its credibility shored up by Stone's own experience in Vietnam, one's critical defences are likely to be lowered even further. Nothing lends itself better than such self-styled 'realism' to ideological mystification or abuse.

The particular danger of a movie like *Platoon*, a danger deriving precisely from its qualities as a movie, is that it permits Oliver Stone, like good old Rambo himself in *First Blood*, to apostrophise each and every spectator with an accusatory finger and ask, 'How do you know what it was like unless you've been there?' And while we are striving to formulate our response, he proceeds to remind us, over and over again, in article upon article, interview upon interview, that he *was* there, that he therefore knows what it was like and that, unless we foolishly want to make something out of it, the matter ought to be closed. And, after all, it would be presumptuous of a spectator to endeavour to question or criticise what he sees on the screen when it all looks and sounds real enough and especially when, in this specific case, that 'realness' would seem to have been conclusively authenticated by the director's active term of service. We are bullied into craven submission.

Moreover, one may even be permitted to entertain doubts as to the very efficacy of such realism at the strictly informational or didactic level, the level at which *Platoon* has been universally accorded validity. For what is served up to us by the film (whose virtuosity it would be unjust to deny) is nothing less than a concentrated version of the kind of gruellingly repetitive imagery with which, during the actual period of hostilities, the American public found themselves bombarded night after night from their television screens; and, as we know, the outcome of such saturation coverage was not so much their ultimate enlightenment as a progressive numbing of their senses.

'On 10 May 1969,' reads an introductory title card, 'troops of the 101st Airborne Division engaged the enemy at the base of Hill 937 in the Ashau Valley. Ten days and eleven bloody assaults later, the troops who fought there called it . . .'

Then the film's own title, *Hamburger Hill*, materialises on the screen to the accompaniment on the soundtrack of helicopter propellers and a breezy radio bulletin.

Hamburger Hill's British-born director, John Irvin, also presents himself, alongside Oliver Stone, as an advocate of the virtues of microscopically raw and grainy filmic realism; and, while a notably less distinctive achievement than Stone's, whose occasional equivocations it compounds by the calculated revisionism of its own response to the meaning of the war, his film is certainly interesting enough to merit brief consideration here.

For cinephiles, of course, its title will recall that of a now largely forgotten Second World War drama, Lewis Milestone's *Pork Chop Hill*, of which Irvin's may be viewed as the near-remake: in both of these movies the central motif of the 'hill' is exploited as an instantly legible image of the Sisyphian irony inherent in even the successes of military action. Irvin's narrative, for instance, chronicles the dogged endeavours by one squad, the Third, First Platoon, from the wellnigh ubiquitous Bravo Company, to capture a certain Hill 937; and it would be fair to say that even a casual reading of the title card quoted above alerts one to the likelihood that, no sooner seized, this Hill 937 will 'ironically' have to be reabandoned to the enemy. So it turns out; such, the movies have warned us again and again, is the tragically absurdist nature of war. Hills in particular, however difficult of access for the soldiers who have been ordered to storm them, have always in the cinema tended to make for disingenuously easy short-cuts to satire or allegory or whatever it is that the screenwriter might have up his sleeve.

A more positive corollary to the use of such a facile symbol is that, because most of the movie's incident takes place on the hill, the screen's imagery seems almost permanently to be pitched at an angle. And even if this angle is not, strictly speaking, cinematic in nature, deriving as it does from the scenic disposition of the land-scape that is being filmed, the effect is as intriguing, unorthodox and 'expressionistic' as though it were. Freed by its chosen setting from the basic physical horizontality of practically every movie ever made, *Hamburger Hill* thereby contrives to avoid what might otherwise have been a visual platitude.

Like the realism of *Platoon*, that of *Hamburger Hill* is articulated most pervasively through its fascination with the small change of the Vietnam experience, with iconographic minutiae that by now have become as familiar to us as those of Flanders' fields: the bobbing white coolie hats of the local peasantry; the incessant jangle of rock music; the flares; the helicopters; the invisible enemy; the untiringly reiterated 'fucking A' (one of the foot soldiers speaks with wry bafflement of how, when on emergency leave home, he shocked his parents by slipping back into the mechanical, barely conscious obscenity of speech that has become second nature to him in Vietnam); the uncanny Voice of America inflections of Hanoi Hannah on a field radio; and, naturally, our old friend, the bawdy, rubber-tongued drill sergeant, who rattles out one of the drollest spiels of any in these movies: 'Some of you think you have problems – because you are against the war, you demonstrated in school, you wear peace symbols on your steel and you have attitudes – "I'm an orphan, my brother's queer, the city of Chicago got the clap from my sister, Mom drinks, Dad coughs blood, I have ringworm and the draft ruined my chances of being a brain surgeon" people. You *have* no problem. Except me.'

Moviegoers, as I say, should now be as acquainted with such notations as with those of cinematic representations of the First World War. But there are individual images in *Hamburger Hill* in which the iconographies of the two wars so vividly coincide that one suspects Irvin was consciously drawing a parallel between them: images of bunkers, of rain-sodden trenches, of jagged, stunted, leafless trees and writhing, mud-caked bodies shuddering into primeval life. There is, too, one oddly memorable shot of a helmet forlornly tumbling downhill, during a scene in which the squad is picked off by friendly fire from circling choppers overhead, that suggests the Lewis Milestone not merely of *Pork Chop Hill* but of *All Quiet on the Western Front*.

A particularity of the second wave of Vietnam films (most conspicuously Stone's) shared by *Hamburger Hill* is the rigour with which Vietnam itself has been sealed off from the external world and, especially, from the political stakes as they are being debated by the two warring nations. As though to underscore the vision of a war devoid of shape or sense, beginning or end, Irvin actually takes the narrative and geographical self-containment of his film to the brink of solipsism by having its action begin *in medias res*. He reinforces the calculated ahistoricism of the film's discourse by the absence (an absence that crucially differentiates it from *Platoon*) of a true centre of gravity, of one witness observing and commenting on and even commemorating events as they occur, guiding the spectator through the labyrinth of what John Updike rather prematurely described as 'the least memorialised of American wars'. Unlike *Platoon* – which, its title notwithstanding, was centred on a hero, on an articulate, individual consciousness (that of Chris), and thus personalised the conflict in a manner different in degree but not in kind from, say, *Rambo* or any number of Second World War movies starring John Wayne or Errol Flynn – *Hamburger Hill* does not shrink from the responsibility of organising its narrative around a group rather than an individual. No single member of the squad is granted precedence over any other. Yet this kind of absolute parity, while respecting one of the most unambiguously admirable qualities of true realism, its *democracy*, does make it difficult for the spectator to care what happens to characters who seldom emerge into clear focus and (among the whites, at least) all seem to resemble Richard Jaeckel, the plucky, crew-cut kid of so many Second World War movies.

As long as *Hamburger Hill* dwells on minutiae, it is an able, competent, not unentertaining film, causing one yet again to marvel at the extraordinary *savoir-faire*, the understated perfectionism of texture and detail, to be found even in Hollywood's *vin ordinaire*: a *savoir-faire* in this case surely not unrelated to the fact that three of the film's creative personnel could, again like Oliver Stone, claim first-hand experience of the war. Irvin was sent there in the late sixties as a documentary cameraman; as was another Englishman,

the production's Special Assignment Photographer (whatever precisely that means), the well-known photo-journalist Don McCullin;
and the scenarist, James Carabatsos (who also scripted Clint
Eastwood's *Heartbreak Ridge*) served with the First Air Cavalry.

It is, though, a truism of Vietnam films that to be merely about
the war (i.e. against it, for it or else warily fence-sitting) is no longer
enough. And part of the problem with *Hamburger Hill* is that it
never arrives at any definitive conclusion as to what its secondary
theme should be (an indecision most likely deriving from the
strictly commercial imperatives that dictated its production in the
first place) and sounds out, along the way, three potentially chal-
lenging and thought-provoking themes which it then allows to
languish undeveloped.

The first of these is the (historically accurate) preponderance of
blacks in the fighting units which served in Vietnam, the consequence, evidently, of the far more generous spectrum of opportunities afforded to those middle-class whites who wished to escape
being drafted. Since this happens to be an issue that no previous
Vietnam movie ever foregrounded, its inclusion here could well
have prompted some useful insights into the war as not merely a
civil but a racial (and, by implication, socio-economic) conflict.
Unfortunately, in view of the trivialising superficiality and patent
insincerity with which it is handled by Carabatsos and Irvin, it is
difficult to avoid the impression that the theme is present in the
movie less out of any deeply felt compulsion to expose injustice
than to spice up a flagging narrative with an occasional conflictual
exchange within the platoon. Even if, to be fair, there is an unusually strong presence of black characters, who are for once more
numerous and less anonymous than their white counterparts, the
only outlet for their grievances would appear to be a cluster of flip,
crass one-liners straight out of the professional screenwriter's stock
barrel. Thus one recruit sullenly mutters that he and his fellow
black grunts must be crazy to be risking their lives for the 'United
States of White America'. Another, to whom a white has ventured
a friendly overture, snaps back at him, 'Don't call me brother. I'm
not your brother!' And so it continues – until (very much as in *The
Boys in Company C*) the simmeringly rebellious black element is
gradually dissolved in the squad's own little melting pot and one

of them, a belated convert to the codified, multiracial American Dream, offers the foolish and degrading opinion that 'We're all good dumb niggers on this hill', as though, even so late into the sixties, blacks still believed that the salvation of their race lay in some humble yet spunky coalition with so-called 'white trash'.

Such allusions to the army's racial imbalance sputter fitfully through the narrative without ever being sufficiently amplified (as Renoir, in *La Grande Illusion*, to take an admittedly crushing example, amplified the theme of class divisions during the First World War) to constitute the film's pivotal theme. And when, halfway through (which is to say, when the squad, despite suffering horrendous casualties, has advanced halfway up the hill), one starts to wonder just what that theme might be, Irvin and Carabatsos identify a brand new enemy within: the media. On their weary return from a combat mission the squad finds itself in the process of being filmed by a TV newsreel crew, whose microphone-toting newscaster is credited with making (to their faces) the outrageously crass comment that 'Senator Kennedy says you guys don't have a chance at all'. For this totally implausible callousness he is excoriated by the squad's sergeant, who remarks, 'At least they take sides, you just take pictures' – a statement, as the critic Nigel Floyd smartly pointed out, that 'might be applied to two of the personnel involved in the production, director Irvin and photographer McCullin'. Having in passing berated the American media for what it perceives as their parasitical kibitzing, however, the film simply drops the subject and moves on in quest of greener pastures.

The last of *Hamburger Hill*'s targets (and, in view of the emotional and ideological burden it is invited to bear, one must suppose that it was always intended to be the most significant of the three) is the antiwar movement. The squad is relaxing during one of the increasingly rare lulls before and after the firestorm. (The movie throughout oscillates lazily between spasms of fierce combat and interludes of becalmed quietude, and the use of successive calendar dates to record and measure the progress of the assault does little to attenuate the monotony that such a construction soon induces.) They loll about, smoke, trade insults, crack jokes, read their mail. One young recruit, who had been discreetly perusing a letter from home, becomes suddenly distraught. It transpires that his girlfriend

has decided she can no longer write to him as her college acquaintances have belatedly advised her of the immorality of the war and
its advocates, who presumably include any hapless grunt who failed
to wriggle out of the draft.

The film's slanderous attack on the peace movement, which was
after all revising the course of modern American history, would be
profoundly offensive if, first, the argument were not so flagrantly
and pathetically loaded (as with that of the TV newsman, the
sadism of the soldier's supposed correspondent seems not much
more than a crude and wholly unconvincing scenaristic device),
and if, second, it were not merely a pinprick of tetchy illiberalism
which the movie's main narrative thrust in no way attempts to
sustain. Frankly, a work as opportunistic as *Hamburger Hill*, which
attempts to pass off a few stray shavings of some vague hawkish
rhetoric as a coherent, firmly held ideological position, has not
earned the right to adopt even the knee-jerk antiwar stance of *The
Green Berets* or the *Rambo* cycle.

Nevertheless, these solecisms taken into account, the movie does
ultimately have something of its own to say, if not precisely about
the Vietnam War itself (on which it can offer nothing but inept
demagoguery), then, indirectly, about the cinema of Vietnam. For,
despite its flaws, despite its fundamental poverty of ambition,
despite, too, the gratuitously elegiac glaze of Philip Glass's soundtrack score, a sort of concerto for heart-strings and orchestra,
Hamburger Hill somehow proves to be an intermittently moving
experience. But it moves one, paradoxically, in the narrative's *temps
morts*, those instants (too infrequent, alas) when Irvin is content to
allow his camera to settle on an unheralded, almost unnoticed
gesture, a weatherworn face, a dying soldier whose last words,
'Remember me', are all the more affecting for not being 'famous',
a pair of black grunts who uplift each other's spirits with some
affectionate mutual palm-slapping and a motto designed to keep
themselves sane: 'It don't mean nothing.'

Because its more grandiose ambitions and half-baked theorising
are quickly discounted as impossible to take seriously, one tends to
pay closer attention here than in some more ambitious and powerful work to those brief, wilfully unprivileged moments when air is
allowed to circulate through the movie and the poignancy and

horror of the grunt's plight is contingent not on anything he does or has done to him but on the mere, intolerable fact of having been drafted, of being in Vietnam. And this in turn assists one towards understanding (as one did with a similarly flawed but not unsympathetic movie like *Go Tell the Spartans*) that, even now, *everything* related to the Vietnam War is capable of moving us; that perhaps one's pity, anger and sorrow need no longer be as partisan or selective as the proximity of the conflict once obliged them to be; and that, if it remains necessary (as I believe) to scrutinise Hollywood's contribution to the historiography of the war with a beadily merciless eye, it is because the subject-matter harbours such a fund of emotion that it strikes one as all the less pardonable that film-makers should so often have squandered its potential.

Hamburger Hill possibly acknowledges that truth with its concluding title card. It is with fairly unconcealed relish that I have itemised in the pages of this book a series of meretricious, self-serving or just plain dumb statements on the war and the American rationale for having waged it, some of which were extracted from movie soundtracks, others quoted verbatim from political notables of the period. So I take especial pleasure in having the opportunity now to reproduce this title card, which apparently formed part of a speech made by one Major Michael Davis O'Donnell on 1 January 1970, in Dak To, Vietnam, and which impresses me, for all its faintly high-flown Biblicisms, as without doubt the most eloquent and touching epitaph (in English) that the war ever inspired. Major O'Donnell is speaking about those ordinary American draftees who found themselves obliged to be brave in Vietnam and who have been cavalierly and insultingly referred to, by those (myself included) who never knew them, as 'grunts', and what he has to say is this: 'If you are able, save for them a place inside of you and save one backward glance when you are leaving for the places they can no longer go. Be not ashamed to say you loved them, though you may or may not have always. Take what they have left and what they have taught you with their dying and keep it with your own. And in that time when men decide and feel safe to call the war insane, take one moment to embrace those gentle heroes you left behind.'

— Chapter 9 —

THE WASTE LAND

Full Metal Jacket was released in the summer of 1987 at a time when its director, Stanley Kubrick, continued to reap the benefit of that privileged phase of a (major) film-maker's career when the expectancy aroused by a new movie and the critical attention it subsequently receives are not invariably proportional to its intrinsic values and ambitions. Bergman, Buñuel and Bresson, to name an alliterative trio, have all at various periods enjoyed its advantages; Coppola, in the wake of the widespread perplexity occasioned by *The Outsiders*, *Rumble Fish* and *The Cotton Club*, would seem to have traversed it; and Peter Greenaway is (at least as I write) smack in the middle.

Where Kubrick is concerned, though, the likelihood is that the 'phase' will coextend with the whole of his professional life, since it is as hard to imagine some forthcoming Stanley Kubrick movie enjoying a modest, unconspicuous release (a release on parole, so to speak) as it is to recall the last title in his filmography of which that was true. (For the record, it was probably his ambitious, low-budget thriller *The Killing*, dating from 1956.) Moreover, the awe, expectancy and wonderment which have always attended his work appear generated as much by the spaces between his films as by the individual films themselves. In the last twenty-five years he has directed only six: *Dr Strangelove, or How I Learned to Stop Worrying and Love the Bomb* (1964), *2001: A Space Odyssey* (1968), *A Clockwork Orange* (1971), *Barry Lyndon* (1975), *The Shining* (1979) and *Full Metal Jacket*; and the four or five years which customarily elapse between one film and its successor in the canon – in short, the *margins* of his oeuvre – tend to have the same vaguely terroristic effect on critics and spectators as the broad and creamy white margins of one of those privately printed volumes of verse whose

168

pages are exquisitely speckled with a mere handful of words. Because each of his films is, in a pedantically literal sense, 'long-awaited' (if only by virtue of the time it takes him to produce it), no sophisticated gimmicks are required from his studio's publicists to translate that literal connotation into an evaluative one. STANLEY KUBRICK'S LONG-AWAITED NEW FILM! screech the posters, and the potential paying customer is already persuaded that here is one movie that absolutely has to be seen.

This marketing operation (which is, in effect, what it becomes once the film is completed) is reinforced by the director's well-publicised distaste for personal publicity. Living somewhere in, and seldom straying from, the English Home Counties, granting very few interviews (and then only when his latest movie is about to be released), assuming complete, autocratic and practically unrestricted (remote) control over every aspect not merely of each movie's production but of its distribution and exhibition, and outwardly indifferent to all the usual endorsements from his 'peers' (his work is systematically ignored by the Hollywood Academy and seldom competes at international festivals), Kubrick is the Howard Hughes of film-makers. As such, not altogether surprisingly, he has had a web of unsubstantiated rumours and insinuations woven about his person, a form of *lèse-majesté* that nevertheless evaporates the moment critics are actually confronted with his movies, with those UFOs (Unidentified Filmic Objects) that descend upon the world every half-decade or so. Even when, as lately, one can detect a slight ebbing of enthusiasm on their part, it has never manifested itself in the tone of flippant condescension adopted by English or American reviewers whenever about to demolish a new film. The critical establishment is, in a word, terrified of Stanley Kubrick. If, here and there, reservations have been voiced, they are mostly in a minor key, and the fundamental legitimacy of Kubrick's vision has never been questioned.

And now, with his most recent work, another co-ordinate has been added to the cunningly orchestrated process of terrorisation – what would seem to be a systematic annexation of *genre*. In the first half of his career Kubrick was superbly oblivious of those dictates of genre to which nearly every other American director is umbilically bound. Notwithstanding certain echoes and overlaps (inevitably, in view of his 'visionary' cast of mind, these are for the most part related to science fiction), each of the movies he made in the sixties and seventies was a self-contained, self-sufficient construct, from whose cult of closure and exclusion (exclusion from genre, from Hollywood, from the mainstream of the American cinema) derived the eerily claustrophobic singularity of purpose that has come to be recognised as one of the dominant traits of his aesthetic identity. Works such as *Lolita*, *Dr Strangelove*, *2001* and *A Clockwork Orange* were truly *sui generis*; and if Kubrick's *Lolita*, though one of his finest films, can scarcely be thought to match Nabokov's, his two other literary adaptations, from Arthur C. Clarke and Anthony Burgess, have long since outranked their models in terms of fame and prestige.

It was with *Barry Lyndon* that Kubrick's ambition finally arched over into megalomania. The point at issue was less one of adaptation (Thackeray's novel is a little-read and reputedly minor romance) than of the eighteenth century, the period in which both novel and movie are set. Had the eighteenth century been filmed before? No matter: Stanley Kubrick was to dazzle the world with *his* eighteenth century, gloatingly brandishing the film's unheard-of numbers of candelabra and costume changes. Five years later, when *The Shining* materialised, an identical question was posed. Had Stephen King been filmed before? Many, many times; but, again, Kubrick's Stephen King could be nothing less than the real McCoy, the definitive article, consigning all earlier efforts to the dustbins of cinema history.

There is a distinct hint of oneupmanship here, and his ploy can be compared to that portrayed in Peter Shaffer's *Amadeus* (a play Kubrick himself might have been tempted to film) whereby Mozart, conceived by Shaffer as a lascivious tot brimming with unearned genius, listens politely to the nice little *morceau d'occasion* composed in his honour by Salieri, begins in his turn to tickle the ivories and ends, to his arch-rival's mortification, by extemporising what was to become the aria 'Non più andrai' in *Figaro*. In a similar fashion, it was almost as though, by belatedly converting to genre, and then devoting his energy to 'improving' the labours of his fellow film-makers, Kubrick were seeking to glorify himself as an Amadeus amid Salieris, a Mozart in a world of mediocrities.

The Waste Land

With *Full Metal Jacket*, then, one's sense of anticipation was predicated entirely on the director's 'vision' – on what was to be, as it were, Kubrick's Vietnam.

Full Metal Jacket is based on *The Short Timers*, a relatively brief (180 pages), unpretentious novel by Gustav Hasford, himself a Vietnam veteran and, along with the director and Michael Herr, the co-author of the film's screenplay. Like the film, Hasford's novel opens at the United States Marine Corps Recruit Depot on Parris Island, South Carolina, on which it expends no more than 30 pages, before switching its location to Vietnam in 1968. The Marine training course, by contrast, occupies just under half of *Full Metal Jacket*'s running time, inevitably inviting us to interpret it as representing the first panel of a 'diptych'. During these forty minutes of narrative the spectator is (in Hitchcock's phrase) 'put through it'. Here, perhaps, more than at any other moment, Kubrick co-opts some already ultra-familiar footage (cf. scenes of basic training from *The Boys in Company C* and Clint Eastwood's *Heartbreak Ridge*) and ingeniously transmutes it into his own 'Non più andrai'.

Behind the credit-titles we are shown a motley group of young recruits, singly, one after the other, all of them as yet unknown to us, their anonymity heightened by the fact that their heads are being shaved; the mild, external desecration of this scalping, we feel, is intended to serve both as a prelude to, and a metaphor for, the brainwashing to follow. For in the course of the movie they will lose not just their hair but their names (the squad's drill sergeant, Hartman, played by a non-professional actor and former Marine, Lee Ermey, who also furnished Kubrick and his co-scenarists with twenty hours of taped parade-ground obscenities, rebaptises them Joker, Cowboy, etc., as deemed appropriate), their clothes and, primarily, their *language*.

Kubrick's approach to language has always been of a reductive and uncompromisingly deterministic nature. He appears to view it as the exclusive product of environmental conditioning, only very marginally influenced by concepts of subjectivity and interiority, by all the whims, shades and modulations of personal expression. One thinks of Lolita's endearing teenybopper crassness, her mother's egregious lower-middlebrow refinement and Clare Quilty's chameleonic slipping in and out of any idiom at will; the reverberations of Dr Strangelove's Hitlerian past spiralling ungovernably out of his crunched and buckled frame as though from the horn of a His Master's Voice phonograph; HAL's quaint, sinister cybernetic pleasantries and unpleasantries in *2001*; the Russian-inflected jargon of the 'Droogs' in *A Clockwork Orange* (coined by Anthony Burgess); and, in *The Shining*, the writer-protagonist's rambling regression into foul-mouthed impenetrability, culminating in the revelation that every single manuscript page of his novel-in-progress has been monopolised by the same infantile message, reiterated in a demoniacally tireless scrawl: 'All work and no play makes Jack a dull boy.'

Normally, in a film, it is through a fairly extensive range of behavioural and linguistic idiosyncrasies that we learn to distinguish one character from another; and also, a point of significance in the context of the star-system, to distinguish an actor's codified mytho-iconography from the variables of personality demanded of him (or her, of course) by any given role. Kubrick, however, will have none of this. Since each of his films is so insular, so hermetically discrete, the dominant tendency in his work is for every character in a particular film to speak alike and for that mode of speech to be so intransigently defined and upheld that no character belonging to one film could possibly be transplanted into another.

In the first half of *Full Metal Jacket* there exist just two modes of speech: Hartman's and that of his recruits. Throughout the forty minutes of his on-screen presence Hartman is never heard to utter a sentence that is not either an insult or else so cankered with sarcasm as to be received as such by his interlocutor. Like all of Kubrick's characters (saving Humbert Humbert and a handful in *Barry Lyndon*), Hartman is in fact inarticulate, practically aphasic; except that, as always, his inarticulacy is camouflaged by the energy and garrulity of a preprogrammed discourse that seems to be controlling him instead of vice versa. And, should one focus one's attention on the film's dialogue, one would be forgiven for suspecting that the scenaristic invention of this section derives from a formal challenge that Kubrick must have set himself: to catalogue,

Cyrano-style, the largest possible number of verbal permutations and variations on the word 'shit', in both its figurative and literal meanings.

Thus, Hartman to one luckless offender: 'I will unscrew your head and shit down your neck!' And, again, when one of his charges has dared to talk back on parade: 'Who said that? Who the fuck said that? Who's the slimy little shit twinkle-toes cocksucker down there who just signed his own death warrant?'

Such excremental rhetoric, it should be added, is not confined to Hartman alone. When the action shifts to Vietnam, it becomes as intensely a part of the movie's local colour as the ubiquitous choppers overhead and the Viet Cong themselves. Later, for instance, during the Tet offensive, when a problem arises for the military, it was obviously considered insufficient to have someone remark 'We're in the shit . . .' or 'The shit's about to hit the fan . . .' or anything so pathetically hackneyed and uninventive. No, Kubrick, Herr and Hasford (doubtless assisted by Ermey's tapes) collectively racked their brains to come up with this gaudy image: 'It's a huge shit sandwich and we're all going to have to take a bite.' (Which, perhaps, as Wilde might have said, is what fiction is all about.)

Hartman's language, then, is the language of chronic verbal incontinence, the confusion, in a way, of logorrhoea and diarrhoea. That assigned to the squad, and from which almost no variation, no relaxation, is authorised (at least, in screen time), coincides almost word for word with the language of the Corps. Designed, as is every other aspect of basic training, to trammel their humanity, to curb their individuality, it is liable to strike the layman as most dispiritingly repressive in its most minor manifestation: the fact that every utterance has to be bookended by the word 'Sir', as in 'Sir, yessir!' Even at that elementary level there exists neither exit nor escape – the possibility of reverie, of reflection, of open-ended communication, is sealed tight as a drum on both sides. Indeed, so all-inclusive does this convention of military address become in the film that, on the rare occasions when it is dropped, as in some brief, insignificant exchange between two of the recruits, the impact on the spectator is genuinely shocking.

Hartman, too, speaks the language of his 'beloved Corps', but enlivens it with the sort of gamy grace-note peculiar to a gunner sergeant. For example, to the assembled recruits: 'If you survive recruit training, you will be a weapon, you will be a minister of death praying for war,' or 'The Marine Corps does not want robots. The Marine Corps wants killers.' That is (one is led to believe) the authentic voice of the United States Marines; and whenever Hartman is allowed the merest hint of extracurricular humanity, of weird, warped drollery, it is characteristic of the movie that it, too, should be expressed through some amusingly worded blasphemy: e.g. 'God has a hard-on for Marines because we kill everything we see.'

As for the recruits, except for those snatches of private, often furtive, conversation, their speech is circumscribed by the Marine discourse in its purest state, purified still further by being recited most of the time in unison. The Marine Corps credo, for instance, which we hear in its totality:

'This is my rifle. There are many like it but this one is mine. My rifle is my best friend. It is my life. I must master it as I must master my life. Without me my rifle is useless. Without my rifle I am useless. I must fire my rifle through. I must shoot straighter than my enemy who is trying to kill me. I must shoot him before he shoots me. I will. Before God I swear this creed: My rifle and myself are defenders of my country. We are the masters of our enemy. We are the saviors of my life. So be it. Until there is no enemy. For peace. Amen.'

These are, in effect, the only forms of language heard in the film, since, with a not very notable exception, *Full Metal Jacket* is (in so far as its speaking parts are concerned) peopled exclusively by military personnel – which, though a typical example of the 'purity', the dark, stark streamlining of subject-matter, that we tend to associate with Stanley Kubrick's cinema, also constitutes a degree of narrative austerity unusual for a Hollywood war movie. (The exception referred to involves a couple of Vietnamese prostitutes who have walk-on roles in the second half and employ an equally codified language, one that sounds a trifle implausible and formulaic on the screen but is probably a fair likeness of the real thing; e.g. 'Me love you long time. Me so horny. Me love you too much.')

Depersonalising language is, however, only part of a more com-

prehensive strategy by which Kubrick does not so much 'dehumanise' his material as emancipate it of every conceivable *mitigating
circumstance*. Thus (we are still in the first section) character psy-
chology is negated by the ethos of the Corps; physical appearances
are subsumed in the standardisation of shaved heads and drab army
uniforms; and, more than once, the narrative itself is allowed to
come close to utter extinction. For what makes this whole training
camp sequence especially creepy and disturbing to watch is that it
appears to be about *absolutely nothing*. During these forty minutes
a heterogeneous cluster of young men (whose heterogeneity Kubrick and his writers have not permitted us to savour) are transformed, first into robots, then into killers, at last into US Marines.
There is, in truth, little more to it than that. And one is reminded
of a documentary, Frederick Wiseman's *Basic Training*, which, de-
tailing the same process, preserves a similarly discreet distance from
its material. That distance, in Wiseman's case, can be defended as
reflecting the discretion proper to all documentaries, where the
camera must be set up far enough from the filmed subject to respect
its privacy and autonomy, yet close enough to it to grant the
spectator access to its inner truth (if any). But, as a work of fiction,
Full Metal Jacket might reasonably have been expected to circulate
among its characters, eavesdrop on their thoughts and feelings,
sensitize their relationship to each other and to their environment
– in short, animate the *tabula rasa* that the white screen represents
for us before a movie is projected on to it. Kubrick's project, per-
versely, would seem to have been to retain that state of *tabula rasa*
for as long as it was possible, to mimic the screen's mint-new
blankness and let only fragments of narrative ruffle its vacuity and
insignificance.

The décor of the Training Depot is predominantly white, as
antiseptic as a clinic, as though the director were petrified that his
imaginative landscape be contaminated by so much as a germ. In
its barren, pristine nowhereness it recalls, possibly deliberately,
both the uterine spacecraft of *2001* (at moments *Full Metal Jacket*
might almost be set in outer space) and the inhumanly unsullied
rooms, salons and corridors of the Overlook Hotel in *The Shining*.
With the methodical, beetle-browed sadism of a child dismember-
ing an insect, Kubrick removes trace after trace of ordinary, decent,

human unkemptness from the micro-society depicted in his film. The visuals look as though they had been disinfected. The sole (and just glimpsed) exteriors are of the scrubby, unprepossessing grounds of the depot. No military personnel superior to Hartman nor any recruits other than those of his squad are allowed to put in an appearance. As for the 'outside world', it remains as out of bounds to the spectator as, apparently, to Cowboy, Joker and Co. This section, in other words, takes place within a scrupulously controlled environment; until we all depart for Vietnam, the development of the narrative is of necessity barely more subtle or complex than that which could be constructed around the predicament of white mice in a laboratory experiment; and *Full Metal Jacket*, in all its mechanical barbarities, might most appropriately be thought of as a drama of *vivisection*.

In such laboratories, of course, an essential prop is the labyrinth. Kubrick's labyrinth, invisible though obscurely perceptible, is composed of the serpentine tracking shots that have been his (second-hand) trademark ever since *Paths of Glory* (1957). In that, his first war movie, the camera elegantly tracked, back and forth, the length and breadth of the trenches of the Western Front; here, at least in theory, since the space is so much more open, accessible and explorable, it could have been let off the leash, permitted to roam freely. Yet the effect remains just as terminal as in the earlier movie, the camera's movements just as tyrannically regimented as those of the young recruits it films. It shunts the cast around like a collie marshalling a flock of sheep: in *Full Metal Jacket*, as though expressly bearing out Hitchcock's infamous maxim, actors *are* cattle. And when, from time to time, the camera does cease to move, Kubrick has unfailing recourse to that cliché of slightly programmatic (and diagrammatic) modernism: symmetry (cf. Peter Greenaway, Chantal Akerman): in wellnigh every shot the spectator's eye is guided ineluctably towards the dead centre of the screen. The trouble is that this centre is also dead in another sense (and perhaps wilfully so). There is nothing *fearful*, in the Blakean sense of the word, about Kubrick's symmetry. It is merely the zero degree of pictorial composition.

But Kubrick's compositions, his advocates would contend, are meant to be a reflection of the concentrationary symmetry of the Marine Corps and of all such military institutions. It is the army, not Kubrick's filming of it, that is totalitarian, just as was the case in Wiseman's documentary. True enough, but with one crucial difference: Wiseman's more modest ambition was to situate his camera unvaryingly at the angle from which the spectator was best positioned to see what was before it. The symmetry of what he filmed was *in front of*, not *inside*, the camera. It constituted Wiseman's subject-matter, not his style. Kubrick, on the other hand, as wholeheartedly espouses the latent ideology of Marine Corps training as did Leni Riefenstahl (and I carefully weigh the analogy) that of the florid Nazi pageantry that she covered during the 1934 Nuremberg Party Convention for her classic documentary *Triumph of the Will*. Riefenstahl's film was no mere objective recording of an autonomous event but its apotheosis and, arguably, its *raison d'être*; and a comparable claim may be made for Kubrick's, except that what is in evidence in *Full Metal Jacket* is a strange and disquieting *annihilation* of the will.

It was Kubrick's fellow director Samuel Fuller (himself a veteran of several feisty war movies) who offered a paradoxical but deadly accurate assessment of *Full Metal Jacket*. He dismissed it as 'a recruitment film'. A recruitment film, this cold, callous chronicle of humiliations and horrors? Yes, in the sense that its fundamental discourse – its 'deep structure', in Noam Chomsky's term – is the Marine Corps' own, insidiously neutralised by the sole, thin sliver of character development generated by the movie.

Startling in its simplicity and even *naïveté*, this involves a recruit whom Hartman nicknames Gomer Pyle, after the bumbling strip cartoon hero. Pyle (Vincent D'Onofrio) is the disgrace and shame of the squad, the sad sack who can do nothing right, who stumbles through the obstacle course, who smuggles (and, naturally, is caught smuggling) a jelly doughnut into his kit. He is, above all, fat, an enormous suety mound of flesh – a malformation that happens to be Kubrick's own invention. In Gustav Hasford's novel the same character is described as a 'skinny redneck'.

It is, to be sure, every film director's prerogative to determine for himself the physical attributes of his characters, even when his film happens to adapt a literary text. But since Pyle's obesity has the incidental effect of compromising narrative credibility (it is inconceivable that someone this fat could have passed the Marine physical), it ought to be worth endeavouring to analyse his motives.

Though one might be tempted, when viewing the first half of *Full Metal Jacket*, to define Stanley Kubrick (the film-maker, not necessarily the private individual) as the ultimate racist, in that it appears to be the entire human race that he despises, it is important, precisely, to make a distinction, as he does, between the humiliation of Gomer Pyle and that suffered by his fellow recruits. First of all, Pyle is, as I have said, fat *where he need not have been*, which may suggest that Kubrick was seeking to revive the old, fascistic connection between physical and mental grossness. Because of his fat-boy bovinity, his lumbering immaturity and general ineptitude, Pyle will find himself singled out as the especial prey of both Hartman's and Kubrick's contempt: among the numerous other indignities to which he is subjected he is ordered to waddle across the parade ground sucking his thumb, his trousers curling around his thick ankles. And when his own inadequacies start to threaten the welfare of the whole squad, his comrades, wielding bars of soap wrapped up in towels, thrash him one night in his bunk. Here Kubrick shamelessly turns the screw by having Joker (Matthew Modine), the recruit assigned by Hartman to oversee Pyle's faltering progress and who was alone in having befriended him, thrash him most soundly of all.

After this incident, Pyle gradually withdraws into himself. Half-demented, he takes to whispering to his rifle. At unguarded moments his big soft mama's boy features coalesce into a mask (one with which certain close-up shots in *A Clockwork Orange* and *The Shining* have already familiarised us) of malignantly simian brutishness. In his training, by contrast, he seems at long last to be displaying a real if somewhat robotic aptitude, and his unexpectedly proficient marksmanship earns even Hartman's grudging approval. He has, in other words, been turned into a clockwork orange (or pumpkin).

But 'a clockwork orange' could equally be interpreted as the definition of a bomb or grenade – and that, as well, Pyle is in the process of becoming. Having somehow contrived to graduate alongside the others, he is discovered by Joker, in the middle of the night, alone in the latrine. He is polishing a loaded rifle with tense, finicky gestures. He treats Joker, in a monstrous close-up, to an almost parodically evil grin. Suspecting that Pyle's neurosis has ended by overbalancing into outright, violent psychosis, Joker endeavours to relieve him of his weapon. Hartman, meanwhile, awakened in his turn by the disturbance, struts into the latrine like a runty little fighting-cock to ascertain its cause. And when, in his own inimitably plain-spoken manner, he also orders Pyle to surrender his rifle, the now deranged young soldier simply opens fire on his tormentor then (fastidiously, almost gracefully, inserting the gun-barrel in his mouth) on himself. With the ecstatic panache of two red roses bursting into flower in time-lapse cinematography, a spew of blood cascades from Hartman's insides, another through the back of Pyle's neck: a fragment of real fiction has finally arrived to muss up Kubrick's antiseptic sets and cut-along-the-dotted-line compositions; and this scene, the film's first example of what has been dubbed (meretriciously) 'lyrical violence' or else (with a veneer of rather complacent irony) 'designer violence', anticipates much of what is to follow in the more sanguinary second half. Kubrick, however, is not done with Pyle. For if, in terms of thematic input, the young soldier's predictable and too insistently tele-graphed act of vengeance is reducible to the proverbial nutshell of 'the worm turning', it is worth noting that even at this ultimate extremity he is not to be spared humiliation, he is not to be allowed to die with his dignity undefiled. Kubrick, who seems to extract as much cruel pleasure as Hartman from baiting him, has him at the moment of his death seated astride a toilet bowl, the blubber fat of his enormous thighs spilling over every which way, his blood and brain tissue streaking the latrine wall behind him like inarticulate graffiti.

The sheer sadism apart, what is significant about the florid ex-cesses of Pyle's treatment is that, when compared to it, the humili-ations which Hartman routinely inflicts on the other recruits *come to appear almost benign.* Diverted by the picturesque spectacle of individual disgrace (the disgrace of someone, moreover, to whom we can all afford to feel superior), we tend to forget that averagely capable and intelligent young men of well-coordinated physiques are also being degraded and that, as Wiseman's cool indictment made clear, it is precisely by the exercise of such degradation that the army functions. That, perhaps, is what Fuller meant when he called *Full Metal Jacket* a recruitment film.

The second panel of the diptych is both more conventionally entertaining and more conventional, period. No further mention is made of either Hartman or Pyle. Joker (who, along with Cowboy, is the sole character to figure in both sections) has been posted to Vietnam as a reporter for the service magazine *Stars and Stripes*. There, he is seconded by someone called Rafterman (Kevyn Major Howard), who proves to be such an anonymous cipher that one wonders why Kubrick bothered to introduce him at all. As in Hasford's novel, the year is 1968, just prior to the surprise offensive launched by the Viet Cong and the North Vietnamese during the Tet cease-fire. But though, by comparison with what has gone before, one now gains the impression of a film almost clogged with incident, not much actually appears to *happen*. Paradoxically, because there is about the action a random, free-floating quality totally (and doubtless deliberately) at variance with the inflexible structures and symmetries of the first half, it generates almost as little narrative tension as did the scenes on Parris Island.

Language loosens up. We hear the language of the grunt in the field, articulated by lots of breezy 'Listen up . . .'s and 'Outstanding!'s. There is the language, too, of the disillusioned grunt in the field, as when one cynical, seen-it-all campaigner, indicating a new arrival, muses enigmatically, 'You know he hasn't been in the shit because he ain't got the stare. The thousand-yard stare. A Marine gets it after he's been in the shit for too long. It's like . . . it's like he's really seen *beyond*.' There is also the language of the grunt cheerfully bemused at finding himself the object of media scrutiny: 'This is Vietnam the Movie!' (An anachronism for the late sixties, surely?) There is the pseudo-euphemistic militarese whose terminology tends to strike sensitive civilian ears as just fractionally grislier than what it is meant to edulcorate, e.g. 'waste' for 'kill'. And, finally, there is the sort of laconically macabre one-liner typical of the whole American war movie tradition, whether the enemy has been the Kraut, the Jap or, as here, 'Charlie'. 'Anyone who runs is a VC. Anyone who stands still is a well disciplined VC,' is one airborne gunner's gleeful rationale as he rakes the placid landscape beneath him with machine-gun fire without troubling to discriminate between Viet Cong and civilians, men, women and children. (This scene is strikingly reminiscent of genuine archive footage included in the opening reel of Chris Marker's documentary *Le Fond de l'air est rouge*.)

Narrative, as well, begins at last to acquire a semblance of shape – or rather (since, whatever the first section lacked, it wasn't shape), begins to instil in the spectator a conviction that, scene by scene, it might be progressively gravitating towards some kind of conclusion. With Rafterman, Joker is dispatched to the beleaguered Hue, where he is reunited with Cowboy (Arliss Howard), now a member of the self-styled 'Lusthog Squad' of the First Platoon, H Company, Second Battalion, Fifth Marine Regiment. In the course of their infiltration of Hue, during a reconnaissance mission (with Kubrick's camera movements at this point characterised by an amazing fluidity, notably in a long, suave virtuoso sequence-shot of the advancing squad, filmed from behind by a slowly forward-tracking Steadicam), the squad's lieutenant is shot dead and Cowboy assumes temporary command. It is then, in a bombed-out and weirdly Piranesian landscape (conjured up by Kubrick's cinematographer, Douglas Milsome, in a lavish, sinisterly delicate palette of steel blues, burnt oranges, pale cloud greys and sunset purples) that Cowboy, Joker, Rafterman and their fellow survivors are confronted with a lone sniper concealed inside an evacuated, dilapidated warehouse.

The first of the soldiers to forge a wary path across its wide-open, rubble-strewn forecourt is the black Eightball (Dorian Harewood), who, picked off almost at once, keels over in slow motion *à la* Peckinpah. Attempting to rescue the still convulsively twitching Eightball from the crossfire, another grunt, who goes for some reason under the name of Doc Jay (John Stafford), meets with a similar fate. Then, following Cowboy's own death during the final advance, the sniper is eventually cornered and fatally wounded. As though in a distorted mirror-image of Pyle in the first-act climax, she (for the sniper is revealed to be a young woman and bears an uncanny resemblance to the actress Shelley Duvall as she appeared in Kubrick's previous film, *The Shining*) turns her agonised features towards the camera. Writhing, she implores the Americans, in a febrile rasp, to give her the *coup de grâce*. It is Joker who, after the lengthiest of pauses, complies. The movie, bizarrely, frustratingly, is over.

Notwithstanding every sort of intellectual misgiving, I dare say I have thrilled as much to (certain species of) lyrical violence, to the glossy pornography of blood, as that potential reader, 'the next man'. It was, however, during this climactic sequence of *Full Metal Jacket* that the worm turned in me, too, and the precise origin of my revulsion, not only from the sequence itself but, by extension, from the movie as a whole, was precisely this shooting of Eightball.

As I say, the incident in question perpetuates a Peckinpah-derived trope of slow-motion violence. In effect, it was the director Sam Peckinpah who, in his 1969 western *The Wild Bunch*, pioneered the notion of romanticising or sentimentalising the bloodier forms of carnage through a self-consciously 'sublime' deployment of slow-motion; and recurrent images (which handily contrived to be both explicit and elegiac) of blood spouting from a rash of freshly drilled bodily orifices in hot Abstract Expressionist washes (by Morris Louis, let's say) were over the years to become virtually his trademark.

In its imitation of Peckinpah's ghoulish mannerisms *Full Metal Jacket* is, of course, far from being the sole offender. But this, remember, is *Kubrick's Vietnam*, this is *Kubrick's violence*, in the hoggingly proprietary sense that we refer to *Fellini-Satyricon* or *Fellini Roma*. Demiurgic creator that he is, the film-maker who singlehandedly propelled his adopted medium into the twenty-first century, Stanley Kubrick could hardly be expected to resign himself to the servile imitation of so patently inferior an artist. He owed it to himself, to his art, to his breathlessly expectant public, to up the ante, to ennoble Peckinpah's invention with 'the Kubrick touch'. And so he does, preparing the terrain well in advance. In an earlier scene (which, with hindsight, strikes one as somewhat uneasily 'planted'), when Eightball is bartering with a pint-sized Vietnamese prostitute and her pimp, Kubrick is careful to have him initially rejected as a client. The black glowers in fretful resentment at the unpalatable notion that even in this God-forsaken hellhole he might have become the victim of racial discrimination – until it transpires that, for the tiny South-East Asian women, American Negroes are reputed to have 'too beaucoup' in their pants. Or, in Joker's earthier vernacular, to be 'packing too much meat'. Whereupon Eightball brashly drops his pants to demonstrate that, if occasioning no cause for modesty, his masculinity has nothing at all freakish about it. And, having underscored by such a pointed clue exactly what it is that Eightball is concealing in his trousers, having called apparently gratuitous but in reality vital attention to that part of his body, the director proceeds, a half-hour later at the movie's end, to confirm the sadistic brio of his sensibility by the fact that when the black is riddled by the sniper's bullets it is, of course, through that same part of the body that he is shot, it is out of his splattered sexual organs that, courtesy of slow-motion, the poor man's blood begins so lyrically to spout. Why had no one thought of that before? Ah, *non più andrai!*

In a sense, as will already be clear, *Full Metal Jacket* is not about Vietnam at all. On either the war's ideological underlay or its hard geopolitical realities (which, aside from the odd date and place name, have been ruthlessly expunged from the film) it offers neither ideas nor intuitions. The first half may be brilliantly filmed, but it shows us nothing we did not already know about the tribalised rigours of Marine training. Nor is the thesis that stern military discipline may transform a big, fat softie of a country boy into a psychopath calculated to afford us too much astonishment. And, for a director who can indeed be credited with having reinvented outer space for the cinema, so that the influence of *2001* is detectable in just about every science-fiction movie to have been released since it first appeared, the Vietnam sequences of *Full Metal Jacket* seem bizarrely cramped and *déjà vu* – not as excruciatingly visceral as those of *Platoon*, for instance, even if Oliver Stone is without question the lesser film-maker.

Why, in that case, should I have devoted a chapter to it in a study purporting to be about 'Hollywood's Vietnam'? The answer lies precisely in the nature of Eightball's death and what it implies not merely for the cinema of Vietnam but for the cinema of war in general and perhaps the American cinema in its entirety.

What is in contention here is whether, as it currently functions, the cinema is in the process of redefining itself as (to paraphrase Lautréamont and the Surrealist ideology that he inspired) 'the chance encounter of a camera and a machine-gun on an editing-table'. Consider, again, the climactic sequence of Kubrick's movie. Since, virtually by definition, a sniper remains unseen until he or she is apprehended and put out of commission, it becomes as though, from the spectator's point of view, Eightball had been killed by Kubrick's camera. But, in a very real sense, if one now enlarges one's field of vision, the sheer impracticality and on occasion downright impossibility of ever framing a cinematic composition so that a killer's gun succeeds in co-existing within the same shot as his victim's flailing body means that it *always* appears to be the camera that is responsible for the shooting. For the American cinema – in which extreme physical violence has become even more prevalent than it is in what is nevertheless known to be an exceptionally violent society – the movie camera has quite simply been metamorphosed into an instrument of mayhem, a machine for killing people.

Naturally, the intimate correlation that exists between these two implements, the gun and the camera, is by no means exclusively confined to the cinema. Alternative examples abound: given the international upsurge of interest in ecology, for instance, and specifically in the often impassioned defence and preservation of endangered species, the formerly rifle-bedecked safari hunter in Africa or India must now content himself with stalking his prey with a telephoto lens; everyone has heard of the irrational fears that seize certain primitive tribes when about to be photographed, believing as they do that the photographer means to abscond with their souls; and so forth. Evidence of such a partial kind, however, cannot begin to explain the predominance of the gun in the history of the cinema, a predominance far in excess of what it has enjoyed in the rival art forms. For why should there be, by comparison, a relative dearth of firearms in (distinguished) novels or poems, plays or operas? And why should one have to ransack one's memory to conjure up the names of even a tiny cluster of 'directors without guns'? (Pagnol? Rohmer? Ozu? Though others have no doubt existed, few spring unbidden to mind.)

For the present, I merely pose these questions, perhaps with the hope that one of the medium's more sociologically minded theorists might eventually undertake to investigate this strange and as yet tantalisingly little-analysed imbalance. My concern here is to indicate just to what extent, as fashions evolve in both cameras and guns, as the crime rate soars even more vertiginously on-screen than off, the movie camera has begun to assimilate the properties of the machine-gun. Directed against an actor, its natural instinct would appear to be to mow him down.

More and more frequently, the (male) film-maker is someone who hunkers down behind his camera with a mentality barely less aggressive, cut-throat and homicidal than that of a soldier behind his gun. Frame by frame, a reel of film is threaded through the camera the way a strip of bullets is fed into a machine-gun; such traditional staples of cinematic terminology as 'shooting' and 'cutting' have come at last to coincide with their most literal and unsavoury connotations; and the notion of an interesting shot seems these days to apply more appositely to some novel and inventive technique for killing off – 'wasting', rather – one's *dramatis personae*. In movie after movie, certainly among those produced in Hollywood, the most emblematic visuals are of death and destruction, of characters 'shot', simultaneously by gun and by camera, and no longer, as was once the case, neatly, cleanly, swiftly, but through the eyes, through the mouth (like Pyle), through the testicles (like Eightball), through any part of the body whose mutilation is calculated to provide the requisitely arresting image.

Stanley Kubrick's 'greatness', his 'uniqueness', are therefore not at all ascribable to his indefatigably promoted and by now near-legendary status as the medium's supreme maverick, the reclusive outsider exploring his own personal, even 'philosophical', preoccupations in cool, Olympian defiance of the American cinema's spurious ideologies and threadbare conventions. On the contrary, if these epithets do apply to him, it is precisely because he is instead, as his latest movie conclusively demonstrates, the absolute embodiment of these same conventions and ideologies, their advance guard and apotheosis, the fastest camera in the West, capable of drawing a bead on a man's penis and shooting its head off from two hundred yards. And the Marine credo, chanted in zombielike chorus by the anonymous recruits of *Full Metal Jacket*, might easily be appropriated, with one obvious, minor adjustment, as the director's own: 'This is my camera. There are many like it but this one is mine. My camera is my best friend. It is my life. I must master it as I must master my life. Without me my camera is useless. Without my camera I am useless. I must fire my camera through.'

— Chapter 10 —

GOODBYE TO ALL THAT

The original edition of this book, as it was published in 1981, ended with the critique of *Apocalypse Now* which currently constitutes its sixth chapter. Nearly a decade later, the film's director, Francis Ford Coppola, was to return to the theme of the Vietnam War with *Gardens of Stone* (based on the novel by Nicholas Proffitt). This curious, confused but not uninteresting postscript to the earlier work could also be viewed as its reverse mirror image, not only in its considerably diminished formal and stylistic ambition but also in the (related) fact that, where *Apocalypse Now* was an unabashedly subjective statement, a testament wrung from the director at great and precisely *personal* expense, *Gardens of Stone* seems to have been essentially a professional chore, no doubt offered to Coppola in the first place because he had been labelled a 'Vietnam' expert. Its existence probably derived from an understandable if sadistically double-edged form of Hollywood typecasting: which is to say, because Coppola had made *Apocalypse Now* it was judged that he would be a suitable candidate for *Gardens of Stone*; and because, again, he had made *Apocalypse Now* (i.e. because the precipitous decline in the fortunes of his maverick Zoetrope operation initially stemmed from the troubled shooting of that film) he was materially obliged to accept the assignment.

For the neatest clue to the distinction which the director himself appears to have made between the two movies one need only consult their respective directorial credits. On the credit titles of *Apocalypse Now* he signs himself, as grandly as in the past, Francis Ford Coppola; on those of *Gardens of Stone*, by contrast, his name has shrunk to the more modest and less resonant 'Francis Coppola'. Now it so happens that, throughout his career, that middle name has appeared, disappeared and reappeared like a moustache; and his devotees, quickly cracking the code, have come to interpret its absence on a film's title as signifying a concomitant absence of any truly personal investment in the project.

Coincidentally, however, the omission of 'Ford' in this instance happens to be an especially ill-timed one. Indeed, it might almost be claimed that the name 'Coppola' would have been the more appropriate one to drop, since *Gardens of Stone*, while bearing only a very oblique relationship to Coppola's earlier work, is indelibly imprinted with the ethos, the ideology and even, to a degree, the iconography of John Ford, with particular reference to the celebrated cavalry trilogy of the forties that comprised *Fort Apache*, *She Wore a Yellow Ribbon* and *Rio Grande*.

But before considering this elegiac Fordian strain, whose obvious but (by virtue of modalities of period, situation and plot) latent presence in the film impresses me as the ultimate measure and meaning of its achievement, it might be worth briefly summarising its narrative.

The year is 1968. In a series of suavely dovetailing medium- and long-shots, the camera panning across the cool, green, freshly mown lawns of the Arlington National Cemetery in Virginia and the flower-bed rows of naïve white tombstones with which they have been planted (the title's 'gardens of stone'), the film's opening sequence depicts a military funeral (already, therefore, one of the quintessentially Fordian rites). Though the spectator has for the moment no way of knowing this, the funeral is that of Jackie Willow (D. B. Sweeney), a former member of the official US Army ceremonial unit, the Old Guard. The ceremony proceeds with an almost monotonous immaculacy of pose and gesture, as the pristine toy soldiers of the Old Guard fire a valedictory salute over the coffin and Willow's young widow, Rachel (Mary Stuart Masterson), herself an 'army brat', is solemnly presented with a furled American flag as a tribute to her husband's loyal and unblemished service. As yet, the funeral is just that, a 'funeral', an inherently melancholic yet comfortingly remote ritual attended by a huddle of anonymous mourners.

At which point Willow, the dead man, off-screen, and possessed of the ultimate in hindsight, begins to narrate his own story.* For Willow, we learn, the posting to Arlington's Fort Myer has been a source of frustration rather than pride. Unencumbered by any very pronounced opinions concerning the legitimacy of the American military intervention in Vietnam, he is clearly first-rate officer material; but, vaguely humiliated by the passive, ceremonial and exhibitionist nature of his duties as a 'tin soldier', unimpressed by his regiment's prestige and history, he becomes increasingly impatient to be sent out to the combat zone. It is, moreover, by this sense of frustration that his case is paralleled by that of a seasoned, mulishly recalcitrant veteran, Sergeant Clell Hazard (James Caan), who takes him under his rugged, much-decorated wing. With an acute consciousness of being ungainfully employed, Hazard has been pestering his superior, the tough, cigar-chomping Captain Homer Thomas (a rather strained Dean Stockwell), to transfer him to a post where he might turn his experience to advantage by preparing new recruits for the enemy they are about to confront.

The film describes Hazard's meeting with Samantha Davis (Anjelica Huston), a sparky *Washington Post* journalist who succeeds, with maybe implausible ease and speed, in reconciling her own antiwar activism with his ingrained sense of professional duty (which is tempered, nevertheless, by a growing unease at the hopelessness of the war). They become lovers. Their encounter, too, finds its mirror image in that of Willow with his childhood sweetheart Rachel, whom he courts and marries in the face both of her initial reluctance to become an army wife (and possibly widow) and her patrician father's distaste for an uncommissioned soldier as a son-in-law.

So the extended military family begins to converge upon, and gravitate about, the central figure of Willow — Hazard in the role of surrogate parent (Willow's father, a former buddy of Hazard's, succumbs to a fatal heart attack in the course of the film's narrative; Hazard himself, we discover, lives separated from his wife and son);

* Though I shall continue to respect the convention that a plot be recounted in the present tense of its own narrative continuum, it is one of the more poignant aspects of *Gardens of Stone* that, its opening and closing scenes apart, the entire movie unfolds in flashback.

Hazard's bluff, ebullient companion-in-arms, the black Sergeant-Major 'Goody' Nelson (James Earl Jones) and his girlfriend Betty Rae (Lonette McKee); Hazard's lover Samantha; and, of course, the patient, tremulous, movingly banal Rachel – until, at long last, the young recruit is granted his commission. He departs for Vietnam (from where he sends back a series of increasingly disillusioned letters), only to return in a body bag twelve months later. In a virtually identical, shot-for-shot reprise of the opening sequence Willow is planted by his comrades in the gardens of stone.

In his review of the film the critic Tom Milne actually referred to the existence of *two* funeral services, failing to realise (in a pardonable lapse for anyone after only a single viewing) that the second was a duplicate of the first. But, if he was mistaken, in a certain sense he was not *wrong*. The point of such a construction, not cyclical but self-referential, is precisely that the two services are different. The first time we see it, Willow's funeral strikes us, as I have said, as being just one among hundreds of others, a military funeral in the abstract, its intrinsic capacity to disturb us eroded by our familiarity with such services on TV news bulletins; the second time, however, the coffin's occupant is no longer the Unknown but (for the spectator, at least) a Known Soldier, a young man with whom we have learned to sympathise during the intervening hundred minutes or so. The structure, moreover, acts as a paradigmatic model for the kind of sequential evolution that is proper to almost all fiction: from the general to the particular, the statistic to the individual, the documentary to the dramatised.

To return now to the question of a Fordian influence: even in so brief and concise a synopsis, even without attempting to reconstruct the film's connective tissue (in other words, its style, its visual tonality, its predominant 'look'), we can already see how pervasive it is. For what both Coppola's and Ford's movies have in common is an enduring preoccupation with the family unit – and here, as so often with Ford, the family unit is represented by the Army. In fact, *Gardens of Stone* bears the same relation to most of Hollywood's Vietnam movies as Ford's elegies for the Fifth Cavalry did to a legion of conventional, action-crammed westerns. Arguably, it is not a war movie at all. For even if, in one guise or another, Vietnam all but monopolises its dialogue, even if its off-screen buzz ends by rendering it as tantalisingly present and ubiquitous as the invisible Kurtz during most of *Apocalypse Now*, it erupts just once into the film's foreground: as newsreel footage on television. And Coppola simultaneously magnifies and distances the implication of that footage for his characters' lives by jerking into extreme close-up the horizontal bars and fuzzily anaemic colours of the electronic signal until they end by coinciding with the cinema screen.

Like Ford before him, Coppola is less interested in the army as a monolithic, smoothly functioning institution than with the private rituals (both official and, as it were, extra-curricular) of the military community: the mutual joshing and the shared nostalgia; the toasts ('To us and those like us. There ain't many of us left. Most of them are dead') and raggings (when Willow finally sports his lieutenant's stripes, each of the three sergeants who had been his superiors takes it in turn to pummel them with his fist); and, perhaps most immediately reminiscent of the Irish-American film-maker, the rambunctious bar-room brawls. Like Ford, too – and no matter how sympathetically he treats Willow's alienation, his panicky dread of being excluded from history – Coppola himself gives the impression of being unrepentantly in thrall to the almost childlike glamour and ostentation of the Old Guard: the operetta-like uni-forms absurdly festooned with ribbons, medals and stripes; the parading soldiers as neatly and regularly spaced as the graves they tend; even the graceful and strangely thrilling glissade, first of the right foot, then of the left, as they advance to the slow, stately pace of a funeral service.

The film is also paced by those domestic rituals most favoured by Ford, such rituals of social communion and conviviality, common to both army and family life, as a wedding, an informal dinner party, the arrival of a letter from an absent loved one, a first nervous meeting with one's future in-laws. Though these tend to be oddly self-contained, the director handling them as so many discrete vignettes, they nevertheless have the cumulative effect of convey-ing a strong sense of intimately interlinked destinies. And the obligatory scenes of drilling and inspection, familiar from practically every Vietnam movie ever made, this time humanise the expected juxtaposition of the drill sergeant's foul-mouthed scurrility and the collective trepidation of his charges with a genuinely felt warmth

and camaraderie that could not be further removed from the
Nazified thuggishness that transformed the Marine barracks of *Full
Metal Jacket* into a crypto-concentration camp.

If to these one adds a few more minor, localised details – the
physical and behavioural resemblance of James Earl Jones to the
Woody Strode of Ford's later westerns (*Sergeant Rutledge, The Horse
Soldiers*), with whom he shares an open, piercing gaze, a resonant
bass voice and the almost stylised negritude of a hero delineated
by some black Homer; the typology of the feminine characters,
from the meekly submissive wife and widow (the Joanne Dru role)
to the spunky, liberated 'spitfire' (the Maureen O'Hara role) – one
might argue, paradoxically, that it is *Gardens of Stone* rather than
The Green Berets which has most movingly and effectively revived
the ethos of understated patriotism and gentle gallantry that John
Wayne had always personified in Ford's cinema.

Withal, the movie is certainly no masterpiece. Were it not for
the extraordinary fluency with which Coppola's camera appropri-
ates (and at the same time 'ventilates') the cramped spatial co-
ordinates of the Fort Myer setting in which most of the action takes
place, were it not, especially, for his quite brilliant direction of
actors (Caan, in particular, a performer often dismissed as bland,
inexpressive and lacking in spirituality, is amazingly touching and
true), the ultra-linear, ultra-conventional dramaturgy of *Gardens of
Stone* and its reluctance ever to take risks or let the most minimal
plot point be less than instantly legible (it is a film fatally devoid
of *mystery*), would easily allow one to mistake it for a superior
made-for-TV movie. On that level, at least, the comparison with
John Ford breaks down. For though Ford's cavalry romances tended
to look like animated Remington paintings and sound like the
gruffer and more sentimental of Kipling's apologiae of the Raj (with
Ford's use of campfire songs to punctuate the narrative echoing
Kipling's fondness for Cockney, aitch-dropping barracks ballads as
chapter-heads), somehow, by some alchemical process of which
the cinema alone continues to guard the secret, they contrived to
add up to rather more than Remington and Kipling combined.
In the finest of Ford's westerns there operated such a perfectly
co-ordinated fusion of style and subject-matter, of the dancer
and the dance, that, viewing a characteristically Fordian shot of

cavalrymen silhouetted against a gorgeously lurid Technicolor sunset, one was no longer in a position to state whether it constituted a narrative 'acteme' designed to further the plot or else a fetishistic image whose primary purpose was to contribute to the film's overall iconography.

In *Apocalypse Now*, flawed as it was, Coppola presided over an equally seamless convergence of the vision and the thing seen, of the reproduction and the reality. For the duration of the film's running time it became impossible for the spectator to construct a mental image of what was happening distinct from the director's own selection of angles of vision. The Vietnam to which it granted us access was the only one of which we were aware as we were watching it: our passive perception of the filmed event was wholly defined and circumscribed by Coppola's active one. With *Gardens of Stone*, by contrast, his concern, visibly, was above all to fulfil his contract, to apply his considerable *savoir-faire* as a director to a project he did not instigate and on which, had he fallen ill, he could have been replaced without undue strain by another, similarly capable craftsman.

And yet . . . All that said, what is most remarkable about the movie is that, though deriving less from an idea than from a contract – a 'package', to employ the current cant expression – it turned out to be not only one of the most moving but also most significant of the entire cinema of Vietnam.

This can be attributed in part to a tragic incident which occurred during the shoot. Coppola, as I have said, makes movies about families, most notably *The Godfather I* and *II* (on the Mafia), *Peggy Sue Got Married* (whose protagonist is given the miraculous opportunity of getting to know her family before she was born) and his back-to-back pair of youth movies, *The Outsiders* and *Rumble Fish* (the pathos of whose young heroes is precisely that they are parentless). But, frequently, the very process of film-making is for him also a family affair. On the credits of *Gardens of Stone*, to look no further, may be seen the name of Roman Coppola, as a member of the technical personnel, as well as that of the director's father, Carmine Coppola, the composer of the film's rather soupy sound-track score. Their presence reflects less nepotism than what one might regard as the director's Italianate or 'Mediterranean' side, the Latin's desire to be surrounded by his family while he prepares either a movie or an enormous bowl of pasta. And, but for a tragic mishap, there would have been yet another Coppola around the table – Francis's own 22-year-old son, and for the occasion his first assistant, Gian-Carlo, who died during the shoot in a sailing accident on Chesapeake Bay.

When analysing a film, most serious critics prefer (rightly enough) to pay little heed to speculatively personal considerations on the grounds that they are gossipy, anecdotal and therefore irrelevant. Even so, it is difficult not to imagine how Coppola must have felt to find the shadow of his own son's death lengthening across this account of the premature death of another man's son ('In a way, the movie paralleled my own life,' he told a *New York Times* interviewer); not too fanciful, either, to suppose that the coincidence of these two deaths, one factual, the other fictional, might have fortuitously provided the impetus for a very much more intense investment of self in the project than his cropped name on the film's credit titles would suggest.

Nevertheless, if there is any truth or validity in such an assertion, it remains solely a matter of (unhappy) circumstance. What really lends *Gardens of Stone* its exemplary, emblematic stature is, again, the movie's relation to John Ford's cavalry romances.

During the thirties and forties, when his sensibility was attuned to the dominantly mythopoeic tendencies of the American cinema in its 'golden age' (an age which, of course, he himself had helped to create), Ford wilfully romanticised the opening up of the American West throughout the nineteenth century. By so doing, to be sure, he pioneered and perpetuated a profoundly racist ideology, one whose pernicious influence has only recently ceased to cling to Hollywood, and retroactively 'purified' a genocide in such a way that, had its victims been Eastern European Jews, let us say, rather than American Indians, he might now find himself bracketed with those neo-Nazi 'historians' whose life's work is the systematic refutation of the Holocaust.

Such an analogy, however, though tempting to a hyper-politicised cast of mind, is specious and misleading. The rapaciously capitalist expansion of the American hinterland did indeed engender what we have come to term a 'genocide'; and Ford himself, to

194

his credit, demonstrated that he had grown fully alert to the genocidal connotations of his favourite genre by making *Sergeant Rutledge* and *Cheyenne Autumn*, revisionist westerns attesting to a radically altered attitude towards both blacks and Indians. But the classic western was also, in a very real sense, an 'innocent' form of moviemaking, whose recurrent racial and social stereotypes, no matter the historical circumstances that had originally produced them, were nurtured within the rigid, on occasion airless, context of a genre that tended to function, more than any other in the cinema, as a controlled environment, with its own cultural autonomy. In consequence, these stereotypes evolved over the years in accordance with the mythic and aesthetic premises underlying the genre rather than in some form of fruitful interaction with the (extra-cinematic) currents of contemporary American history. And, by the fifties, when such premises seemed no longer tenable, the once rigorously codified western attempted for a brief period to accommodate the increasing fragmentation of ideas and ideologies by which, like every other genre, it was being bombarded – e.g. the 'elegiac' western (Sam Peckinpah's *Ride the High Country*), the 'psychological' western (Edward Dmytryk's *Warlock*), the 'liberal' western (Delmer Daves's *Broken Arrow*) – before atrophying and disappearing altogether, a hopeless anachronism. In the case of the Vietnam War movie, however, it is not impossible that this same process will be reversed; in short, that the genre, if such it is, will *only now* begin to enjoy the kind of consensual support of which, for obvious reasons, it has been deprived in the past. (It is surely not without significance that the second wave of Vietnam movies have been, on the whole, more commercially successful than the first.)

The result of such a development is not yet visible. Whatever might be their various qualities, their very distinct ideologies, it has been almost a constant of Vietnam movies, from *The Green Berets* to *Apocalypse Now*, from *Rambo* to *Full Metal Jacket*, that, precisely because Hollywood has always been ill-at-ease with ideas that to any degree smacked of the abstract or conceptual, they have concentrated above all in conveying the combat experience in as pressing and visceral a manner as possible, in making the spectator feel that *he is there*. The consequence of this concern – this resolve, as it were, to bring the war into extreme close-up – is that we have been frustrated of any truly reflective or comprehensive overview of the event, any angle of vision aspiring to more than a 'grunt's-eye-view'. (It has been little commented upon, for instance, that, by contrast with filmic representations of the First and Second World Wars, Hollywood's Vietnam has never been a war of *officers*. In the vast majority of films cited in this book the officer is either absent or else a marginal and frequently antipathetic figure.) *Gardens of Stone* does not provide such an overview. But, in its Fordian reverberations, its relative serenity and warmth, its absence of horrors, its melancholic detachment from the pain and passion of the period that it depicts and, above all, its indifference to the hyper-realist aesthetics of *being there*, it differs crucially from every other movie on the subject. *Platoon*, to take only the most obvious example, may be set in 1969 – which is to say, two decades before the film itself was made – yet its narrative material is handled by Oliver Stone as directly, as dynamically, as urgently, as though it had in reality been shot in the late sixties. Its narrative 'tense' – at least, as we are watching it – strikes us as a very unequivocal present. Not for one instant are we encouraged to distance ourselves from these young men in the jungles of South-East Asia, from their fears, their hopes and aspirations – as we are in Coppola's film and, indeed, in *She Wore a Yellow Ribbon*.

The significance of *Gardens of Stone*, then, whatever its failings, is that it is perhaps the first of the Vietnam movies *to be set in the past*, the first, in short, to acknowledge that the war is over.

APPENDIX I

Two recent films to have tackled the subject of the Vietnam War were Stephen Frears's *Saigon – Year of the Cat* (1983) and Roland Joffé's *The Killing Fields* (1984), neither of which was made in Hollywood (even if the latter was part-financed by a major American studio).

I do not intend to deal at any length with Frears's film, since it was British, shot for television and never theatrically released. Yet what makes it of interest here is that, anticipating *The Killing Fields*, it was the first Vietnam work to call attention to one of the most unsavoury moments of the war: its culmination. With the fall of Saigon and the appallingly hasty and undignified retreat of US ambassadorial and military personnel, thousands of Vietnamese employees, sympathisers and informers, who had been promised an eventual safe passage out of the country, were abandoned to the Viet Cong.

It has to be said first, unfortunately, that there was about the film a humdrum bedrock Britishness; if Frears already possessed a sensibility, he had not yet acquired a style to embody it. And, as often in British 'political' films, both its director and scenarist (David Hare, the dramatist of *Plenty* and *Map of the World* and future director of *Wetherby*) seemed incapable of divorcing the political dimension of their narrative from the personal – in this case, a fairly stereotyped romance between an American officer and an expatriate English spinster – as though no great event could be regarded as comprehensible unless filtered through the perceptions of one quiveringly sensitive, invariably middle-class protagonist. Where it did impress, however, was in its nervy reconstruction of the eleventh-hour American withdrawal from the doomed capital.

If, on paper, few situations appear to lend themselves more

readily to cinematic treatment than the 'fall' of a city, it tends to prove an especially tricky concept to render plausible. Any single observer of such a débâcle is liable to feel like Stendhal's Fabrice at the Battle of Waterloo – obscurely aware of some monumental convulsion heaving up just beyond his own restricted field of vision. And one may recall the grotesque climax to Anthony Mann's *The Fall of the Roman Empire*, in which the imperial power expired with the jarring brusqueness of an elevator arriving at street level: one minute, it seemed, there was a Roman Empire, and in the next minute it was gone. But the collapse of Saigon (also, in *The Killing Fields*, of Phnom Penh) was, in a narrowly literal sense, an overnight occurrence. The American occupiers, having obstinately, misread all the available signs over a period of months, even years, were left with a mere twenty-four hours to shred documents, pack up whatever belongings they could carry off and scramble to safety. In *Saigon – Year of the Cat* these scenes are (but then, they could scarcely fail to be) acutely distressing to watch, as the embassy's guards bolt door after door behind them in their frantic scurry to catch the last helicopter, forsaking a vacant compound to the defenceless hordes of their Vietnamese 'collaborators' (a callous description, perhaps, under the circumstances).

Even more effective was the equivalent sequence in *The Killing Fields*. Joffé's film (one of David Puttnam's personal productions) was based on a *New York Times Magazine* article 'The Death and Life of Dith Pran' by the Pulitzer Prize-winning war correspondent Sydney Schanberg. As Schanberg himself wrote in that article: 'I began the search for my friend Dith Pran in April of 1975. Unable to protect him when the Khmer Rouge troops ordered Cambodians to evacuate their cities, I had watched him disappear into the interior of Cambodia, which would become a death camp for millions. Dith Pran had saved my life the day of occupation, and the shadow of my failure to keep him safe – to do what he had done for me – was to follow me for four-and-a-half years. . . .'

Schanberg (played in the film, a trifle monotonously, by Sam Waterston) travelled to Cambodia in 1972 as a correspondent for the *New York Times* to cover the war between the revolutionary army of the Khmer Rouge and the government of Lon Nol. His assistant was a locally born man, Dith Pran, whose professional relationship with the American journalist evolved over their years together into one of mutual affection. But, when Phnom Penh fell in 1975, their friendship was put to a decisive test, a test that Schanberg ever after believed he had failed. By persuasively arguing their case with an officer of the Khmer Rouge, Pran had managed to save not only Schanberg's life but those of several other foreign correspondents isolated in the capital after the American withdrawal. Subsequently, however, when the population of Phnom Penh was herded *en masse* out into the countryside, and the administrative staff of the French Embassy, in which Pran had sought refuge, was ordered to surrender to the occupying forces all Cambodian nationals, Schanberg was unable in his turn to prevent his friend (and saviour) from being engulfed by the collective fate of his compatriots. And what ensued in Cambodia was, even for the history of the twentieth century, a holocaust of truly awesome dimensions: from a population of seven million inhabitants, an estimated three million were either massacred by the Khmer Rouge or else perished of hunger and disease. (The 'killing fields' of the movie's title refer to what was virtually the sole harvest of these terrible years.)

As for Schanberg, he had ignored his editor's advice by his decision to remain in the fallen city, thereby subsequently acquiring for himself a number of awards for 'international reporting at great risk'. Yet, as was brought home to him upon his return to the United States, by 'scrupulously' allowing poor Dith Pran to decide for himself whether he ought to be ferried out with his family or risk a precarious future at his colleague's side, he had in effect tacitly coerced him into staying. And in its latter half, dividing the narrative in two, the film proceeds to juxtapose Pran's dogged resolve, at first merely to survive, then to escape into Thailand, with Schanberg's increasingly desperate attempts to expiate a perhaps ineradicable sense of guilt – until their climactic, emotional reunion in a camp for displaced persons.

As one can see, *The Killing Fields* is a film simply bursting with subject-matter – with narrative, thematic and even political ideas. And my necessarily laconic précis does scant justice to the textural richness of what is, on the whole, and in spite of a few pivotal flaws, an impressive work.

It is impressive on three counts: first, visually, in that, notwith-standing a facile reliance on what one supposes to be an ironic pictorialism (as though the horror of Cambodia's devastation were somehow measurable by the luxuriance of its scenic splendour prior to the war) and a dry, self-denyingly impersonal approach to *mise en scène* (we know as little of Joffé's preoccupations as a film-maker by the end as at the beginning), the movie succeeds again and again in evoking the kind of classic news photograph which, through the visceral immediacy and kinetic dynamism of its (often fortuitous) composition, remains as securely lodged in one's memory as a great painting. And, whether intentionally or not, it is one of the themes of *The Killing Fields* that the source of the war's obscenity can be traced to the irreducible fact that the US Army's hardware, both its aircraft and ground craft, was simply too *big*, too massive and ponderous, for a country so small in scale and proportion, just as the American soldiers themselves, with their healthy, strapping, corn-fed bodies and straight, four-square features, appeared to tower over the more frailly built enemy. (This disparity was, to be sure, no fault of the Americans, but it is only right, as an integral element of the Vietnam War's iconography, that it should attract the attention of Joffé's camera.)

Second, it is impressive directorially, in that, though Joffé is, as I have suggested, slightly overwhelmed by the weight of his subject-matter, he does on occasion bring off a striking *coup de théâtre* (or *cinéma*). One such is the precipitous flight of American diplomatic VIPs (and Pran's family) towards the already impatiently buzzing and whirring helicopters, a scene that is lent still further urgency by his use of a single long take of real virtuosity. He has, moreover, the ability to tie a cluster of thematic loose ends into one brilliantly incisive 'cartoon', as it were, exemplified by the conceit of encapsulating Pran's prospective status as a 'non-person' by the heart-rending manner in which his portrait snapshot fades utterly from the false passport concocted for him by Schanberg and a photographer friend; or the (perhaps more dubious) moment when, to the accompaniment of Puccini's *Turandot* on his record-player, Schanberg inserts a video tape into his Betamax and subjects newsreel footage of the war to the humiliating attentions of the fast-forward button on his remote-control unit.

And also it impresses intellectually, in that the movie's contemplation of the war is as impartial as it is unflinching. Though it refuses to spare the mindless thuggery of the Khmer Rouge, whose conditioned response to almost any problem is simply to gun down the person or persons who happen to have posed it, and though its most shocking image is of a ditchful of human remains stretching to the horizon like some Brobdingnagian carcass, it nevertheless tempers its indictment by reminding the spectator (through Schanberg's voice) that, if one has ruthlessly and indiscriminately sought to bombard a nation 'into the Stone Age', in Curtis LeMay's infamous phrase, one should not, afterwards, be self-righteous about being confronted with cavemen. Thus it takes full account of what, when all is said and done, the word 'aftermath' really means: a period so indelibly scarred by whatever upheaval preceded it that it can only be assessed and understood within its own specific context. An obvious given, you would think, yet it has been systematically disregarded by all those partisans of American involvement whose mortification at the war's outcome has since been qualified by a gleeful, I-told-you-so interpretation of its consequences for much of South-East Asia.

As for the movie's flaws, apart from those cited above, they are mostly contingent on the awkward narrative split in its second half. Whereas the story of Pran (movingly played by a non-actor, Haing S. Ngor, himself a former victim of the Khmer Rouge) cannot help but make an impact as (possessing the strength, not of an iron bar, but of an apparently fragile yet in reality unbreakably taut wire) he clings to life itself as though to a lifebuoy, that of the guilt-ridden Schanberg peddling his tortured brow Stateside is far less absorbing. And it must be said that *The Killing Fields* truly 'blows' its ending, which ought to have been the most poignant moment of all, with the maudlin and irrelevant 'Imagine' elbowing its way on to an otherwise irreproachable soundtrack.

APPENDIX II

Filmography

Alice's Restaurant

USA, 1969, director: Arthur Penn. *Production company*: Florin Corporation, *producer*: Hillard Elkins, Joe Manduke, *associate producer*: Harold Leventhal, *script*: Venable Herndon, Arthur Penn. Based on the song 'The Alice's Restaurant Massacree' by Arlo Guthrie, *photography*: Michael Nebbia, *colour process*: DeLuxe, *editor*: Dede Allen, *production designer*: Warren Clymer, *leading players*: Arlo Guthrie (*Arlo*), Pat Quinn (*Alice*), James Broderick (*Ray*), Michael McClanathan (*Shelly*), Geoff Outlaw (*Roger*), Tina Chen (*Mari-Chan*), Kathleen Dabney (*Karin*), William Obanhein (*Officer Obie*), Seth Allen (*Evangelist*), Judge James Hannon (*Himself*), Pete Seeger (*Himself*). 110 mins.

American Graffiti

USA, 1973, director: George Lucas. *Production company*: Lucasfilm/Coppola Company. For Universal, *producer*: Francis Ford Coppola, Gary Kurtz, *script*: George Lucas, Gloria Katz, Willard Huyck, *photography*: Ron Eveslage, Jan D'Alquen, Techniscope, *colour process*: Technicolor, *editor*: Marcia Lucas, *visual consultant*: Haskell Wexler, *leading players*: Richard Dreyfuss (*Curt Henderson*), Ronny Howard (*Steve Bolander*), Paul Le Mat (*John Milner*), Charlie Martin Smith (*Terry Fields*), Cindy Williams (*Laurie*), Candy Clark (*Debbie*), Mackenzie Phillips (*Carol*), Wolfman Jack (*Disc Jockey*), Harrison Ford (*Bob Falfa*). 110 mins.

Apocalypse Now

USA, 1979, director: Francis Coppola. *Production company*: Omni Zoetrope, *producer*: Francis Coppola, *co-producer*: Fred Roos, Gray Frederickson, Tom Sternberg, *script*: John Milius, Francis Coppola. Based on the novel *Heart of Darkness* by Joseph Conrad. *Photography*: Vittorio Storaro, Technovision, *colour process*: Technicolor, *2nd Unit photography*: Stephen H. Burum, *insert photography*: Caleb Deschanel, *aerial photography*: David Butler, *editor*: Walter Murch, Gerald B. Greenberg, Lisa Fruchtman, *production designer*: Dean Tavoularis, *music*: Carmine Coppola, Francis Coppola, *Playmate show choreography*: John Calvert, *commentary*: Michael Herr, *narrator*: Martin Sheen, *leading players*: Marlon Brando (*Colonel Walter E. Kurtz*), Robert Duvall (*Lt Colonel Bill Kilgore*), Martin Sheen (*Captain Benjamin L. Willard*), Frederic Forrest (*Hicks, 'Chef'*), Albert Hall (*Chief Phillips*), Sam Bottoms (*Lance B. Johnson*), Larry Fishburne ('*Clean*'), Dennis Hopper (*Photo-journalist*), G. D. Spradlin (*General Corman*), Harrison Ford (*Colonel Lucas*), Jerry Ziesmer (*Civilian*), Scott Glenn (*Captain Richard Colby*), Francis Coppola (*Director of TV Crew*), Ifugao people of Banaue,

Philippine Islands (*Montagnard Tribesmen*). 141 mins (70mm). 35mm version with end title sequence: 153 mins.

Big Bounce, The

USA, 1968, director: Alex March. Warner Bros. *Production company*: Greenway, *producer*: William Dozier, *script*: William Dozier. Based on the novel by Elmore Leonard. *Photography*: Howard R. Schwartz, Panavision, *colour process*: Technicolor, *editor*: William Ziegler, *music*: Michael Curb, *leading players*: Ryan O'Neal (*Jack Ryan*), Leigh Taylor-Young (*Nancy Barker*), James Daly (*Ray Ritchie*), Robert Webber (*Bob Rogers*), Lee Grant (*Joanna*), Van Heflin (*Sam Mirakian*). 102 mins.

Big Wednesday

USA, 1978, director: John Milius. *Production company*: A-Team. For Warner Bros. *Producer*: Buzz Feitshans (surfing sequences) Greg MacGillivray, *script*: John Milius, Dennis Aaberg, *photography*: Bruce Surtees; (surfing sequences) Greg MacGillivray, Panavision, *colour process*: Metrocolor, *editor*: Robert L. Wolfe; Tim O'Meara, *production designer*: Charles Rosen, *music*: Basil Poledouris, *leading players*: Jan-Michael Vincent (*Matt Johnson*), William Katt (*Jack Barlow*), Gary Busey (*Leroy Smith, known as 'The Masochist'*), Patti D'Arbanville (*Sally Johnson*), Lee Purcell (*Peggy Gordon*), Darrell Fetty (*Jim King, known as 'Waxer'*), Sam Melville (*'The Bear'*), Gerry Lopez (*Himself*), Hank Warden (*'Shopping Cart'*), Joe Spinell (*Psychologist*). 119 mins.

Billy Jack

USA, 1971, director: T. C. Frank [Tom Laughlin]. Warner. *Production company*: National Student Film Corporation, *producer*: Mary Rose Solti, *script*: Frank and Teresa Christina [Tom Laughlin and Delores Taylor], *photography*: Fred Koenekamp, John Stephens, *colour process*: Technicolor, *editor*: Larry Heath, Marion Rothman, *music/music director*: Mundell Lowe, *Indian snake ceremony*: Rolling Thunder of Shoshone Nation, *Wokova friendship dance*: Andy Vidovich of Paiute Nation, *Hapkido Karati*: Bon Soo Han of Korea, *leading players*: Tom Laughlin (*Billy Jack*), Delores Taylor (*Jean Roberts*), Clark Howat (*Sheriff Cole*), Bert Freed (*Stuart Posner*), Julie Webb (*Barbara*), Ken Tobey (*Deputy Sheriff Mike*), Victor Izay (*Doctor*), Debbie Schock (*Kit*). 113 mins.

Birdy

USA, 1984, director: Alan Parker. *Production company*: A & M Films. For Tri-Star-Delphi III Productions. *Producer*: Alan Marshall, *script*: Sandy Kroopf, Jack Behr. Based on the novel by William Wharton. *Photography*: Michael Seresin, *colour process*: Metrocolor, *aerial photography*: David Butler, *editor*: Gerry Hambling, *production designer*: Geoffrey Kirkland, *flying effects*: Bob Harman, *ornithopter*: Ken Johnson, *music*: Peter Gabriel, *leading players*: Matthew Modine (*Birdy*), Nicolas Cage (*Al Columbato*), John Harkins (*Doctor Weiss*), Sandy Baron (*Mr Columbato*), Karen Young (*Hannah Rourke*), Bruno Kirby (*Renaldi*), Nancy Fish (*Mrs Prevost*), George Buck (*Birdy's Father*), Dolores Sage (*Birdy's Mother*). 120 mins.

A traumatised young veteran (whose nickname, Birdy, derives from a lifelong fascination with ornithology) is eventually rehabilitated with the support of a childhood buddy, who is himself recuperating from (more strictly physical) wounds received in combat. Parker's film – as meretriciously shot as is customary with this director – is interesting in that, though on the whole a faithful adaptation of William Wharton's much-admired first novel, it has elected to update the action from the post-Second World War period to that of Vietnam's aftermath.

Boys in Company C, The

Hong Kong, 1977, director: Sidney J. Furie. *Production company*: Golden Harvest/Good Times Films, *executive producer*: Raymond Chow, *producer*: André Morgan, *script*: Rick Natkin, *photography*: Godfrey Godar, Panavision, *colour process*: Technicolor, *editor*: Michael Berman, Frank J. Urioste, Alan Pattillo, James Benson, *music*: Jaime Mendoza-Nava, *leading players*: Stan Shaw (*Tyrone Washington*), Michael Lembeck (*Vinnie Fazio*), James Canning (*Alvin Forster*), Craig Wasson (*Dave Bisbee*), Andrew Stevens (*Billy Ray Pike*), Noble Willingham (*Sgt Curry*), James Whitmore Jnr (*Lt Archer*), Scott Hylands (*Capt. Collins*), Lee Ermey (*Sgt Leroy Loyce*). 128 mins.

Braddock: Missing in Action III

USA, 1988, director: Aaron Norris. *Production company*: Cannon Films/ Cannon International, *producer*: Menahem Golan, Yoram Globus, *script*: James Bruner, Chuck Norris. Based on characters created by Arthur Silver, Larry Levinson, Steve Bing. *Photography*: Joao Fernandes. In colour. *Editor*: Michael J. Duthie, Ken Bornstein, *music*: Jay Chattaway, *leading players*: Chuck Norris (*Colonel James Braddock*), Aki Aleong (*General Quoc*), Roland Harrah III (*Van Tan Cang*), Miki Kim (*Lin Tan Cang*), Yehuda Efroni (*Reverend Polanski*), Ron Barker (*Mik*), Floyd Levine (*General Duncan*), Jack Rader (*Littlejohn*). 103 mins.

This third instalment in the adventures of Rambo's rival is a rancid brew of Amerasian orphans, saintly missionaries (Father Polanski!), sadistic Viet Cong and conniving CIA officers. Worthless on every conceivable level.

Cacciatore II (The Last Hunter)

Italy, 1980, director: Anthony M. Dawson [Antonio Margheriti]. *Production company*: Flora Film/Gico Cinematografica, *producer*: Gianfranco Couyoumdjian, *script*: Dardano Sacchetti, *story*: Gianfranco Couyoumdjian, *photography*: Riccardo Pallottini, *colour process*: Technicolor, *editor*: Alberto Moriani, *leading players*: David Warbeck (*Harry E. Morris*), Tisa Farrow (*Jane Foster*), Tony King, Bobby Rhodes. 96 mins.

This inept pastiche of Hollywood's Vietnam (e.g. a charismatically mad major modelled on Robert Duvall's characterisation in Apocalypse Now; *a lip-smacking relish for Viet Cong atrocities à la* The Green Berets *and* The Deer Hunter; *a journalist heroine whose name, Jane Foster, was no doubt intended to evoke that of the leading actress of* Coming Home) *is included here as representing a rare stab at what might be (or might have been) called the spaghetti Vietnam War movie.*

Carry It On (UK, Joan)

USA, 1970, directors: James Coyne, Robert Jones, Christopher Knight. *Production company*: The New Film Company, *associate producer*: Robert

Silverthorne, *script/photography/editor*: James Coyne, Robert Jones, Christopher Knight, *music/songs*: 'Carry It On' by G. I. Turner, 'Last Thing on My Mind' by Tom Paxton, 'Hickory Wind' by Graham Parson and Bob Buchanan, 'Suzanne' by Leonard Cohen, 'Miller's Cave' by Jack Clemente, 'Land of a Thousand Dances' by Chris Kenner, 'Cinammon Girl' by Neil Young, 'Down So Low' by T. Nelson, 'Mother Earth' by Memphis Slim, 'Oh Happy Day' arranged by Edwin Hawkins, 'We Shall Overcome' by Pete Seeger, Guy Carowan, Zilphia Horten and Frank Hamilton, 'All I Have to Offer You Is Me' by Dallas Frazier and Alan Range, *sung and played by*: Joan Baez, *featuring*: Joan Baez, David Harris. 95 mins.

Cease Fire

USA, 1985, director: David Nutter. *Production company*: Double Helix Films/ELF Productions, *producer*: William Grefe, *script*: George Fernandez, *photography*: Henning Schellerup. In colour. *Editor*: Ralph R. Clemente, David Nutter, *music*: Gary Fry, *leading players*: Don Johnson (*Tim*), Lisa Blount (*Paula*), Robert F. Lyons (*Luke*), Richard Chavez (*Badman*), Rick Richards (*Robb*), Chris Noel (*Wendy*), Christina Wilfong (*Ellen*), Josh Segal (*Ronnie*). 98 mins.

The originality of Cease Fire, *an otherwise muddily undistinguished drama, is that the alienation of its Vietnam vet protagonist forms the real substance of its narrative and is not opportunistically co-opted into serving as an alibi for thrillerish violence and criminality. 'Not death but surviving,' as one of the characters remarks, 'is the real hell.'*

Clay Pigeon (UK, Trip to Kill)

USA, 1971, directors: Tom Stern, Lane Slate. *Production company*: Tracom, *producer*: Tom Stern, *script*: Ronald Buck, Buddy Ruskin, Jack Gross Jnr, *story*: Buddy Ruskin, Jack Gross Jnr, *photography*: Alan Stensvold, *colour process*: Metrocolor, *editor*: Danford Greene, *music supervisor*: Gavin Murrell, *leading players*: Tom Stern (*Joe Ryan*), Telly Savalas (*Frank Redford*), Robert Vaughn (*Henry Neilson*), Jeff Corey (*Free Clinic Doctor*), Peter Lawford (*MacGregor*), Marilyn Akin (*Angeline*), John Marley (*Police Captain*), Marlene Clark (*Saddle*), Burgess Meredith (*Freedom Lovelace*). 91 mins.

Coming Home

USA, 1978, director: Hal Ashby. *Production company*: Jerome Hellman Enterprises/Jayne Productions, *producer*: Jerome Hellman, *script*: Waldo Salt, Robert C. Jones, *story*: Nancy Dowd, *photography*: Haskell Wexler, *colour process*: DeLuxe, *editor*: Don Zimmerman, *production designer*: Michael Haller, *leading players*: Jane Fonda (*Sally Hyde*), Jon Voight (*Luke Martin*), Bruce Dern (*Captain Bob Hyde*), Robert Carradine (*Billy Munson*), Penelope Milford (*Vi Munson*), Robert Ginty (*Sgt Dink Mobley*), Charles Cyphers (*Pee Wee*), Tresa Hughes (*Nurse De Groot*), Mary Jackson (*Fleta Wilson*). 128 mins.

Cutter and Bone (UK, Cutter's Way)

USA, 1981, director: Ivan Passer. *Production company*: Gurian Entertainment. For United Artists. *Producer*: Paul R. Gurian, *script*: Jeffrey Alan Fiskin. Based on the novel *Cutter and Bone* by Newton Thornburg. *Photography*: Jordan Cronenweth, *colour process*: Technicolor, *editor*: Caroline Ferriol, *art director*: Josan

Russo, *music*: Jack Nitzsche, *leading players*: Jeff Bridges (*Richard Bone*), John Heard (*Alex Cutter*), Lisa Eichhorn (*Maureen Cutter, 'Mo'*), Ann Dusenberry (*Valerie Duran*), Stephen Elliott (*J. J. Cord*), Arthur Rosenberg (*George Swanson*), Nina Van Pallandt (*Woman in Hotel*), Patricia Donahue (*Mrs Cord*), Geraldine Baron (*Susie Swanson*). 109 mins.

Deer Hunter, The

USA, 1978, director: Michael Cimino. *Production company*: EMI Films, *producer*: Barry Spikings, Michael Deeley, Michael Cimino, John Peverall, *script*: Deric Washburn, *story*: Michael Cimino, Deric Washburn, Louis Garfinkle, Quinn K. Redeker, *photography*: Vilmos Zsigmond, Panavision, *colour process*: Technicolor, *editor*: Peter Zinner, *art director*: Ron Hobbs, Kim Swados, *music*: Stanley Myers; main title theme performed by John Williams, *leading players*: Robert De Niro (*Michael Vronsky*), John Cazale (*Stan, 'Stosh'*), John Savage (*Steven*), Christopher Walken (*Nikanor Chevotarevich, known as Nick*), Meryl Streep (*Linda*), George Dzundza (*John*), Chuck Aspegren (*Axel*), Shirley Stoler (*Steven's Mother*), Rutanya Alda (*Angela*), Pierre Segui (*Julien*). Choir of St Theodosius Cathedral, Cleveland, Ohio. 182 mins.

Easy Rider

USA, 1969, director: Dennis Hopper. Columbia. *Production company*: Pando Company, in association with Raybert Productions, *executive producer*: Bert Schneider, *producer*: Peter Fonda, *script*: Peter Fonda, Dennis Hopper, Terry Southern, *photography*: Laszlo Kovaks, *colour process*: Technicolor, *editor*: Donn Cambren, *art director*: Jerry Kay, *leading players*: Peter Fonda (*Wyatt*), Dennis Hopper (*Billy*), Antonio Mendoza (*Jesus*), Phil Spector (*Connection*), Mac Mashourian (*Body Guard*), Warren Finnerty (*Rancher*), Tita Colorado (*Rancher's Wife*), Luke Askew (*Stranger*), Luana Anders (*Lisa*), Jack Nicholson (*George Hanson*). 95 mins.

Edge, The

USA, 1968, director: Robert Kramer. *Production company*: Blue Van Alpha-60, *producer*: Robert Machover, *script*: Robert Kramer, *photography*: Robert Machover, *editor*: Norm Fruchter, *leading players*: Jack Rader (*Dan*), Tom Griffin (*Tom*), Howard Loeb Babeuf (*Bill*), Jeff Weiss (*Max*), Anne Waldman March (*Didi*), Sanford Cohen (*Peter*), Paul Hultberg (*Sinclair*), Catherine Merrill (*Sally*), Russell Parker (*Michael*), Gerald Long (*Gerry*), Theodora Bergery (*Anne*). 98 mins.

Exterminator, The

USA, 1980, director: James Glickenhaus. *Production company*: Interstar Corporation, *producer*: Mark Buntzman, *script*: James Glickenhaus, *photography*: Robert M. Baldwin, *colour process*: Movielab, *editor*: Corky Ohara, *production designer*: William de Seta, *music*: Joe Renzetti, *leading players*: Christopher George (*Detective James Dalton*), Samantha Eggar (*Dr Megan Stewart*), Robert Ginty (*John Eastland*), Steve James (*Michael Jefferson*), Tony Di Benedetto (*Chicken Pimp*), Dick Boccelli (*Grino Pontivini*), Patrick Farrelly (*CIA Agent Shaw*), Roger Grimsby (*Himself*), Judy Licht (*Herself*), Stan Getz (*Himself*). 102 mins.

Exterminator 2

USA, 1984, director: Mark Buntzman. *Production company*: Cannon, *executive producer*: Menahem Golan, Yoram Globus, *producer*: Mark Buntzman, William Sachs, *script*: Mark Buntzman, William Sachs, *photography*: Bob Baldwin, Joseph Mangine, *colour process*: TVC, *editor*: George Norris, Marcus Manton, *music*: David Spear, *leading players*: Robert Ginty (*John Eastland*), Deborah Geffner (*Caroline*), Mario Van Peebles (*X*), Frankie Faison (*Be Gee*), Scott Randolph (*Eyes*), Reggie Rock Bythewood (*Spider*), Bruce Smolanoff (*Red Rat*), David Buntzman (*Head Mafioso*). 90 mins.

Eyewitness (UK, The Janitor)

USA, 1981, director: Peter Yates. *Production company*: 20th Century-Fox, *producer*: Peter Yates, *script*: Steve Tesich, *photography*: Matthew F. Leonetti, *colour process*: Technicolor; prints by DeLuxe, *editor*: Cynthia Scheider, *production designer*: Philip Rosenberg, *music*: Stanley Silverman, *leading players*: William Hurt (*Daryll Deever*), Sigourney Weaver (*Tony Sokolow*), Christopher Plummer (*Joseph*), James Woods (*Aldo Mercer*), Irene Worth (*Mrs Sokolow*), Kenneth McMillan (*Mr Deever*), Pamela Reed (*Linda Mercer*), Albert Paulsen (*Mr Sokolow*), Steven Hill (*Lieutenant Jacobs*). 108 mins.

First Blood

USA, 1982, director: Ted Kotcheff. *Production company*: Carolco. For Anabasis. *Producer*: Buzz Feitshans, *script*: Michael Kozoll, William Sackheim, Sylvester Stallone. Based on the novel by David Morrell. *Photography*: Andrew Laszlo, Panavision, *colour process*: Technicolor, *editor*: Joan Chapman, *production designer*: Wolf Kroeger, *music*: Jerry Goldsmith, *leading players*: Sylvester Stallone (*John Rambo*), Richard Crenna (*Colonel Trautman*), Brian Dennehy (*Sheriff Will Teasle*), David Caruso (*Mitch*), Jack Starrett (*Galt*), Michael Talbott (*Balford*), David Crowley (*Shingleton*), Chris Mulkey (*Ward*), Don Mackay (*Preston*). 93 mins.

Four Friends (UK, Georgia's Friends)

USA, 1981, director: Arthur Penn. *Production company*: Filmways. A Cinema 77/Geria film. A Florin production. *Producer*: Arthur Penn, Gene Lasko, *script*: Steven Tesich, *photography*: Ghislain Cloquet, *colour process*: Technicolor, *editor*: Barry Malkin, Marc Laub, *production designer*: David Chapman, *music/music director*: Elizabeth Swados, *leading players*: Craig Wasson (*Danilo Prozor, 'Danny'*), Jodi Thelen (*Georgia Miles*), Michael Huddleston (*David Levine*), Jim Metzler (*Tom Donaldson*), Scott Hardt (*Young Danilo*), Elizabeth Lawrence (*Mrs Prozor*), Miklos Simon (*Mr Prozor*), Michael Kovacs (*Prozors' Neighbour*), Beatrice Fredman (*Mrs Zoldos*). 115 mins.

Full Metal Jacket

Great Britain, 1987, director: Stanley Kubrick. *Production company*: Warner Bros. A Natant film. *Producer*: Stanley Kubrick, *script*: Stanley Kubrick, Michael Herr, Gustav Hasford, based on the novel *The Short Timers* by Gustav Hasford, *photography*: Douglas Milsome, in colour, *editor*: Martin Hunter, *production designer*: Anton Furst, *music*: Abigail Mead, *technical adviser*: Lee Ermey, *leading players*: Matthew Modine (*Private Joker*), Adam Baldwin (*Animal Mother*),

Vincent D'Onofrio (*Leonard Lawrence, Private Gomer Pyle*), Lee Ermey (*Gunnery Sergeant Hartman*), Dorian Harewood (*Eightball*), Arliss Howard (*Cowboy*), Kevyn Major Howard (*Rafterman*), Ed O'Ross (*Walter J. Schinoski, Lieutenant Touchdown*), John Terry (*Lieutenant Lockhart*). 116 mins.

Gardens of Stone

USA, 1987, director: Francis Coppola. *Production company*: Tri-Star-ML Delphi Premier Productions, *producer*: Michael I. Levy, Francis Coppola, *script*: Ronald Bass. Based on the novel by Nicholas Proffitt. *Photography*: Jordan Cronenweth, *colour process*: DeLuxe, *electronic cinema staff*: Gian-Carlo Coppola, Murdo Laird, Roman Coppola, Gus Carpenter, *editor*: Barry Malkin, *production designer*: Dean Tavoularis, *art director*: Alex Tavoularis, *music*: Carmine Coppola, *leading players*: James Caan (*Sergeant Clell Hazard*), Anjelica Huston (*Samantha Davis*), James Earl Jones (*Sergeant-Major 'Goody' Nelson*), D. B. Sweeney (*Jackie Willow*), Dean Stockwell (*Captain Homer Thomas*), Mary Stuart Masterson (*Rachel Feld*), Dick Anthony Williams (*Slasher Williams*), Lonette McKee (*Betty Rae*), Sam Bottoms (*Lieutenant Webber*), Elias Koteas (*Pete Deveber*), Larry Fishburne (*Flanagan*). 112 mins.

Getting Straight

USA, 1970, director: Richard Rush. Columbia. *Production company*: The Organization, *producer*: Richard Rush, *script*: Robert Kaufman. Based on the novel by Ken Kolb. *Photography*: Laszlo Kovacs, *colour process*: Eastman Colour, *editor*: Maury Winetrobe, *music*: Ronald Stein, *leading players*: Elliott Gould (*Harry Bailey*), Candice Bergen (*Jan*), Robert F. Lyons (*Nick*), Jeff Corey (*Dr Wilhunt*), Max Julien (*Ellis*), Cecil Kellaway (*Dr Kasper*), John Lormer (*Vandenburg*), Leonard Stone (*Lysander*), William Bramley (*Wade Linden*), Harrison Ford (*Jake*). 125 mins.

Glory Boy (UK, My Old Man's Place)

USA, 1971, director: Edwin Sherin. *Production company*: Philip Waxman-Jerome Minskoff Productions, *producer*: Philip A. Waxman, *script*: Stanford Whitmore. Based on the novel *The Old Man's Place* by John Sanford. *Photography*: Richard C. Glouner, *colour process*: Eastman Colour, *editor*: Ferris Webster, *music*: Charles Gross, *leading players*: Arthur Kennedy (*Walter Pell*), Mitchell Ryan (*Sgt Martin Flood*), William Devane (*Jimmy Pilgrim*), Michael Moriarty (*Trubee Pell*), Topo Swope (*Helen*), Lloyd Gough (*Dr Paul*), Ford Rainey (*Sheriff Coleman*). 103 mins.

Good Guys Wear Black

USA, 1977, director: Ted Post. *Production company*: Action One Film Partners, a Mar Vista production, *producer*: Allan F. Bodoh, *script*: Bruce Cohn, Mark Medoff, *story*: Joseph Fraley, *photography*: Bob Steadman, *colour process*: CFI, *editor*: William Moore, Millie Moore, *music/music director*: Craig Safan, *martial arts choreography*: Chuck Norris, Aaron Norris, *leading players*: Chuck Norris (*John T. Booker*), Anne Archer (*Margaret*), James Franciscus (*Conrad Morgan*), Lloyd Haynes (*Murray Saunders*), Dana Andrews (*Edgar Harolds*), Jim Backus (*Doorman*). 95 mins.

Good Morning, Vietnam

USA, 1987, director: Barry Levinson. *Production company*: Touchstone. In
association with Silver Screen Partners III. A Rollins, Morra and Brezner
production. *Producer*: Mark Johnson, Larry Brezner, *script*: Mitch Markowitz,
photography: Peter Sova, *colour process*: DeLuxe, *editor*: Stu Linder, *production
designer*: Roy Walker, *music*: Alex North, *leading players*: Robin Williams (*Airman
Adrian Cronauer*), Forest Whitaker (*Private Edward Garlick*), Tung Thanh Tran
(*Tuan*), Chintara Sukapatana (*Trinh*), Bruno Kirby (*Lieutenant Steven Hauk*),
Robert Wuhl (*Marty Lee Dreiwitz*), J. T. Walsh (*Sergeant-Major Dickerson*), Noble
Willingham (*General Taylor*), Richard Edson (*Private Abersold*), Juney Smith (*Phil
McPherson*), Richard Portnow (*Dan 'The Man' Levitan*), Cu Ba Nguyen (*Jimmy
Wah*). 108 mins.

*It has always been Barry Levinson's gift (a singular one in the context of contemporary
American cinema) to be capable of filming the Word. In* Diner, Tin Men *and now* Good
Morning, Vietnam *it is less by any act that they might perform than by the parameters
of their oral discourse that his characters tend to define themselves – be it by the
mazily meandering free-association exchanges of the two former movies or the deliriously
unbridled extemporisations that the disc-jockey Adrian Cronauer practises in the
latter (basically a stylised, lightning-streak version of the same, wittingly droll where
the prattle of Levinson's earlier heroes was unwittingly so). In consequence, the best, most
enjoyable and most purely* cinematic *sequences of* Good Morning, Vietnam *– about
an irreverent DJ posted to South-East Asia in the late sixties – are those in which Cronauer/
Williams (the actor apparently improvised his monologues) simply unfurls his tongue
and lets rip into the microphone. And though they were widely criticised as redundant,
the glimpses we are afforded of his public convulsed with laughter are essential to the
film's premise, which is that Cronauer is funny not for basic generic reasons – i.e. because*
Good Morning, Vietnam *happens to be a comedy (as characters in Neil Simon
comedies rattle off one-liner upon one-liner without ever contemplating making a living
out of it) – but because, were an objective existence to be projected for the world that
the film conjures up, he would* still *be funny.*

Unfortunately, and unlike either Diner *or* Tin Men, Good Morning, Vietnam
*has been burdened with a real plot; and Levinson's plotting instincts resemble so
many homing pigeons: to whatever exotic locale he may dispatch them, they swiftly
wing their way back to the stock barrel from which they first fluttered forth. Cronauer
befriends a young Vietnamese woman, with whom he becomes romantically involved,
and her brother who, it transpires, works in league with the Viet Cong; and this betrayal
of confidence (as Cronauer sees it) leads to a maudlin confrontation between the two
men, with the supposedly 'subversive' disc-jockey actually regurgitating the American
military's own rationale for the war: 'We're here to help you people!' And later when,
unceremoniously escorted out of the country (precisely for having fraternised with a
VC sympathiser), he briefly stops off to play a little baseball with his new Vietnamese
acquaintances, and even the two MPs accompanying him join in, the impression is
conveyed that, if only the war's architects had an ounce of Cronauer's wit, charm and
gregarity, the cultural imperialism that they camouflaged by the publicly stated ambition
of conquering 'hearts and minds' would have been a pushover.*

Go Tell the Spartans

USA, 1977, director: Ted Post. United Artists. *Production company*: Mar Vista Productions, a Spartan Company production, *producer*: Allan F. Bodoh, Mitchell Cannold, *script*: Wendell Mayes. Based on the novel *Incident at Muc Wa* by Daniel Ford. *Photography*: Harry Stradling Jnr, *colour process*: CFI, *editor*: Millie Moore, *music/music director*: Dick Halligan, *leading players*: Burt Lancaster (*Major Asa Barker*), Craig Wasson (*Corporal Stephen Courcey*), Jonathan Goldsmith (*Sergeant Oleonowski*), Mar Singer (*Captain Al Olivetti*), Joe Unger (*Lieutenant Raymond Hamilton*), Dennis Howard (*Corporal Abraham Lincoln*), David Clennon (*Lieutenant Stanley Wattsberg*), Evan Kim (*Cowboy*). 114 mins.

Green Berets, The

USA, 1968, directors: John Wayne, Ray Kellogg. Warner-Pathé. *Production company*: Batjac, *producer*: Michael Wayne, *script*: James Lee Barrett. Based on the novel by Robin Moore. *Photography*: Winton C. Hoch, Panavision, *colour process*: Technicolor, *editor*: Otho Lovering, *music*: Miklos Rozsa, *leading players*: John Wayne (*Col. Mike Kirby*), David Janssen (*George Beckworth*), Jim Hutton (*Sgt Petersen*), Aldo Ray (*Sgt Muldoon*), Raymond St Jacques (*Doc McGee*), Jack Soo (*Col. Cai*), Bruce Cabot (*Col. Morgan*), George Takei (*Capt. Nim*), Patrick Wayne (*Lt Jamison*), Luke Askew (*Sgt Provo*), Irene Tsu (*Lin*). 141 mins.

Greetings

USA, 1968, director: Brian De Palma. *Production company*: West End Films, *producer*: Charles Hirsch, *script*: Charles Hirsch, Brian De Palma, *photography*: Robert Fiore, *colour process*: Eastman Colour, *editor*: Brian De Palma, *music/songs*: The Children of Paradise, *leading players*: Jonathan Warden (*Paul Shaw*), Robert De Niro (*Jon Rubin*), Gerrit Graham (*Lloyd Clay*), Megan McCormick (*Marina*), Ashley Oliver (*Bronx Secretary*), Cynthia Peltz (*Divorcee*), Ruth Alda (*Linda*). 88 mins.

Hail, Hero!

USA, 1969, director: David Miller. Warner-Pathé. *Production company*: Halcyon Productions, *producer*: Harold D. Cohen, *script*: David Manber. Based on the novel by John Weston. *Photography*: Robert Hauser, *colour process*: Technicolor, *editor*: Jack McSweeney, *music*: Jerome Moross, *leading players*: Michael Douglas (*Carl Dixon*), Arthur Kennedy (*Albert Dixon*), Teresa Wright (*Santha Dixon*), John Larch (*Mr Conklin*), Charles Drake (*Senator Murchiston*), Mercer Harris (*Jimmy*), Deborah Winters (*Becky*), Peter Strauss (*Frank Dixon*). 97 mins.

Hair

USA, 1979, director: Milos Forman. *Production company*: United Artists, a CIP Film productions feature, *producer*: Lester Persky, Michael Butler, *script*: Michael Weller. Based on the musical play by Galt MacDermot (music), Gerome Ragni, James Rado (book and lyrics), *photography*: Miroslav Ondricek; Richard Kratina, Jean Talvin, *colour process*: Technicolor, *editor*: Stanley Warnow, Alan Heim, *production designer*: Stuart Wurtzel, *puppet creations*: Larry Reehling, *choreography*: Twyla Tharp; Kenneth Rinker, *leading players*: John Savage (*Claude*), Treat Williams (*Berger*), Beverly D'Angelo (*Sheila*), Annie Golden

(*Jeanie*), Dorsey Wright (*Hud*), Don Dacus (*Woof*), Cheryl Barnes (*Hud's Fiancée*), Richard Bright (*Fenton*), Nicholas Ray (*General*), Charlotte Rae (*Lady in Pink*), Miles Chapin (*Steve*), Fern Tailer (*Sheila's Mother*), Charles Denny (*Sheila's Father*). 121 mins.

Hamburger Hill

USA, 1987, director: John Irvin. *Production company*: RKO Pictures, *producer*: Marcia Nasatir, James Carabatsos, *script*: James Carabatsos, *photography*: Peter MacDonald, *colour process*: Rank; prints by Technicolor, *editor*: Peter Tanner, *production designer*: Austen Spriggs, *music*: Philip Glass, *leading players*: 3rd Squad, 1st Platoon: Anthony Barrile (*Languilli*), Michael Patrick Boatman (*Motown*), Don Cheadle (*Washburn*), Michael Dolan (*Murphy*), Don James (*McDaniel*), Dylan McDermott (*Sergeant Frantz*), M. A. Nickles (*Galvan*), Harry O'Reilly (*Duffy*), Daniel O'Shea (*Gaigin*), J. C. Palmore (*Healy*), Tim Quill (*Beletsky*), Tommy Swerdlow (*Bienstock*), Courtney B. Vance (*Doc*). 110 mins.

Hanoi Hilton, The

USA, 1987, director: Lionel Chetwynd. *Production company*: Cannon, *producer*: Menahem Golan, Yoram Globus, *script*: Lionel Chetwynd, *photography*: Mark Irwin, *editor*: Penelope Shaw, *music*: Jimmy Webb, *leading players*: Michael Moriarty (*Lieutenant Commander Williamson*), Paul Le Mat (*Captain Hubman*), Jeffrey Jones (*Major Fisher*), Lawrence Pressman (*Colonel Cathcart*), Stephen Davies (*Captain Robert Miles*), David Soul (*Major Oldham*), Rick Fitts (*Captain Turner*), Aki Aleong (*Major Ngo Doc*), Gloria Carlin (*Paula*). 130 mins.

Hard Ride, The

USA, 1970, director: Burt Topper. An Anglo-EMI Presentation. *Production company*: American International/Burwalt Productions, *producer*: Charles Hanawalt, *script*: Burt Topper, *photography*: Robert Sparks, *colour process*: Movielab, *editor*: Kenneth Crane, *music/music director*: Harley Hatcher, *leading players*: Robert Fuller (*Phil*), Sherry Bain (*Sheryl*), Tony Russel (*Big Red*), William Bonner (*Grady*), Marshall Reed (*Father Tom*), Mikel Angel (*Ralls*), Biff Elliot (*Mike*). 90 mins.

Heroes

USA, 1977, director: Jeremy Paul Kagan. *Production company*: Turman-Foster Company. For Universal. *Producer*: David Foster, Lawrence Turman, *script*: James Carabatsos, *photography*: Frank Stanley, *colour process*: Technicolor, *editor*: Patrick Kennedy, *production designer*: Charles Rosen, *music*: Jack Nitzsche, *leading players*: Henry Winkler (*Jack Dunne*), Sally Field (*Carol*), Harrison Ford (*Kenny Boyd*), Val Avery (*Bus Driver*), Olivia Cole (*Jane Adcox*), Hector Elias (*Dr Elias*), Dennis Burkley (*Gus*), Tony Burton (*Chef*). 113 mins.

Hi, Mom!

USA, 1969, director: Brian De Palma. *Production company*: West End Films, *producer*: Charles Hirsch, *script*: Brian De Palma, *story*: Charles Hirsch, Brian De Palma, *photography*: Robert Elfstrom, *colour process*: Movielab, *editor*: Paul Hirsch, *music/music director*: Eric Kaz, *leading players*: Robert De Niro (*Jon Rubin*),

Jennifer Salt (*Judy Bishop*), Lara Parker (*Jeannie Mitchell*), Gerrit Graham (*Gerrit Wood*), Nelson Peltz (*Playboy*), Charles Durnham (*Superintendent*), Allen Garfield (*Joe Banner*), Paul Bartel (*Uncle Tom Wood*). 86 mins. (16mm).

Ice

USA, 1969, director: Robert Kramer. *Production company*: Monument Film Corporation/American Film Institute, *producer*: David C. Stone, *photography*: Robert Machover, *leading players*: Robert Kramer (*Robert*), Tom Griffin. 132 mins (35 and 16mm).

Joe

USA, 1970, director: John G. Avildsen. *Production company*: Cannon Productions, *producer*: David Gil, *script*: Norman Wexler, *photography*: John G. Avildsen, *colour process*: DeLuxe, *editor*: George T. Norris, *music/music director*: Bobby Scott, *leading players*: Dennis Patrick (*Bill Compton*), Peter Boyle (*Joe Curran*), Susan Sarandon (*Melissa Compton*), Patrick McDermott (*Frank Russo*), Audrey Caire (*Joan Compton*), K. Callan (*Mary Lou Curran*). 107 mins.

Just a Little Inconvenience

USA, 1977, director: Theodore J. Flicker. *Production company*: Fawcett-Majors/Universal TV, *producer*: Allan Balter, *script*: Theodore J. Flicker, Allan Balter, *photography*: Duke Callaghan, *colour process*: Technicolor, *editor*: Bernard J. Small, *music*: Jimmie Haskell, *leading players*: Lee Majors (*Frank Logan*), James Stacy (*Kenny Briggs*), Barbara Hershey (*Nikki Klausing*), Lane Bradbury (*Doctor*), Jim Davis (*Dave Erickson*), Charles Cioffi (*Major Bloom*), Bob Hastings (*Harry*). 97 mins.

Since there can hardly be two Theodore J. Flickers, one is forced to conclude that the director of this embarrassingly foolish melodrama – about the gradual rehabilitation of an embittered Vietnam War amputee – is none other than the founder of The Premise Theater of satirical improvisation and amiable auteur of The Troublemaker and The President's Analysis. When that little poser has been fully mulled over, however, virtually nothing remains to engage the spectator's intelligence. All in all, the principal source of visual stimulation is Lee Majors' mobile left eyebrow, which contrives to steal every scene from the rest of his face.

Killing Fields, The

Great Britain, 1984, director: Roland Joffé. *Production company*: Goldcrest Films and Television, an Enigma (First Casualty) production, *producer*: David Puttnam, *script*: Bruce Robinson, *photography*: Chris Menges, *colour process*: Eastman Colour, *editor*: Jim Clark, *production designer*: Roy Walker, *music*: Mike Oldfield, *leading players*: Sam Waterston (*Sydney Schanberg*), Doctor Haing S. Ngor (*Dith Pran*), John Malkovich (*Al Rockoff*), Julian Sands (*John Swain*), Craig T. Nelson (*Military Attaché*), Spalding Gray (*US Consul*), Bill Paterson (*Doctor MacEntire*), Athol Fugard (*Doctor Sundesval*), Graham Kennedy (*Dougal*), Katherine Kragum Chey (*Ser Moeun, Pran's Wife*), Oliver Pierpaoli (*Titony, Pran's Son*). 142 mins.

Limbo

USA, 1972, director: Mark Robson. *Production company*: The Filmmakers Group for Universal, *producer*: Linda Gottlieb, *script*: Joan Silver, James Bridges. From a story by Joan Silver. *Photography*: Charles Wheeler, *editor*: Dorothy Spencer, *music*: Anita Kerr, *leading players*: Kate Jackson (*Sandy Lawton*), Katherine Justice (*Sharon Dornbeck*), Stuart Margolin (*Phil Garrett*), Hazel Medina (*Jane York*), Kathleen Nolan (*Mary Kaye Buell*), Russell Wiggins (*Alan Weber*), Joan Murphy (*Margaret Holroyd*), Kim Nicholas (*Kathy Buell*). 112 mins.

Losers, The

USA, 1970, director: Jack Starrett. MGM-EMI. *Production company*: Fanfare Film Prods, *producer*: Joe Solomon, *script*: Alan Caillou, *photography*: Nonong Rasca, *colour process*: Eastman Colour, *editor*: James Moore, Richard Brockway, *music/music director*: Stu Phillips, *leading players*: Daniel Kemp (*Major Thomas*), William Smith (*Link Thomas*), Bernie Hamilton (*Captain Jackson*), Adam Roarke (*Duke*), Houston Savage (*Dirty Denny*), Gene Cornelius (*Speed*), Paul Koslo (*Limpy*). 95 mins.

M*A*S*H

USA, 1969, director: Robert Altman. *Production company*: Aspen/20th Century-Fox, *producer*: Ingo Preminger, *script*: Ring Lardner, Jnr. Based on the novel by Richard Hooker. *Photography*: Harold E. Stine. Panavision, *colour process*: DeLuxe, *editor*: Danford B. Greene, *art director*: Jack Martin Smith, Arthur Lonergan, *music*: Johnny Mandel, *leading players*: Donald Sutherland (*Hawkeye Pierce*), Elliott Gould (*Trapper John McIntyre*), Tom Skerritt (*Duke Forrest*), Sally Kellerman (*Major Hot Lips*), Robert Duvall (*Major Frank Burns*), Jo Ann Pflug (*Lt Dish*), René Auberjonois (*Dago Red*), Roger Bowen (*Col. Henry Blake*), Gary Burghoff (*Radar O'Reilly*), David Arkin (*Sgt Major Vollmer*), Fred Williamson (*Spearchucker*), Michael Murphy (*Me Lay*). 116 mins.

Medium Cool

USA, 1969, director: Haskell Wexler. Paramount. *Production company*: H & J Pictures, *producer*: Tully Friedman, Haskell Wexler, *script*: Haskell Wexler, *photography*: Haskell Wexler, *colour process*: Technicolor, *editor*: Verna Fields, *music*: Mike Bloomfield; The Mothers of Invention, *leading players*: Robert Forster (*John*), Verna Bloom (*Eileen*), Peter Bonerz (*Gus*), Marianna Hill (*Ruth*), Harold Blankenship (*Harold*), Sid McCoy (*Frank Baker*), Christine Bergstrom (*Dede*), Robert McAndrew (*Pennybaker*). 111 mins.

Milestones

USA, 1974, directors: Robert Kramer, John Douglas. *Production company*: A David C. Stone and Barbara Stone production, *producer*: David C. Stone, Barbara Stone, *script*: Robert Kramer, John Douglas, *photography*: John Douglas, *colour process*: Color, *editor*: Robert Kramer, John Douglas, *leading players*: Helen Grace Paley (*Helen*), David C. Stone (*Joe*), John Douglas (*John*), Laurel Berger (*Laurel*), Mary Chapelle (*Mama*), Bobby Buechler (*Jamie*), Liz Dear (*Liz*), Jay Foley (*Terry*), Suey Hagadora (*Suey*), Harvey Quintal (*Harvey*), Tina Shepherd (*Elizabeth*). 195 mins.

Missing in Action

USA, 1984, director: Joseph Zito. *Production company*: Cannon Productions, *producer*: Menahem Golam, Yoram Globus, *script*: James Bruner, *story*: John Crowther, Lance Hool. Based on characters created by Arthur Silver, Larry Levinson, Steve Bing. *Photography*: Joao Fernandes, *colour process*: Metrocolor, *editor*: Joel Goodman, Daniel Loewenthal, *leading players*: Chuck Norris (*Colonel James Braddock*), M. Emmett Walsh (*Tuck*), David Tress (*Senator Porter*), Leonore Kasdorf (*Ann*), James Hong (*General Iran*), Ernie Ortega (*Colonel Vinh*), Pierrino Mascarino (*Jacques*), E. Erich Anderson (*Massucci*). 101 mins.

One of a (to date) three-episode series in which Chuck Norris seems to be playing Michelin Man Rambo with some of the hot air let out, this is actually the sequel to Missing in Action 2, which was the first to be filmed but the second to be released.

Missing in Action 2 – The Beginning

USA, 1984, director: Lance Hool. *Production company*: Cannon, *producer*: Menahem Golan, Yoram Globus, *script*: Arthur Silver, Larry Levinson, Steve Bing, *photography*: Jorge Stahl, *colour process*: TVC, *editor*: Mark Conte, Marcus Manton, *music*: Brian May, *leading players*: Chuck Norris (*Colonel James Braddock*), Soon-Teck Oh (*Colonel Yin*), Steven Williams (*Captain David Nester*), Bennett Ohta (*Colonel Ho*), Cosie Costa (*Lieutenant Anthony Mazilli*), Joe Michael Terry (*Corporal Lawrence Opelka*). 95 mins.

Or Missing in Action Ditto. Comparing Missing in Action to Rambo: First Blood, Part II, Chuck Norris was pleased to claim that 'My version is a little more positive than Stallone's – it's less anti-government.'

Model Shop

USA, 1968, director: Jacques Demy. *Production company*: Columbia, *producer*: Jacques Demy, *script*: Jacques Demy, *English dialogue*: Jacques Demy, Adrien Joyce, *photography*: Michel Hugo, *colour process*: Technicolor, *editor*: Walter Thompson, *production designer*: Kenneth A. Reid, *music/songs*: Spirit, *leading players*: Anouk Aimée (*Lola*), Gary Lockwood (*George Matthews*), Alexandra Hay (*Gloria*), Carol Cole (*Barbara*), Severn Darden (*Portly Man*), Tom Fielding (*Gerry*), Neil Elliot (*Fred*). 92 mins.

More American Graffiti

USA, 1979, director: B. W. L. Norton. *Production company*: Lucasfilm, *executive producer*: George Lucas, *producer*: Howard Kazanjian, *script*: B. W. L. Norton. Based on characters created by George Lucas, Gloria Katz, Willard Huyck. *Photography*: Caleb Deschanel, *colour process*: Technicolor, *editor*: Tina Hirsch, *leading players*: Candy Clark (*Debbie Dunham*), Bo Hopkins (*Little Joe*), Ron Howard (*Steve Bolander*), Paul Le Mat (*John Milner*), Mackenzie Phillips (*Carol, 'Rainbow'*), Charles Martin Smith (*Terry 'the Toad' Fields*), Cindy Williams (*Laurie Bolander*), Anna Bjorn (*Eva*), Richard Bradford (*Major Creech*), John Brent (*Ralph*), Country Joe McDonald (*Himself*). 111 mins.

Norwood

USA, 1969, director: Jack Haley Jnr. *Production company*: Paramount, *producer*: Hal B. Wallis, *script*: Marguerite Roberts. Based on the novel by Charles Portis. *Photography*: Robert B. Hauser, *colour process*: Technicolor, *editor*: Warren Low, John W. Wheeler, *music director*: Al DeLory, *leading players*: Glen Campbell (*Norwood Pratt*), Kim Darby (*Rita Lee Chipman*), Joe Namath (*Joe William Reese*), Carol Lynley (*Yvonne Phillips*), Pat Hingle (*Grady Fring*), Tisha Sterling (*Marie*), Dom De Luise (*Bill Bird*), Leigh French (*Vernell Bird*), Jack Haley Snr (*Mr Reese*), Cass Daley (*Mrs Remley*). 95 mins.

Odd Angry Shot, The

Australia, 1979, director: Tom Jeffrey. *Production company*: Samson Productions. In association with the Australian Film Commission and the New South Wales Film Corporation. *Producer*: Sue Milliken, Tom Jeffrey, *script*: Tom Jeffrey. Based on the novel by William Nagle. *Photography*: Don McAlpine, *colour process*: Eastman Colour, *editor*: Brian Kavanagh, *music*: Michael Carlos, *leading players*: Graham Kennedy (*Harry*), John Hargreaves ('*Bung' Holey*), John Jarratt (*Bill*), Bryan Brown (*Rogers*), Graeme Blundell (*Dawson*), Richard Moir (*Medic*), Ian Gilmore (*Scott*), John Allen (*Lt Golonka*), Brandon Burke (*Isaacs*). 92 mins.

Three foot soldiers are united in a close friendship during their twelve months of active service with Australia's Special Air Service Regiment in the late sixties. Prior to 1972 no fewer than 60,000 such Australian 'grunts' found themselves stationed in Vietnam in support of the US forces, and this film attempts to convey the experience of a 'typical' cross-section. Most nearly approaching The Boys in Company C *in its ineffectually anti-authoritarian tendencies and (antipodean) melting-pot dramatis personae, it also shares with its American counterparts a wholly evasive attitude to its country's involvement in the conflict. 'What are we doing here?' is a question posed by one of the trio of protagonists. 'Well, everyone's got to be somewhere . . .' is the answer he receives.*

Platoon

USA, 1986, director: Oliver Stone. *Production company*: Hemdale Film Corporation, *producer*: Arnold Kopelson, *script*: Oliver Stone, *photography*: Robert Richardson, *colour process*: CFI, *editor*: Claire Simpson, *production designer*: Bruno Rubeo, *music*: Georges Delerue, *leading players*: Tom Berenger (*Sergeant Barnes*), Willem Dafoe (*Sergeant Elias*), Charlie Sheen (*Chris Taylor*), Forest Whitaker (*Big Harold*), Francesco Quinn (*Rhah*), John C. McGinley (*Sergeant O'Neill*), Richard Edson (*Sal*), Kevin Dillon (*Bunny*), Reggie Johnson (*Junior*), Keith David (*King*), Johnny Depp (*Lerner*), David Neidorf (*Tex*), Mark Moses (*Lieutenant Wolfe*), Chris Pedersen (*Crawford*). 120 mins.

P.O.W. The Escape

USA, 1986, director: Gideon Amir. *Production company*: Cannon, *producer*: Menahem Golan, Yoram Globus, *script*: Jeremy Lipp, James Bruner, Malcolm Barbour, John Langley, *story*: Avi Kleinberger, Gideon Amir, *photography*: Yechiel Ne'eman, *colour process*: TVC, *editor*: Roy Watts, Michael J. Duthie, Alain Jakubowicz, *music supervisor*: Michael Linn, *leading players*: David Carradine

(*Colonel Jim Cooper*), Charles R. Floyd (*Sparks*), Mako (*Captain Vinh*), Steve James (*Jonston*), Phil Brock (*Adams*), Daniel Demorest (*Thomas*), Tony Pierce (*Waite*). 89 mins.

Directed by Joseph Zito's assistant on Missing in Action, P.O.W. The Escape *is to that film what it was to* Rambo – *a pale stencil.*

Rambo: First Blood, Part II

USA, 1985, director: George Pan Cosmatos. *Production company*: Carolco. For Anabasis. *Producer*: Buzz Feitshans, *script*: Sylvester Stallone, James Cameron, *story*: Kevin Jarre. Based on characters created by David Morrell. *Photography*: Jack Cardiff. Panavision. *Colour process*: Technicolor, *editor*: Mark Goldblatt, Mark Helfrich; Gib Jaffe, Frank E. Jimenez, Larry Bock, *production designer*: Bill Kenney, *music*: Jerry Goldsmith, *leading players*: Sylvester Stallone (*John Rambo*), Richard Crenna (*Colonel Trautman*), Julie Nickson (*Co Bao*), Charles Napier (*Marshall Murdock*), Steven Berkoff (*Lieutenant Podovsky*), Martin Kove (*Ericson*), Andy Wood (*Banks*), George Kee Cheung (*Sergeant Tay*), William Ghent (*Captain Vinh*). 96 mins.

Revolutionary, The

USA, 1970, director: Paul Williams. United Artists. *Production company*: Pressman-Williams Enterprises, *producer*: Edward Pressman, *script*: Hans Koningsberger. Based on his own novel. *Photography*: Brian Probyn, *colour process*: Technicolor, *editor*: Henry Richardson, *production designer*: Disley Jones, *music/music director*: Michael Small, *leading players*: Jon Voight (*A*), Jennifer Salt (*Helen Peret*), Seymour Cassel (*Leonard*), Robert Duvall (*Despard*), Collin Wilcox-Horne (*Anne*), Lionel Murton (*Professor*), Reed de Rouen (*Mayor*), Warren Stanhope (*A's Father*), Mary Barclay (*A's Mother*), Richard Pendry (*NCO*). 101 mins.

Rolling Thunder

USA, 1977, director: John Flynn. *Production company*: American International Pictures, *producer*: Norman T. Herman, *script*: Paul Schrader, Heywood Gould, *story*: Paul Schrader, *photography*: Jordan Cronenweth, *colour process*: DeLuxe; prints by Movielab, *editor*: Frank P. Keller, *music*: Barry De Vorzon, *leading players*: William Devane (*Major Charles Rane*), Tommy Lee Jones (*Johnny Vohden*), Linda Haynes (*Linda Forchet*), Lisa Richards (*Janet*), Dabney Coleman (*Maxwell*), James Best (*Texan*), Cassie Yates (*Candy*), Luke Askew (*Automatic Slim*). 99 mins.

Saigon

USA, 1988, director: Christopher Crowe. *Production company*: 20th Century-Fox. In association with American Entertainment Partners. *Producer*: Alan Barnette, *script*: Christopher Crowe, Jack Thibeau, *photography*: David Gribble, *colour process*: DeLuxe, *editor*: Douglas Ibold, *production designer*: Dennis Washington, *music*: James Newton Howard, *leading players*: Willem Dafoe (*Buck McGriff*), Gregory Hines (*Albaby Perkins*), Fred Ward (*Sergeant

Benjamin Dix), Amanda Pays (*Nicole*), Kay Tong Lim (*Lime Green*), Scott Glenn (*Colonel Dexter Armstrong*), David Alan Grier (*Rogers*), Keith David (*Maurice*), Raymond O'Connor (*Staff Sergeant Flowers*), Richard Brooks (*Preacher*). 102 mins.

In a movie like Saigon *– the account of two detectives, with the US Army's Criminal Investigations Detachment in that city in 1968, who have been assigned to identify the murderer of a local prostitute – the question of Vietnam has been completely normalised, South-East Asia complacently exoticised and the war itself made no longer even a background but a* backdrop, *a dull offscreen rumble only very marginally intersecting with the narrative. There is nothing inherently reprehensible in such an evolution (it was bound to occur sooner or later), except on those occasions when the film-makers find themselves, as one might have predicted, unable to resist picking at the dry, flaky scab of the American 'civilising mission'. In one scene, when the detectives are rescued from an irate mob by a phalanx of US air power, their saviour apostrophises the locals: 'When will you people learn that we are never outgunned?' – and it is difficult not to be sensitive to the nuance of 'outgunned' (which the North Vietnamese were) in lieu of 'beaten' (which of course they were not).*

Secret Honor

USA, 1984, director: Robert Altman. *Production company*: Sandcastle 5. In co-operation with the University of Michigan (Department of Communication), Los Angeles Actors' Theater. *Producer*: Robert Altman, *script*: Donald Freed, Arnold M. Stone. Based on their own play. *Photography*: Pierre Mignot, *colour process*: Movielab, *editor*: Juliet Weber, *music*: George Burt, *leading player*: Philip Baker Hall (*Richard Milhous Nixon*). 90 mins.

Robert Altman's Secret Honor *occupies a somewhat marginal position in the cinema of Vietnam. The filmic transposition of a one-act play by Donald Freed and Arnold M. Stone (directed by Altman himself off-Broadway), it is a witty, tendentious character study of Richard Milhous Nixon, who is the play's (and the film's) sole protagonist and who, in the course of its ninety minutes, commits to a tape-recorder some whimsical musings on his life, career and ultimate disgrace. The last, and also most startlingly speculative of his confessions, is that the secret of his presidency (the so-called Committee of a Hundred, the Californian power brokers who had masterminded his political ascension, forced him to prolong the Vietnam War in order to safeguard their schemes for economic expansion in South-East Asia) had become so unendurable that he wilfully brought it to its ignominious conclusion by exploiting Watergate as a cover for his more consummate treason.*

Slaughter

USA, 1972, director: Jack Starrett. An Anglo-EMI presentation. *Production company*: American International Pictures/Slaughter United Partnership, *producer*: Monroe Sachson, *script*: Mark Hanna, Don Williams, *photography*: Rosalio Solano. Todd-AO 35, *colour process*: DeLuxe, *editor*: Renn Reynolds, *music/music director*: Luchi de Jesús, *leading players*: Jim Brown (*Slaughter*), Stella Stevens (*Ann Cooper*), Rip Torn (*Dominick Hoffo*), Don Gordon (*Harry Bastoli*), Cameron Mitchell (*A. W. Price*), Marlene Clark (*Kim Walker*). 90 mins.

Slaughter's Big Rip-Off

USA, 1973, director: Gordon Douglas. *Production company*: American
International Pictures, *executive producer*: Samuel Z. Arkoff, *producer*: Monroe
Sachson, *script*: Charles Johnson. Based on the character created by Don
Williams. *Photography*: Charles Wheeler. Todd-AO 35, *colour process*: Movielab,
editor: Christopher Holmes, *music*: James Brown, Fred Wesley, performed by
James Brown and the J.B's, *leading players*: Jim Brown (*Slaughter*), Ed
McMahon (*Duncan*), Brock Peters (*Reynolds*), Don Stroud (*Kirk*), Gloria Hendry
(*Marcia*), Richard Williams (*Joe Creole*). 93 mins.

Small Circle of Friends, A

USA, 1980, director: Rob Cohen. *Production company*: Small Circle of Friends
Inc. For United Artists. *Producer*: Tim Zinnemann, *script*: Ezra Sacks,
photography: Michael Butler, *colour process*: Technicolor, *editor*: Randy Roberts,
production designer: Joel Schiller, *music*: Jim Steinman, *leading players*: Brad Davis
(*Leonardo DaVinci Rizzo*), Karen Allen (*Jessica Bloom*), Jameson Parker (*Nick
Baxter*), Shelley Long (*Alice*), John Friedrich (*Alex Haddox*), Gary Springer
(*Greenblatt*), Craig Richard Nelson (*Harry Norris Winthrop*), Harry Caesar
(*Jimmy*), Nan Martin (*Mrs Baxter*), Dan Stern (*Crazy Kid*). 112 mins.

Some Kind of Hero

USA, 1981, director: Michael Pressman. *Production company*: Paramount,
producer: Howard W. Koch, *co-producer*: James Kirkwood, *script*: James
Kirkwood, Robert Boris. Based on the novel by James Kirkwood. *Photography*:
King Baggot, *colour process*: Movielab, *editor*: Christopher Greenbury, *music*:
Patrick Williams, *leading players*: Richard Pryor (*Eddie Keller*), Margot Kidder
(*Toni Donovan*), Ray Sharkey (*Vinnie DiAngelo*), Ronny Cox (*Colonel Powers*), Lynne
Moody (*Lisa Keller*), Olivia Cole (*Jessie Keller*). 97 mins.

Southern Comfort

USA, 1981, director: Walter Hill. *Production company*: Phoenix. For Cinema
Group Venture. *Producer*: David Giler, *script*: Michael Kane, Walter Hill,
David Giler, *photography*: Andrew Laszlo, *colour process*: DeLuxe, *editor*: Freeman
Davies, *production designer*: John Vallone, *music arranged by* Ry Cooder, *leading
players*: Keith Carradine (*Rifleman Lee Spencer*), Powers Boothe (*Rifleman Charles
Hardin*), Fred Ward (*Rifleman Lonnie Reece*), Franklyn Seales (*Rifleman Cleotis
Simms*), T. K. Carter (*Rifleman Tyrone Cribbs*), Lewis Smith (*Rifleman Earl Stuckey*),
Les Lannom (*Corporal Claude Casper*), Peter Coyote (*Sergeant Crawford Poole*). 106
mins.

Strawberry Statement, The

USA, 1970, director: Stuart Hagmann. M-G-M. *Production company*:
Chartoff-Winkler Productions, *producer*: Irwin Winkler, Robert Chartoff, *script*:
Israel Horovitz. Based on the book *The Strawberry Statement: Notes of a College
Revolutionary* by James Simon Kunen. *Photography*: Ralph Woolsey, *colour
process*: Metrocolor, *editor*: Marje Fowler, Fredric Steinkamp, Roger J. Roth,
music: Ian Freebairn Smith, *leading players*: Bruce Davison (*Simon*), Kim Darby
(*Linda*), Bud Cort (*Elliot*), Murray MacLeod (*George*), Tom Foral (*Coach*), Danny
Goldman (*Charlie*), Kristina Holland (*Irma*), Bob Balatan (*Elliot*), Kristin Van

Buren (*Meg*), Israel Horovitz (*Dr Benton*), James Kunen (*Chairman*), James Coco (*Grocer*). 109 mins.

Stunt Man, The

USA, 1978, director: Richard Rush. 20th Century-Fox. *Production company*: Melvin Simon Co, *producer*: Richard Rush, *script*: Lawrence B. Marcus. Based on the novel by Paul Brodeur. *Adaptation*: Richard Rush, *photography*: Mario Tosi, *colour process*: Metrocolor, *editor*: Jack Hofstra, Caroline Ferriol, *music*: Dominic Frontiere, *leading players*: Peter O'Toole (*Eli Cross*), Barbara Hershey (*Nina Franklin*), Steve Railsback (*Cameron*), Sharon Farrell (*Denise*), John Garwood (*Gabe, Eli's Cameraman*), Allen Goorwitz (*Sam*), Alex Rocco (*Jake*), Phillip Bruns (*Ace*), Chuck Bail (*Chuck Barton*), Adam Roarke (*Raymond Bailey*). 130 mins.

Summer Soldiers

Japan, 1971, director: Hiroshi Teshigahara. *Production company*: Teshigahara, *producer*: Yukio Tomizawa, *script*: John Nathan, *photography*: Hiroshi Teshigahara. In colour. *Editor*: Fusako Shuzui, *music*: Toru Takemitsu, *leading players*: Keith Sykes (*Jim*), Lee Reisen (*Reiko*), Kazuo Kitamura (*Tachikawa*), Toshiro Kobayashi (*Mrs Tachikawa*), Shoichi Ozawa (*Tanikawa*). 103 mins.

Summertree

USA, 1971, director: Anthony Newley. *Production company*: Bryna Productions, *producer*: Kirk Douglas, *script*: Edward Hume, Stephen Yafa. Based on the play by Ron Cowen. *Photography*: Richard C. Glouner, *colour process*: Eastman Color, *editor*: Maury Winetrobe, *music*: David Shire, *leading players*: Michael Douglas (*Jerry McAdam*), Jack Warden (*Herb*), Brenda Vaccaro (*Vanetta*), Barbara Bel Geddes (*Ruth*), Kirk Callaway (*Marvis Johnson*), Bill Vint (*Tony*), Jeff Siggens (*Bennie*), Rob Reiner (*Don*). 89 mins.

Taking Off

USA, 1971, director: Milos Forman. *Production company*: Universal/ Forman-Crown-Hausman, *producer*: Alfred W. Crown, *script*: Milos Forman, John Guare, Jean-Claude Carrière, John Klein, *photography*: Miroslav Ondricek, *colour process*: Movielab, *editor*: John Carter, *art director*: Robert Wightman, *leading players*: Lynn Carlin (*Lynn Tyne*), Buck Henry (*Larry Tyne*), Linnea Heacock (*Jeannie Tyne*), Georgia Engel (*Margot*), Tony Harvey (*Tony*), Audra Lindley (*Ann Lockston*), Paul Benedict (*Ben Lockston*), Vincent Schiavelli (*Mr Schiavelli*), David Gittler (*Jamie*), The Ike and Tina Turner Revue (*Themselves*). 93 mins.

Taxi Driver

USA, 1976, director: Martin Scorsese. *Production company*: Italo-Judeo. A Bill Phillips production. *Producer*: Michael Phillips, Julia Phillips, *script*: Paul Schrader, *photography*: Michael Chapman, *colour process*: MGM, *visual consultant*: David Nichols, *editor*: Tom Rolf, Melvin Shapiro, *art director*: Charles Rosen, *music*: Bernard Herrmann, *leading players*: Robert De Niro (*Travis Bickle*), Cybill Shepherd (*Betsy*), Jodie Foster (*Iris*), Peter Boyle (*Wizard*), Leonard Harris (*Charles Palantine*), Harvey Keitel (*Sport*), Martin Scorsese (*Passenger Watching Silhouette*),

Steven Prince (*Andy, Gun Salesman*), Diahnne Abbot (*Concession Girl*), Frank Adu (*Angry Black Man*). 114 mins.

Tracks

USA, 1976, director: Henry Jaglom. *Production company*: Rainbow Pictures, *executive producer*: Bert Schneider, *co-producer*: Howard Zuker, Irving Cohen, Ted Shapiro, *script*: Henry Jaglom, *photography*: Paul Glickman. In colour. *Editor*: George Folsey Jnr, *music consultants*: Robert Ragland, Robert Rosene, *leading players*: Dennis Hopper (*Sergeant Jack Falen*), Taryn Power (*Stephanie*), Dean Stockwell (*Mark*), Topo Swope (*Chloe*), Michael Emil [Michael E. Jaglom] (*Emile*), Zack Norman (*Gene*). 92 mins.

Uncommon Valor

USA, 1983, director: Ted Kotcheff. *Production company*: Paramount, *producer*: John Milius, Buzz Feitshans, *script*: Joe Gayton, *photography*: Stephen H. Burum, *colour process*: Movielab, *editor*: Mark Melnick, *production designer*: James L. Schoppe, *music*: James Horner, *leading players*: Gene Hackman (*Colonel Jason Rhodes*), Robert Stack (*Hugh MacGregor*), Fred Ward (*Wilkes*), Reb Brown (*Blaster*), Randall 'Tex' Cobb (*Sailor*), Patrick Swayze (*Scott*), Harold Sylvester (*Johnson*), Tim Thomerson (*Charts*), Lau Nga Lai (*Lai Fun*), Kwan Hi Lim (*Jiang*). 105 mins.

Visitors, The

USA, 1972, director: Elia Kazan. *Production company*: United Artists, *producer*: Chris Kazan, Nick Proferes, *script*: Chris Kazan, *photography*: Nick Proferes, *editor*: Nick Proferes, *music*: Johann Sebastian Bach, *leading players*: Patrick McVey (*Harry Wayne*), Patricia Joyce (*Martha Wayne*), James Woods (*Bill Schmidt*), Chico Martinez (*Tony Rodrigues*), Steve Railsback (*Mike Nickerson*). 90 mins.

Who'll Stop the Rain? (UK, Dog Soldiers)

USA, 1978, director: Karel Reisz. *Production company*: The Dog Soldiers Co. For United Artists. *Producer*: Herb Jaffe, Gabriel Katzka, *associate producer*: Roger Spottiswoode, Sheldon Schrager, *script*: Judith Rascoe, Robert Stone. Based on the novel by Robert Stone. *Photography*: Richard H. Kline, *colour process*: Technicolor; prints by MGM, *editor*: Chris Ridsdale, Mark Conte, Carlos Puente Portillo, *production designer*: Dale Hennesy, *music*: Laurence Rosenthal, *leading players*: Nick Nolte (*Ray Hicks*), Tuesday Weld (*Marge Converse*), Michael Moriarty (*John Converse*), Anthony Zerbe (*Antheil*), Richard Masur (*Danskin*), Ray Sharkey (*Smitty*), Gail Strickland (*Charmian*), Charles Haid (*Eddie Peace*), David Opatoshu (*Bender*). 126 mins.

Winter Soldier

USA, 1972. *Production company*: Winterfilm. In association with Vietnam Veterans Against the War. Made by the Winterfilm-Collective. *With*: Rusty Sachs, Scott Camil, Ken Campbell, Scott Shimabukuro, Steve Pitkin, John Kerry, Joe Bangert, Jonathan Birch, Charles Stevens, Fred Nienke, Nathan Hale, Michael Hunter, Murphy Llody, Carl Rippberger, Robert Clark, Gordon Stewart, Curtis Windgrodsdy, Gary Kayes, Allan Akers, Bill Hatton, Edmund Murphy, James

Duffy, Scott Moore, Mark Lenix, Thomas Heidtman, Dennis Caldwell, James Henry, Evan Haney. 99 mins. (16mm).

Year of the Dragon

USA, 1985, director: Michael Cimino. *Production company*: Dino De Laurentiis Corporation. For MGM/UA. *Producer*: Dino De Laurentiis, *script*: Oliver Stone, Michael Cimino. Based on the novel by Robert Daley. *Photography*: Alex Thomson, *colour process*: Technicolor; prints by Metrocolor, *editor*: Françoise Bonnot, *production designer*: Wolf Kroeger, *music/music director*: David Mansfield, *leading players*: Mickey Rourke (*Captain Stanley White*), John Lone (*Go Joey Tai*), Ariane (*Tracy Tzu*), Leonard Termo (*Angelo Rizzo*), Ray Barry (*Louis Bukowski*), Caroline Kava (*Connie White*), Eddie Jones (*William McKenna*), Joey Chin (*Ronnie Chang*), Victor Wong (*Harry Yung*), K. Dock Yip (*Milton Bin*), Pao Han Lin (*Fred Hung*). 134 mins.

Zabriskie Point

USA, 1969, director: Michelangelo Antonioni. *Production company*: M-G-M, *producer*: Carlo Ponti, *script*: Michelangelo Antonioni, Fred Gardner, Sam Shepard, Tonio Guerra, Clare Peploe, *photography*: Alfio Contini. Panavision. *Colour process*: Metrocolor, *editing assistant*: Franco Arcalli, *production designer*: Dean Tavoularis, *music*: The Pink Floyd, *leading players*: Mark Frechette (*Mark*), Daria Halprin (*Daria*), Rod Taylor (*Lee Allen*), Paul Fix (*Café Owner*), G. D. Spradlin (*Lee Allen's Associate*), Bill Garaway (*Morty*), Kathleen Cleaver (*Kathleen*), and the Open Theatre of Joe Chaikin. 110 mins.

Index